$0.95

DISCARDED

DATE DUE

JAN 15 2013	
	PRINTED IN U.S.A.

"The complexity of warfare is staggering. Attacks against the United States are all too often framed only in terms of a kinetic strike against military forces, infrastructure, or most recently, a cyber-attack. Kevin Freeman goes right to the heart of the issue: the strength of the United States lies in the U.S. economy, it has been attacked, and such attacks can cripple us. Some believe this undoable, unimaginable, or unthinkable. Our adversaries are using every tool to defeat us, and we must protect ourselves."

—**David G. Reist**,
BGen. USMC (Ret.), Vice President of the Potomac Institute for Policy Studies

"When nations contend for power, they use all the means at their disposal. If they are building weapons and making threats of war, there are likely to be other things going on, too. This would include economic things, things designed to upset the wealth and therefore the power of their potential enemies. This is an old way of fighting, even if the means of prosecuting it are new. Kevin has suggested what some of these new ways are. It makes a chilling story."

—**Larry P. Arnn**,
President of Hillsdale College

"Kevin Freeman's detailed analysis of the 2008 U.S. economic market downturn is the elephant in the room with regards to America's financial and national security troubles. His exposure of the U.S. markets' continuing vulnerabilities to hostile foreign entities is chilling and requires study and due diligence by those charged with defending America's financial system. This book is another major indicator that America's enemies are fighting a total war and our national security apparatus is asleep at the wheel."

—**John Guandolo**,
*Vice President of the Strategic Engagement Group and
former Special Agent in the FBI Counterterrorism Division*

"*Secret Weapon* is an incredibly informative look into the financial crisis of September 2008. Terrorism takes on many forms, and Kevin Freeman has exposed the threat of financial terrorism to our economic system. This groundbreaking work is a must-read for all Americans to fully grasp the extent of the economic warfare being waged against the United States."

—**E. J. Kimball**,
*President of the Strategic Engagement Group and
former Foreign Policy Counsel to U.S. Congresswoman Sue Myrick*

"Forget against whom our nation has declared war. Recall with renewed commitment who has sworn war *against us*. Kevin Freeman's witness to the latter is a quantum leap in national security threat analysis."

—Patrick Maloy,
Major USMC (Ret.)

"Understanding the serious implications to our country's national security and our economic system, Kevin Freeman has undertaken a personal crusade to inform our policymakers, lawmakers, and military leaders at his own expense. I personally have accompanied Mr. Freeman to numerous meetings to inform them of the existence of the study and its implications. These meetings included members or their senior staffs of Congress (both the House of Representatives and the Senate), the Inspector General of the Security Exchange Commission, and several former high government officials who had served in previous presidential administrations."

—Steve Zidek,
Assistant Professor at Mercyhurst College Intelligence Studies program and former Deputy National Intelligence Officer at the National Intelligence Council

"As we confront the threat in the War on Terror, the national security focus has been almost exclusively on boots on the ground fighting jihadists over there. The problem is, the enemy has always known that he won't win the war over there—but he can win it here by attacking other centers of power. One of those centers of power, already weakened, is the financial markets. Kevin Freeman does an excellent job of fleshing out the realities of this threat with uncomforting clarity. For those who fancy themselves defenders of the homeland, this is a must read."

—Stephen Coughlin,
Vice President of the Strategic Engagement Group and former consultant to the Joint Chiefs of Staff

"Kevin D. Freeman courageously bucked the establishment in revealing new dangers posed by economic warfare and other non-military forms of attack. This book is must reading."

—Bill Gertz,
bestselling author of The Failure Factory *and national security columnist for the* Washington Times

"Kevin Freeman's *Secret Weapon* is the scariest book you'll read all year. We're not just endangered by those at home who mismanaged the market; we're endangered by those abroad who took advantage of it. If we don't start thinking creatively, as Freeman argues, we'll be in serious trouble."

—**Ben Shapiro**,
bestselling author of Primetime Propaganda

"When Kevin Freeman, after an impressive career in finance, began investigating the possibility that terrorists are manipulating our markets, he suddenly found himself inside a real world spy novel. There is so much smoke surrounding his study of economic warfare that the only question is not whether there is a fire, but rather how far it has spread."

—**Kevin Hassett, Ph.D.**,
Director of Economic Policy Studies at the American Enterprise Institute and former Senior Economist at the Board of Governors of the Federal Reserve System

"Kevin has the courage to talk about a sensitive topic that few are willing to address. He has proven to be a detailed researcher, not willing to leave any stone unturned as he educates the public about the real risk of financial terrorism. We need more people like him who will highlight the risks of non-traditional warfare within the financial markets."

—**Jeffrey Roach, Ph.D.**,
Chief Economist at Investment Committee Chair Horizon Investments and former Senior Economist at the Bank of America

"Osama bin Laden stated that one of his principal goals was to bankrupt America. We ignore the economic threat posed by radical Islam at our peril. *Secret Weapon* by Kevin Freeman is a must read for Americans who want to understand the critical role that financial warfare plays in our ongoing struggle with radical Islam and other forces hostile to American interests."

—**Tom Pauken**,
former Reagan administration official and author of Bringing America Home

"Kevin Freeman is a voice that needs to be heard. His knowledge is unsurpassed and his research is impeccable. Bottom line: Mr. Freeman knows what he's talking about and the rest of us ignore him at great risk."

—**Everett Piper**,
President of Oklahoma Wesleyan University

"Kevin Freeman is one of the few people with serious credentials in the financial and investment community who take economic warfare seriously. A longstanding art of statecraft, economic warfare—whether conducted offensively or defensively—is rarely studied, rarely taught, and due to lack of knowledge and willful blindness, rarely considered in the high councils of government. Yet today, new techniques, the digital revolution, and the integration of economic statecraft with strategic and tactical deception, combine to render our economy and national security unusually vulnerable. Mr. Freeman raises both unpleasant realities and even less pleasant possibilities that deserve serious scrutiny by those who would defend our country and civilization."

—**John Lenczowski**,
Founder and President of The Institute of World Politics and
former Director of European and Soviet Affairs at
the National Security Council

"Kevin Freeman has been warning America's leadership of the dangers of financial terrorism for the last three years. It is happening now and Kevin provides the evidence in his book *Secret Weapon*. Every American needs to understand how our financial markets have been manipulated by people who want to destroy the nation and how they can do even greater damage in the future. This book is a critical read for everyone."

—**William G. Boykin**,
Lt. Gen. USA (Ret.), former Commander of U.S. Army Special Forces and found-
ing member of Delta Force

"Incredibly, the potential coordinated actions of foreign entities to disrupt the U.S. financial industry seem to be ignored by most. Some hostilities could be state-sponsored, while others could be initiated and executed by small groups. Such threats are real and demand immediate evaluation of vulnerabilities, examination of available means, and solution-oriented thinking to address them to minimize the yet unanticipated catastrophic effects. While our policy makers ignore the looming perfect storm, Kevin Freeman does his best to wake us up."

—**Dr. Rachel Ehrenfeld**,
Director of Economic Warfare Institute and
author of Funding Evil: How Terrorism Is Financed—and How to Stop It

"In his 2009 study for the U.S. Department of Defense, 'Economic Warfare: Risks and Responses,' Kevin Freeman warned of dangerous gaps in our financial regulatory environment that expose us to the risks of a future economic meltdown. Given the even weaker state of global markets today, the next meltdown will make 2008 look like a walk in the park. This time, let's hope governments around the globe are not only listening to Freeman's advice, but also acting upon it."

—**H. T. Narea**,
author of The Fund *and adjunct professor at the Graduate School of Foreign Service at Georgetown University*

SECRET WEAPON

SECRET WEAPON

HOW ECONOMIC TERRORISM BROUGHT DOWN THE U.S. STOCK MARKET AND WHY IT CAN HAPPEN AGAIN

KEVIN FREEMAN

Since 1947
**REGNERY
PUBLISHING, INC.**
An Eagle Publishing Company • Washington, DC

Cataloging-in-Publication data on file with the Library of Congress

ISBN 978-1-59698-794-4

Published in the United States by
Regnery Publishing, Inc.
One Massachusetts Avenue NW
Washington, DC 20001
www.Regnery.com

Manufactured in the United States of America
10 9 8 7 6 5 4 3 2 1
Books are available in quantity for promotional or premium use. Write to Director of Special Sales, Regnery Publishing, Inc., One Massachusetts Avenue NW, Washington, DC 20001, for information on discounts and terms, or call (202) 216-0600.

Distributed to the trade by
Perseus Distribution
387 Park Avenue South
New York, NY 10016

Humbly dedicated by faith to God Almighty that by His Spirit because of His Grace, He might be glorified.

"Whether therefore ye eat, or drink, or whatsoever ye do, do all to the glory of God."

—I Corinthians 10:31 (King James Version)

CONTENTS

INTRODUCTION

merica stands on the brink.

It stands on the brink because of government overspending and our colossal national debt. It stands on the brink because of manipulation, failed regulations, and predatory trading on our financial markets. It stands on the brink because of terrorism threats and covert moves against us by hostile foreign powers.

But to take down our economy and eliminate the United States as a superpower—as many of our enemies seek to do—all these things will have to come together in a perfect storm. Something close to that occurred in September 2008, when our enemies hammered the U.S. economy in a stealth financial attack.

That attack—and the likelihood that we'll be hit again in the near future—is the story of *Secret Weapon*.

For too long, the warning signs have been clear. On September 11, 2001, our enemies hit the American homeland—and some evidence suggests they preceded that attack by short selling U.S. airlines and other financial stocks. This was merely the latest and most obvious attack on the economic infrastructure of the United States. After all, Osama bin Laden had been vowing for years to take down the American economy—and he targeted the World Trade Center buildings precisely because of their importance, both actual and symbolic, in the financial world.

This strategy was nothing new. For hundreds of years, nations as well as terrorist groups have understood the importance of attacking their enemies' economies. The United States is no exception—we engaged in economic warfare against the Soviet Union during the Cold War, against the British during the Suez Canal crisis in 1956, against the Germans and the Japanese during World War II, and against the South during the Civil War. Our enemies did the same. Economic warfare is as real—and can be just as devastating to a nation's security—as a shooting war.

Our enemies' attempts to wage economic warfare against us, however, never met with much success. Certainly, financial terrorism never did—at least not until September 2008, when America's financial infrastructure took a major hit and then crumbled. Over the course of the next few months, an estimated $50 trillion of global wealth simply evaporated, with more than a quarter of that sum disappearing from the United States. The media rushed to assign blame for the resulting economic crisis. Liberals pointed the finger at Wall Street fat cats, while conservatives faulted federal regulations that pressured financial companies to undertake risky loans. Democrats blamed Republicans; Republicans blamed Democrats.

Nobody blamed the true culprits: America's foreign enemies.

Many Americans believe that our physical infrastructure may be vulnerable to terrorism, but that our economy is somehow immune from attack. We like to think our stock market is just that—*our* stock market—and that our banks are American-made, American-funded, and American-run. No foreign enemy could sabotage our entire economy—that's the conventional wisdom.

Not only is that perspective dangerously naïve, it's downright wrong. Today's global economy is deeply interconnected, and like all interconnected industries and modes of technology—airlines, trains, the Internet—it can be exploited by terrorists and other malevolent actors. History is filled with examples of financial attacks on companies, industries, and nations for both economic and non-economic ends.

In the coming pages, we will pull the curtain back on the greatest untold scandal of the twenty-first century—the September 2008 financial attack on America. We begin by discussing the 9/11 atrocity and the little-known financial and economic aspects of the attacks. As authors Phillip J. Cooper and Claudia Maria Vargas observe, al Qaeda envisioned 9/11 as "a serious attack intended to produce massive casualties and serious damage to the economy, but it was also very much designed to be a symbolic assault—one that would strike the symbols of U.S. economic, political, and military power."[1]

We then recount my involvement with the issue of economic warfare and financial terrorism, and how I was recruited by the Pentagon to author a report on the possibility of such action being taken against the United States. As a longtime financial industry insider, my interest in this topic was virtually nil—until I discovered signs that short selling was being used as a market weapon prior to the financial collapse of September 2008.

From there, we proceed to the biggest question of the last decade: Who was behind that collapse? In any crime, prosecutors look for three elements: motive, means, and opportunity. We will examine each in turn. America has many enemies, both foreign and domestic, and all have motive to take down the economy. Our enemies range from Islamic terrorist groups to Muslim state actors to China and Russia and Venezuela. They also include "piggybackers" like George Soros—people who profited from the collapse, but whose role in the affair remains murky. All may have been involved in the bear raids that destroyed the economy in September 2008. As we will demonstrate, some certainly were.

Then we will look at the means our enemies used to assault the economy, including oil manipulation, bear raids, credit default swaps, naked short selling, currency and debt manipulation, double- and triple-short ETFs, machinations by sovereign wealth funds, algorithmic trading, rogue trading, dark markets, dark pools, sponsored access, and Islamic-compliant arboons. We will explain why understanding all these terms is crucial for protecting your wealth and for recognizing the hidden hands operating within our markets.

Next, we will look at opportunity. Our government has provided ample opportunity for our enemies to exploit these tools. Regulatory authorities have looked the other way, assuming that all participants in our financial markets are rational actors who want the market to succeed, and that the last thing any participant wants to do is to destroy the market itself. This is eminently false—some players are happy to exploit the freedom and openness of our markets to take down those very markets. We will also explain the dire consequences of our failure of imagination in the lead-up to September 2008, and how U.S. authorities were blind to the signs that our enemies were changing and improving their methods of attack.

We will trace the full-scale meltdown of the U.S. economy step by step: Phase One was the rapid rise in oil prices that squeezed our economy; Phase Two was led by the mysterious bear raids that took down Bear Stearns, Lehman Brothers, and other once-great financial institutions. We now face Phase Three. Because we have done almost nothing to rectify the vulnerabilities that existed prior to September 2008—through policies such as inflating our currency and raising our debt, we have actually worsened them—we are susceptible to another use of the secret weapon. That possibility is becoming a probability as the warnings you read here are ignored day after day by the federal government. Although we are making some breakthroughs in acknowledging what really happened in September 2008 and in defending ourselves from another financial attack, they are far too slow in coming—and some powerful players have an interest in stifling the story completely.

Finally, we will explore what the next attack will look like. How will it go down? Who will be behind it? And how can you protect yourself?

Our enemies are using a secret weapon—the weapon of economic warfare and financial terrorism—designed to take the United States down once and for all. Knowledge is the first step in fighting back. That is *our* secret weapon.

CHAPTER ONE

THE WRITING ON THE WALL

A t 8:46 a.m. Eastern Time on September 11, 2001, five al Qaeda hijackers flew American Airlines Flight 11 into the north tower of the World Trade Center. The building burst into smoke and flame, clouding the bright blue sky in ash. Seventeen minutes later, five more al Qaeda hijackers crashed United Airlines Flight 175 into the south tower. Less than two hours after that, both towers collapsed. Meanwhile, in Washington, D.C., five more al Qaeda hijackers crashed American Airlines Flight 77 into the Pentagon. The Capitol building nearby was the likely target of a fourth hijacked plane, United Airlines Flight 93, whose heroic passengers forced their jihadist captors to prematurely crash the plane in a field in Shanksville, Pennsylvania. Around 3,000 American lives were lost in the attacks.

The 9/11 plot also caused untold economic damage, with estimates ranging up to $500 billion.[1] In the immediate aftermath of the attacks, job losses reached 143,000 per month in New York City, where the terrorist onslaught may have cost the city as much as $60 billion in revenue.[2] Building losses reached $34 billion, and America's airline industry took over five years to recover from the carnage. One study suggests that when you factor in the costs of new homeland security measures, additional defense spending for the wars in Afghanistan and Iraq, additional veterans' benefits, and servicing the additional debt over the next decade, the total cost of 9/11 approaches $5 trillion.[3]

That, of course, was Osama bin Laden's strategy. For years, he had announced his intent to target the economy of the United States. Bin Laden understood that attacking our physical infrastructure would deal a blow to America, but it was the resulting economic damage that could really bring the country to its knees. His astute insights should come as no surprise; contrary to his popular image as a cave-dwelling barbarian, bin Laden studied economics and business administration at Saudi Arabia's King Adulaziz University. He was the wealthy and sophisticated scion of an opulent family that grosses about $5 billion annually. Osama was set to inherit a good deal of that wealth, but due to his radicalism, his family allegedly disowned him, and the Saudi government stripped him of his citizenship. Still, he managed to hold on to a decent fortune originally estimated at $300 million. These estimates were lowered in 2004 to about $50 million, which would still make Osama a rich fellow.

Many of bin Laden's associates are similarly wealthy. This is not unexpected, although it contradicts the popular myth that poverty breeds terrorism. According to economist Alan Krueger, who did research on 129 *shahids* (martyrs), terrorists are less likely to be poor than their peers, and more likely to have at least a high school education. "Terrorists tend to be drawn from well-educated, middle-class or high-income families," Krueger found.[4]

Consistent with his education and wealth, in the mid-1990s bin Laden reportedly began playing on foreign stock exchanges, a habit that appears to have continued right up to 9/11. An Italian newspaper reported that al Qaeda may have been "using a Milan stockbroker firm to operate on Europe's money markets."[5] Notably, shortly before the 9/11 attacks there were reports of unusual activity on the Milan stock exchange.[6]

There are many other indications that bin Laden and his collaborators were active on the financial markets in the days leading up to 9/11. For example, the amount of U.S. currency in circulation increased dramatically between June and August 2001. According to economist William Bergman of the Federal Reserve Bank of Chicago, "The August increase alone was the third largest single monthly increase since 1947, trailing only December 1999 (with pre-Y2K concern as well as terrorism threats) and January 1991 (the onset of US military action in Iraq, and an important enforcement month in the BCCI money laundering scandal).... The above-average growth in currency in July and August 2001 totaled over $5 billion." Bergman drew a shocking conclusion from these facts: "[Anyone] mindful that their financial assets might be seized or otherwise at risk after the attacks converted their bank accounts to a more liquid asset before the attacks. Under money laundering and other laws, including those applied in a time of war or a declared national emergency, assets in the banking system can be frozen and seized."[7]

Bergman theorized that this "wartime hoarding" prior to September 11 was undertaken by foreign governments and entities like al Qaeda that had foreknowledge of the attacks.

Bergman's work, unfortunately, has been hijacked by the repulsive 9/11 Truthers, who claim the attacks were part of some bizarre conspiracy by the U.S. government to murder its own citizens. As a result, many terrorism analysts and theorists reflexively discount indications that insider trading occurred in the lead-up to 9/11. It's a shame that analyses like Bergman's have been tainted by the Truthers, since these reports reveal strange and suspicious financial activity that raises very serious questions.

One of the few studies of Bergman's findings was done by the Federal Reserve, which attributed the rising number of dollars in circulation to a financial crisis in Argentina.[8] Similarly, the 9/11 Commission appointed by the U.S. Congress did investigate charges of insider trading and unusual option activity occurring before 9/11. According to the commission, "The investigation found absolutely no evidence that any trading occurred with foreknowledge of 9/11. The transparency of the U.S. securities markets almost ensures that any such trading would be detectable by investigators."[9] The commission's faith in market transparency, however, was later questioned in peer-reviewed academic research conducted at the University of Illinois, University of Zurich, Hong Kong Baptist University, University of Wisconsin, National University of Singapore, and Charles Sturt University in Australia.[10] Furthermore, as we shall see in later chapters, what transparency did exist in 2001 largely disappeared over the next few years, making it even easier for a person, group, or government to launch a covert financial attack on the United States.

Notwithstanding the 9/11 Commission's blinkered findings, the 9/11 attacks were surrounded by highly unusual circumstances on the financial markets aside from the currency increase noted by Bergman. For example, on August 2, 2001, the Federal Reserve Board of Governors sent a non-routine supervisory letter to all of its member banks. Without explaining why it was being sent, the letter instructed recipients to keep an eagle eye on Suspicious Activity Reports (SARs). Investigating SARs, the Reserve said, "provides useful information on suspicious activity being identified by the reporting institutions." The Reserve encouraged banks to "continue to conduct a thorough and timely review of all material SARs filed by supervised financial institutions in their districts." It continued, "This review is an integral component of the supervisory function. A periodic, comprehensive review of SARs will assist Reserve Banks in identifying suspicious or suspected criminal activity occurring at or through supervised financial institutions; provide the information necessary to assess the procedures and controls used by the reporting institutions to identify, monitor, and report violations and suspicious illicit activities; and assist in the assessment of the adequacy of anti-money laundering programs."[11]

And "suspicious illicit activities" were certainly evident on the markets. Shortly before the 9/11 attacks, Reuters later reported, there was a spike in airline options activity. German bankers told reinsurer Munich Re they were seeing a significant uptick in airline options activity, a way of betting against the airlines. "We have received reports that those associated with the terrorist activities of last week may have sought to exploit our securities markets to profit from those activities," explained Stephen Cutler, the top enforcement officer at the SEC, on September 20, 2001. "We are vigorously pursuing all credible leads, but at this time, we have drawn no conclusions." One market maker on the Chicago Board Options Exchange told Reuters there had been heightened activity on United Airlines—whose planes were used in two of the four airborne attacks on 9/11—for the September 30 and October 30 "puts"; in other words, somebody was shorting huge amounts of United Airlines stock, perhaps anticipating it would take a hit after 9/11. "They bought them before (the attacks) and the month before, September 6 and August 6, the October and September 30 puts," he stated.[12]

Munich Re was the source of many of the borrowed stocks used for the short selling, a practice in which a trader typically borrows shares of some stock and later sells them at the current price, making a profit if the price falls. One banker reported that several major French banks had made inquiries about borrowing extensive numbers of shares of Munich Re. "These inquiries were very big in size and they only asked about one share, and for that reason it stood out," he averred. One German banker outside Munich Re reported there were inquiries for millions of shares. "If somebody would be looking for that many," he told Reuters, "it would be super-obvious. The share price would go through the floor. . . . Even at 500,000 we would be immediately looking into the company to see if there was something fundamental going on, a takeover or some news." Remarkably, volatility in United Airlines shares increased dramatically—by 30 percent—between September 4 and September 7.[13]

All this certainly looks like terrific, high-level financial manipulation. Prior to September 11, September and October 30 United Airlines puts—meaning the puts' owners could sell them at $30 per share—were very low. (The stock was already trading well above $30, so the right to sell at $30 wasn't useful.) After the terrorist attacks, the puts climbed rapidly as stock prices dropped to $20 per share. The options were "worth at least five times their pre-attack price."[14] This begs an important question: Did bin Laden make a bundle of money from the attack?

On September 19, CBS reported that on September 10, the put trading for American Airlines—whose planes were used in the other two attacks on 9/11—exceeded the call trading. This meant that people were short selling—and doing it so much that sources had "never seen that kind of imbalance before." Furthermore, CBS found that on September 6 the put and call trading for United was also "extremely imbalanced." The network reported, "Now US investigators want to know whether Osama bin Laden was the ultimate inside trader; profiting from a tragedy he's suspected of masterminding to finance his operations." George Constantinides of the University of Chicago observed, "It's hard to attribute it to chance. So something is definitely going on." Columbia University law professor John Coffee and Professor James Cox of Duke University School of Law agreed. [15]

This is not conclusive, of course; there have been high put/call ratios in the past that had nothing to do with terrorism or insider trading. As Allen Poteshman of the University of Illinois writes, "It is clear both that there is a good deal of prima facie evidence that the terrorists or their associates traded in the option market ahead of the September 11 attacks, but at the same time that there are a number of reasons to suspect its probative value." Nonetheless, after investigating the numbers in great detail, Poteshman declared, "I conclude that option market activity does provide evidence that is consistent with the terrorists or their associates having traded ahead of the September 11 attacks.... It does appear that significant abnormal option market positions were established that would profit from the decline of one of the airline stocks most directly affected by the attacks."[16]

The Investment Dealers Association of Canada told its members that the SEC identified a total of thirty-eight companies whose shares were traded at a far higher level than usual in the weeks prior to 9/11. The AP reported that the companies included General Motors, Raytheon, Continental, Delta, Northwest, Southwest, U.S. Airways, Boeing, and Lockheed

Martin. The *Wall Street Journal* also revealed that the government was investigating the high-volume buying of five-year Treasury notes, which are typically picked up when people expect a recession, a war, or both. "The Journal," reported the *San Francisco Chronicle*, "said agents of the U.S. Secret Service…have contacted a number of bond traders regarding the unusually large purchases, including one $5 billion transaction." "We will do everything within our power to track those people down and bring them to justice," railed SEC Chairman Harvey Pitt to Congress.[17]

Dr. Hugh McDermott, senior lecturer in law enforcement at the Charles Sturt University Australian Graduate School of Policing, explains how terrorists can easily exploit the markets to profit from their plots:

> When terrorists have "inside information" about an imminent attack, they purchase financial derivatives before the attack and make millions from the subsequent market movements…. Global financial markets reacted swiftly to the news of the terrorist attacks on New York (2001), Madrid (2004) and London (2005), with a general flight to quality. Gold, bonds and defence stock strengthened and investors flocked to highly liquid, developed markets. In contrast, less mature markets suffer as do stocks such as reinsurance and aviation. American Airlines' share price dropped 39 per cent after the 9/11 attacks and United Airlines dropped 42 per cent. Even a novice trader can see the windfall that could be achieved in shorting these stocks before a terrorist attack.[18]

Derivatives on Munich Re were trading at double their usual volume in the days before 9/11, according to the German Stock Market Commission, and the firm's share price fell 22 percent after the attacks. On September 7, 2001, put options on British Airways were four times the usual; its stock dropped 42 percent after the attacks. On September 10, 285 times the normal volume of United Airlines put options were bought. The International

Organisation of Securities Commissions said that all this amounted to "the most important crime of insider trading ever committed." In light of these facts, McDermott dismisses as "implausible" the 9/11 Commission's assertion that there was "no evidence that anyone with advance knowledge of the terrorist attacks profited through securities transactions." As McDermott notes, "Short selling was up 11 percent on airlines due to the global downturn following the 'dot com bust,' but it was up around 40 percent on United and American Airlines. Surges in call options on gold and oil were also not explained."[19]

Profiting from attacks is not merely a theory—many traders did it as the 9/11 assault occurred. David Yarrow, managing director of the British hedge fund Clareville Capital, made spectacular profits by shorting airline stocks after the first plane hit the World Trade Center.[20] Rogue trader Jérôme Kerviel, who was prosecuted in 2009 by the French government for nearly bankrupting financial services giant Société Générale, said that September 11, 2001 marked "the best trading day in the history of Société Générale.... It seems that profits were colossal that day."[21]

If these traders could make money by reacting quickly to the 9/11 attacks, then bin Laden and his accomplices could certainly exploit their foreknowledge of the atrocity to similar ends. And they even had religious sanction to do so; chapter eight of the Koran instructs, "Enjoy, therefore, the good and lawful things which you have gained in war, and fear Allah." Later in the same chapter, the Koran states, "The unbelievers shall expend their riches in debarring others from the path of Allah. Thus they dissipate their wealth: but they shall rue it, and in the end be overthrown. The unbelievers shall be driven into hell."

September 11, of course, was not the first Islamist attempt to attack the U.S. economy, nor would it be the last. The World Trade Center had long been their ideal target. According to the 9/11 Commission Report, "Like [Ramzi] Yousef, KSM [al Qaeda terrorist Khalid Sheikh Mohammed] reasoned he could best influence U.S. policy by targeting the country's economy. KSM and Yousef reportedly brainstormed together about what drove the U.S. economy. New York, which KSM considered the economic capital of the United States, therefore became the primary target." Later, as we know, the approved target list came to include "the White House, the U.S. Capitol, the Pentagon, and the World Trade Center." The 9/11 attack "was to be a serious attack intended to produce massive casualties and serious damage to the economy, but it was also very much designed to be a symbolic assault—one that would strike the symbols of U.S. economic, political, and military power."[22]

In 2000, al Qaeda terrorists in Yemen attacked the USS *Cole*. Although the ship was "capable of simultaneously tracking hundreds of incoming missiles or aircraft more than two hundred miles away," according to Lawrence Wright in *The Looming Tower*, it was not prepared for a low-tech terrorist attack. When a fiberglass boat carrying two smiling and waving jihadists approached, the *Cole* did nothing. Then the boat exploded, blowing out the side of the ship and causing shock waves over two miles away. In typical fashion, bin Laden viewed the attack through the prism of the American economy. After the explosion he crowed, "The destroyer represented the capital of the West, and the small boat represented Mohammed."[23]

Of course, symbolism wasn't enough for al Qaeda—its leaders were determined to attack the U.S. economy directly. Secretary of Defense Donald Rumsfeld worried, "The cost-benefit ratio is against us! Our cost is billions against the terrorists' costs of millions."[24] Said bin Laden, "Every dollar of al Qaeda defeated a million [U.S.] dollars.... We are continuing this policy in bleeding America to the point of bankruptcy. Allah willing, and nothing is too great for Allah." Bin Laden boasted about his ability to create massive defense spending per terrorist: "All that we have to do is to send two mujahedeen to the furthest point east to raise a piece of cloth on which is written al Qaeda, in order to make generals race there to cause America to suffer human, economic and political losses without their achieving anything of note other than some benefits for their private corporations." Bin Laden always focused specifically on the economy—all his thoughts seemed geared toward it.[25]

Following a failed assassination attempt on Pakistani President Pervez Musharraf in 2004, Pakistani security agencies arrested numerous al Qaeda operatives. One of those was Abu Musab al-Baluchi, the nephew of notorious 9/11 planner Khalid Sheikh Mohammed and the cousin of Ramzi Yousef, the 1993 World Trade Center bomber. Baluchi's capture in turn led to the apprehension of Muhammad Naeem Noor Khan, a Pakistani tasked with delivering communications to al Qaeda operatives. When the Pakistani agencies arrested Khan, they found a cache of computer disks and a laptop that contained pictures of financial institutions throughout the United States. In response, the United States raised its terror alert status, especially with regard to "financial sectors in New York, Washington and Newark."[26]

In one of bin Laden's final tapes released prior to his death, he called on people everywhere to stop buying U.S. goods and U.S. dollars. Attempting to garner leftist support for his agenda, he also ripped America's inaction on global warming. "George Bush junior, preceded by Congress, dismissed the [climate change] agreement to placate giant corporations," bin Laden spat. "And they are themselves standing behind speculation, monopoly and soaring living costs.... Noam Chomsky was correct when he compared the US policies to those of the Mafia. They are the true terrorists and therefore we should refrain from dealing in the US dollar and should try to get rid of this currency as early as possible. I am certain that such actions will have grave repercussions and huge impact."[27] If bin Laden had the means, is there any doubt he would have pursued this strategy—as would other enemies of the United States?

★ ★ ★

Here are the facts: first, with foreknowledge of the 9/11 attacks, al Qaeda terrorists could have turned a big profit by trading in advance of the operation. Second, according to press reports, as early as 1995, bin Laden and al Qaeda were active in financial markets. Third, Osama came from a wealthy family and was educated in economics and business. Fourth, in the run-up to 9/11, there were unusual and suspicious activities on the financial markets, including the short selling of stocks of airlines involved in 9/11. And fifth, as a result of this short selling shortly after the attacks, the international press and German regulators widely speculated that the perpetrators may have been behind these trades.

Osama bin Laden always focused on hitting the U.S. economy, and he got his wish on September 11. It would not be the last time. When bin Laden was killed, U.S. forces found plans to directly attack Europe's economy—on September 6, 2011, Pakistani police arrested Younis al-Mauritani, an aide to bin Laden, who was planning to attack Europe's economic infrastructure by using speedboats to bomb pipelines, tankers, and dams.[28]

Regarding the topic of this book—the threat of financial terrorism since the market collapse of 2008—it doesn't really matter if al Qaeda exploited the markets to cash in on 9/11; even if it didn't, the financial fall-out of 9/11 made it obvious that terrorists could manipulate the markets. The Dow never opened on September 11, 2001, but when it did reopen on September 17, it suffered theretofore its worst single-day point decline in history, dropping 684 points.[29] Terrorists, like everyone else, surely noticed that anyone who shorted the market before the attacks stood to make a huge profit. And in fact, suspicious trading patterns surrounded the attacks, prompting various investigations of possible stock manipulations. Although the 9/11 Commission eventually rejected reports of stock manipulations—a conclusion some analysts have strongly disputed—at a minimum, analysts and the authorities generally agreed that the reports should be investigated. Oddly, when indications arose in late 2008 that someone had carried out a far more concentrated attack on the U.S. economy itself, almost no one investigated the reports—the puzzle pieces were all in plain sight, but no one fit them together.

Whether terrorists traded in advance of 9/11 or not, they were made aware afterward that such activity would have been profitable and that they could cash in on a future attack. As we will see, after 9/11 the American homeland did not suffer another large-scale terrorist attack until 2008. But when it came, it was much more sophisticated than 9/11 itself and caused far more damage to the American economy. It plunged the entire world into near depression—and bin Laden and his associates couldn't have been happier.

CHAPTER TWO

A BRIEF HISTORY OF
ECONOMIC WARFARE

Financial terrorism seems like a fantasy to many folks, who naively believe that nobody could manipulate the markets and sink America's major financial institutions while covering their tracks. Historically, however, economic warfare, including financial terrorism, has been a common tactic. The difference between economic warfare and financial terrorism is that economic warfare is state-sponsored action taken against another state's economy to coerce its government into certain activity, while financial terrorism is secret, behind-the-scenes manipulation of a nation's economy by state or non-state actors.

If war, as Clausewitz said, is the continuation of politics by other means, then economic warfare and financial terrorism are simply war by other means. There are no bullets, bombs, or battles. There are only money and resources used to push states to pursue or not to pursue certain policies. While many attempts at economic warfare and financial terrorism are ineffective, at their extreme these tactics can provoke shooting wars and cripple a national economy. In the near future, it's not inconceivable that these types of asymmetrical warfare could wipe entire countries from the globe.

Traditional economic warfare involves measures such as blockades, tariffs, currency manipulation, and embargoes. As this chapter will demonstrate, these were the primary economic weapons used throughout the last century. In the 1930s, currency and trade wars dominated the international scene, contributing to the outbreak of World War II. In the 1940s, the Nazis routinely counterfeited foreign currency as a wartime tactic. During the Cold War, the United States and the Soviet Union regularly attacked each other's economies, for example, by creating restraints of trade to prevent the other side from funding its military weapons programs. In recent decades, Arab states have repeatedly resorted to economic warfare to coerce the West into pressuring Israel.

Economic warfare, in fact, began long before the twentieth century; as long as there has been warfare, there has been economic warfare, and as long as there has been terrorism, there has been financial terrorism. What makes the current version so dangerous is the sophistication and intricacy of today's financial weaponry—derivatives, hidden orders, high-frequency trading, anonymity, and the interconnectedness of the markets.

What follows is a short collection of case studies outlining the history of economic warfare over the last few centuries and showing how it has influenced some of the world's key conflicts.

THE BASICS: FROM THE SEVEN YEARS' WAR TO THE CIVIL WAR

During the 1700s and 1800s, the chief version of economic warfare was the blockade, undertaken largely by Great Britain, the great naval power of the time. Opposing powers eventually hit upon a clever way to avoid such blockades: they used neutral countries to transport their products. The Dutch, then the other great naval power, became the blockade-runner of choice. The rule was "free ships, free goods": if a neutral power ran the ships, the goods on the ships were considered neutral, even if they were intended for enemies of Britain.

All that changed during the Seven Years' War. British jurists invented the "Rule of the War of 1756," which decreed that "a neutral has no right to deliver a belligerent from the pressure of his enemy's hostilities, by trading with his colonies in time of war in a way that was prohibited in time of peace." This established the concept that what you do matters just as much as who you are—a notion that hedge fund traders and executives would be wise to take into account these days as they funnel cash from America's enemies onto U.S. markets.

The British heavily engaged in other forms of trade war as well. Due to the popularity of mercantilist economics—which emphasized state-sponsored economic activity such as imposing tariffs, establishing colonies, subsidizing exports, and restricting wages and domestic consumption— many states began embroiling themselves in fierce trade competition. According to scholar Tor Egil Førland in the *Journal of Peace Research*, "Seeing the volume of international trade (and of gold and silver) as more or less static, nations considered they could enrich themselves only by taking over the trade of other countries. One way of accomplishing this was wrestling colonies from competitors through wars, simultaneously taking over the carrying trade.... In the seventeenth and eighteenth centuries the application of mercantilist theory led to a series of colonial wars involving Britain, France, Spain and lesser powers."[1]

Napoleon employed economic warfare to great effect against the British. He prevented the import of British goods into French-controlled territory, while simultaneously exporting tremendous amounts of French goods into Britain. The British, he said, were free to buy as much French merchandise as they wanted, so long as they paid in gold. Napoleon's policy did hurt the British, though it failed to achieve its goal of destroying the British economy as a prelude to a French invasion of Britain. Moreover, his efforts created a serious problem: by eradicating British imports, Napoleon effectively raised the price French subjects paid for many goods. As Førland points out, "Napoleon's weapon of economic warfare turned out to be a boomerang."[2]

During the Civil War, the Confederacy also attempted to levy indirect economic warfare on Britain and France; the goal was to coerce them into joining the war against the North by cutting off their supply of cotton. This, too, ended in failure, as the Confederates cost themselves a great deal of cash sorely needed for the war effort.[3]

These examples show that economic warfare is often a two-edged sword: it sometimes achieves the desired ends, but almost invariably, it cuts the initiator to the bone.

THE OLD-FASHIONED BLOCKADE: PEARL HARBOR AND OIL

In the late 1800s and early 1900s, the Japanese used traditional mercantilist policies to rapidly industrialize and militarize their island nation. As Winston Churchill noted, "In less than two generations, with no background but the remote past, the Japanese people advanced from the two-handed sword of the Samurai to the ironclad ship, the rifled cannon, the torpedo, and the Maxim gun; and a similar revolution took place in industry."[4]

Around the turn of the century, after defeating Russia and China in wars, Japan secured resource bases in Taiwan, Korea, and Sakhalin. After World War I, in which the Japanese fought on the side of the allies, Japan's militaristic regime was emboldened by the nation's military triumphs and growing economy. In 1931, the Japanese invaded Manchuria, a situation depicted with some accuracy in the movie *The Last Emperor*. Fearing a possible conflict with the Soviet Union, they then signed a defense treaty with Nazi Germany. In another belligerent move, the Japanese blockaded ports in East Asia as they attempted to bring vast swathes of the continent under Japanese control in an area euphemistically called the Greater East Asia Co-Prosperity Sphere.

Alarmed at the extent of Japan's aggression, the United States seemed to be on a collision course with Emperor Hirohito's army. In Europe, America was covertly backing Britain against Japan's ally, Nazi Germany. After Japan, encouraged by the Nazis, began creeping into French Indochina, President Roosevelt imposed an embargo on steel and scrap metal supplies to Japan. The Japanese responded by pushing farther into Indochina, and FDR countered by freezing all Japanese assets in the United States.

Days later, Roosevelt delivered the decisive blow, ordering an oil embargo against Japan that effectively cut off 90 percent of the empire's oil supply and extinguished three-quarters of its foreign trade.[5] Churchill recounted the events:

> For several months the British and American Governments had been acting towards Japan in close accord. At the end of July the Japanese had completed their military occupation of Indo-China. By this naked act of aggression their forces were poised to strike at the British in Malaya, at the Americans in the Philippines, and at the Dutch in the East Indies. On July 24 President Roosevelt asked the Japanese Government that, as a prelude to a general settlement, Indo-China should be neutralized and the Japanese troops withdrawn. To add point to these proposals, an executive order was issued freezing all Japanese assets in the United States. This brought all trade to a standstill. The British Government took simultaneous action, and two days later the Dutch followed. The adherence of the Dutch meant that Japan was deprived at a stroke of her vital oil supplies.[6]

This threw Japan's war machine into crisis, forcing its Navy to rely on its precarious oil reserves. Recognizing the choice that had been thrust upon the Japanese, Churchill commented, "It was evident that this was a stranglehold, and that the choice before them was either for Japan to reach an agreement with the United States or go to war."[7]

The Japanese requested a meeting between their prime minister and Roosevelt, ostensibly to propose a deal: Japan would give up certain assets—

but not all of them—in Indochina and China in exchange for an end to the U.S. oil blockade. The United States refused the request, believing with some credibility that the Japanese would interpret such a deal as a sign of appeasement. On November 27, 1941, the United States told the Japanese that it would only sell them oil if they left Indochina and China forthwith—and that it would only send enough oil for civilian needs. Furthermore, the United States sent Japan a ten-point note demanding that China remain under the full control of General Chiang Kai-Shek, who was fighting both the Japanese and Mao Tse Tung's Communist guerrillas. Secretary of State Cordell Hull fumed that Churchill had gotten his way—the United States would be forced into war. "The diplomatic part in our relations with Japan is now virtually over," he said. "The matter will now go to the officials of the Army and Navy, with whom I have talked…. Japan may move suddenly and with every possible element of surprise."[8]

On December 7, Hull's predictions came true. The Japanese, who planned to seize the oil fields of the Indies but knew the move would provoke an armed conflict with the United States, decided to strike first by attacking Pearl Harbor.[9]

Here's the point: economic warfare often leads to real warfare. This was the case during World War II, although of course, Japan itself provoked U.S. sanctions by rampaging across Asia and allying with Hitler.

During wartime, the United States doubled down on its economic warfare policies. FDR instituted a Board of Economic Warfare tasked with securing the resources necessary to pursue the war—and to preventing our enemies from doing the same. Dean Acheson, assistant Secretary of State during World War II, explained the strategy: "We waged economic war on foes and friends within their grasp alike, spreading deprivation with even-handed harshness."[10]

As part of this policy, the United States economically bludgeoned neutral states that aided the Germans. The campaign yielded some benefits, but neutral countries often refused to bend to the Allies' will. In August 1943, for example, the Allies proposed to make concessions to the Swiss in return for the Swiss cutting off arms supplies to the Germans. Switzerland indicated it was interested. According to Acheson, however, when the Swiss opened their books, the Allies "learned the shocking truth that, instead of reducing exports to Germany in the second quarter of 1943, the Swiss had actually increased them over the first quarter by from fifty to a hundred percent. They also withheld the figures from the British and ourselves until after the agreement was made." The Allies threatened "postwar retaliation and cancellation of all import permits" and even threatened to blacklist some Swiss firms, but the Swiss would not budge.

In sum, although economic warfare is a powerful weapon that can even provoke a shooting war, the tactic is not always successful—especially when the target faces more immediate threats, like sharing a border with Nazi Germany.[11]

THE SOPHISTICATED GAME: OPERATION BERNHARD

In 1939, members of Adolf Hitler's Security Service (*Reichsicherheitsdienst*) proposed that the Germans destroy the British currency by counterfeiting millions of pounds worth of banknotes. By deceitfully inflating the British currency, the value would collapse, hindering the Brits from buying the goods and services needed to win the war. At first Hitler rejected the plan as "dishonorable," but eventually he embraced part of it, instructing his underlings to begin paying German spies and fellow travelers with forged notes. This would serve the dual purpose of allowing Germany *not* to pay these operatives and allowing these individuals to become dispensing points for fake British currency.

Major Bernhard Krueger, after whom the operation was named, led the German Security Service's Forgery Division, creating fake papers for its operatives. Forging banknotes on this scale was an immense task—after all, banknotes are the most highly scrutinized pieces of paper in the world. Fortunately, Krueger had the ultimate supply of cheap labor hidden away in concentration camps all over Europe. Jewish inmates were selected for the job and rewarded with better living conditions.

Krueger began by having his slaves create five-pound banknotes. He mixed up the paper from Turkish flax obtained through Italy, ensuring that every detail of the notes, down to the way the ink absorbed into the paper, was accurate. He even sent a batch of counterfeited currency to Switzerland to see if bankers could tell it was fake—and they could not. Even the Bank of London was fooled.

Every month, Krueger's men turned out over £500,000 worth of currency to be distributed in Britain. Soon, with demand by his distributors outstripping supply, they began asking for £50 notes. Over the course of the year, Krueger expanded his operation and increased his staff to number nearly 150. His team created millions' worth of banknotes each month and even branched out to print U.S. dollars. The fakes were so good that they circulated quite normally; in fact, Krueger's agents began receiving their own forged notes when trading other currencies. In a noteworthy move, Krueger asked for—and received—medals for his prisoners.

Krueger's operation was so successful that it forced the Bank of England to withdraw all notes larger than £5 from circulation during the war and to change the paper on which the £5 note was printed. Near the end of the war, the Bank of England banned all pound notes from £10 to £1,000. Krueger's scheme only ended when the war drew to a close. The prisoners were lucky enough to escape.[12]

Despite its vast scale, Operation Bernhard wasn't nearly comprehensive enough to truly damage the British currency—and because it was launched late in the war, it did not have much time to achieve its objectives. However, examining Operation Bernhard is instructive. If the operation had succeeded, it would have knocked the British out of the war. Adding hundreds of millions of pounds into the British economy could have seriously undermined Britain's floating currency.

It's a lesson well worth learning, especially when we consider the many weaknesses of the U.S. dollar today. Here's one example: the North Korean regime runs its own version of Operation Bernhard aimed at the United States. According to David Rose of *Vanity Fair*, North Korea is home to a secret agency called Office 39, directly overseen by the nation's dictator,

Kim Jong Il. That office used messengers to launder counterfeit "super-notes" worth millions of dollars through the casinos in Las Vegas. According to Rose, "Most of the notes have ended up in general circulation." David Asher, head of the State Department's Illicit Activities Initiative from 2003 to 2005, further explains, "In one sense, Office 39 is like an investment bank. It provides the money for the stuff Kim needs. Like any organized-crime syndicate, you've got a don, and you've got accountants, and it's a very complicated business, keeping track of all this money and making sure the boss gets paid. But when members of the organization don't deliver, they get killed."

Office 39, not coincidentally, handles Kim Jong Il's personal bank accounts in Switzerland and sells missiles to foreign countries. Overall, Office 39 rakes in between $500 million and $1 billion per year or more. That's not enough to substantially damage U.S. currency holdings, but it spreads uncertainty that can create risks. As Rose reports, "In 2004, Taiwan's central bank issued a warning that supernotes had been turning up on the island. This caused a panic, and the Taiwanese banks were overwhelmed by customers seeking to return $100 bills totaling hundreds of millions of dollars, most of them perfectly genuine."[13]

The high-quality counterfeits are essentially indistinguishable from the real bills. The United States has even had to force the shutdown of foreign banks that act as distributors for the North Korean supernotes. And the scale of the counterfeiting does not seem to be diminishing: in 2007, the North Koreans bought enough paper to print $2 billion.[14]

THE BIG GAME: THE COLD WAR

Shortly after World War II, with the Soviet Union seizing large swaths of Eastern Europe, the United States began slapping economic sanctions on Moscow. In March 1948, the Department of Commerce restricted exports to the Soviets and their satellite states. Under the Export Control Act of 1949, the United States refrained from sending any sort of strategic materials to the Soviets. We followed this up with the 1951 Battle Act, designed to punish countries helping the Soviets import strategic materials, including oil drilling equipment.[15]

Such trade restrictions became de rigueur during the Cold War. Before the communist takeover of Cuba, for example, the United States was the largest buyer of Cuban sugar, purchasing nearly 60 percent of Cuba's exports. Once Castro seized power, America instituted an embargo that nearly crippled the industry, after which the Soviet Union filled the gap. Over time, the Soviets spent more and more money on Cuba, effectively relieving it of the need to compete on the world market. In the late 1980s, the Soviets bought up between 50 and 60 percent of Cuba's sugar exports at an insane markup—in 1987, the Soviet Union paid Cuba a whopping forty-two cents per pound for sugar, even though the average world price was just six cents per pound. That was actually the low water mark for the 1980s—during the decade as a whole, more than 80 percent of Cuban sugar was exported to the Soviet Union. Meanwhile, the Soviets sent oil so cheaply to Cuba that Castro began re-exporting it at prevailing world prices. This largess turned Cuba into a reliable Soviet ally, but over time it became an increasing burden on the Soviet economy.

During the 1970s, the United States loosened some of its anti-Soviet trade restrictions, lowering barriers especially to wheat exports in reaction to a Soviet grain crisis. These conciliatory moves only encouraged more belligerence among Soviet leaders. Leonid Brezhnev told senior party officials in 1972, "We communists have to string along with the capitalists for a while. We need their credits, their agriculture and their technology. But we are going to continue massive military programs, and by the mid-1980s, we will be in a position to return to an aggressive foreign policy designed to gain the upper hand with the West."[16]

After his election as president in 1980, Ronald Reagan changed the American strategy against the Soviets from a policy of containment to one pursuing victory. The core of this strategy was economic warfare. Exploiting the inherent weakness of the Soviet economy (which was smaller than the economy of California alone), Reagan turned the dollar into a weapon, subjecting the Soviet economy to unrelenting pressure. He began by forging an alliance with Saudi Arabia and convincing the desert kingdom to increase its oil production, thereby lowering world oil prices. This move undercut the Soviets' chief economic export—oil—and forced them to ramp up production to compete.[17]

Reagan also pushed for a technological embargo on the Soviet Union, but he arranged for the Soviets to get hold of one particular type of technology. According to Thomas Reed, who was a member of Reagan's National Security Council, the United States allowed the Soviets to steal technology specifically designed to malfunction. This was a clever maneuver, especially because the Soviets were planting Soviet intelligence officers into all their supposedly friendly delegations—for example, every Soviet cosmonaut who worked with the Apollo/Soyuz flight was a KGB officer. "Within a few months, the shipments began," Reed recalled. "'Improved'—that is to say, erratic—computer chips were designed to pass quality-acceptance tests before entry into Soviet service. Only later would they sporadically fail, frazzling the nerves of harried users." Used to sabotage the Soviet oil and fuel system, these chips caused the largest natural gas explosion in world history—a blast along a trans-Siberian pipeline so large that measuring agencies thought a 3-kiloton nuclear device had been detonated.[18]

The program was called "Farewell," and as Reed pointed out, the "campaign was cold-eyed economic warfare, put in place to inflict a price on the Soviet Union for corrupting the lofty ideals of détente. While there were no physical casualties from the pipeline explosion, there was significant damage to the Soviet economy. Its ultimate bankruptcy, not a bloody battle or nuclear exchange, is what brought the Cold War to an end."[19]

THE SUEZ CANAL: HOW THE UNITED STATES USED ECONOMIC WARFARE AGAINST OUR ALLIES

The United States employed economic warfare not just against our Cold War rivals, but against our own allies as well. In 1956, the United States cut off Egypt's arms supply, fearing Egyptian leader Gamal Abdel Nasser would attack Israel. Nasser then turned to the Soviet Union for his weapons, prompting the U.S. to withdraw financial support for Egypt's Aswan Dam project. Nasser reacted by nationalizing the Suez Canal, which had been under European control.

After encouraging Israel to encroach into the Sinai, the British and the French used the resulting Israeli-Egyptian clash as a pretext to send their troops to regain control of the canal. The move provoked Soviet threats, a Syrian oil embargo, and most damaging for the French and British, the opposition of the United States. CIA Director Allen Dulles denounced the invasion as "the straight old-fashioned variety of colonialism of the most obvious sort." Agreeing with Dulles, President Eisenhower decided to intervene on Egypt's behalf.

Eisenhower realized that Britain's currency was vulnerable. This was a legacy of World War II, which had devastated the British economy. The Brits rebuilt largely by exporting tremendous amounts of products all over the world, building up their balance of payments. According to historian James Hubbard, "British officials saw that half the world's trade was still conducted in sterling and the Treasury imagined that sterling's international role could be enhanced further. The Treasury loosened controls on the sterling balances held in London and inched towards full convertibility of sterling."

Normally, when a country moves toward convertibility, it attempts to centralize enough foreign currency to trade back for its own currency, thus preventing the currency from collapsing. If, for example, the United States wants to allow the dollar to be traded easily with other currencies, we will hold large amounts of foreign capital in store so that we can always get our own currency back. If we did not hold such amounts, people could trade our currency for less and less foreign currency, driving down its value.

That is precisely what happened in Britain during the Suez crisis. Britain didn't have enough reserves to stem a run on sterling, so the Chancellor of the Exchequer asked the United States for help. But instead of assisting our erstwhile ally, America itself began selling sterling, declaring that we would only prevent a currency crisis if Britain withdrew its troops from the Suez.[20] Overall, $650 million was sucked out of British reserves to deal with the crisis, making Britain utterly dependent on other European countries for financial support. The United States increased the pressure by suspending its oil shipments to Europe, creating massive European pressure that helped force France and Britain to capitulate to Eisenhower's demands. As historian D. B. Kunz explained, "Economic diplomacy defined the course of the Suez crisis from beginning to end." In the end, the IMF had to bail out the British to the tune of $1.3 billion, with the United States eventually lending Britain an additional $500 million.[21]

To make matters worse for Britain, after the Europeans succumbed to the pressure and withdrew from the Suez, Nasser's renewed control of the canal gave him a new form of leverage. Not only was he able to control shipments through the canal, but he also became the de facto leader of the Arab world. From that position he urged Arab nations to reduce oil exports, eventually forcing Britain to introduce gas rationing.[22] It was the first of many oil manipulation schemes used by Middle Eastern countries as a weapon against the West.

If Middle Eastern nations have learned from the Suez experience, the Chinese likely have, too. Holding more than $1 trillion in U.S. currency and treasury bonds, Beijing may one day use these resources against us in the same way we used our sterling holdings against the Brits during the Suez crisis.

FULL-SCALE ECONOMIC WARFARE: OPEC IN 1973

After joining the United States in cutting off oil supplies to Europe during the Suez crisis, the Muslim Middle East began to feel its oats. The region was further empowered in 1960 by the creation of OPEC, originally including Iran, Iraq, Kuwait, Saudi Arabia, and Venezuela, and later taking in Libya, the United Arab Emirates, and Qatar, among others. Over time, as

OPEC came to control a greater and greater share of world oil production, its members began to realize they could strongly affect international affairs.

OPEC threw its weight around the U.S. economy during the Nixon administration, when the United States disconnected the dollar from the price of gold and allowed the currency to float freely against other currencies. The dollar quickly lost value, and OPEC, which priced oil in dollars, cut supply, driving up prices. The result was a stagnating U.S. economy—an "oil shock" that prompted the Nixon administration to intervene much more directly in the economy. Fatefully, Nixon also ended oil quotas, setting the stage for America to import massive quantities of oil from OPEC nations. According to Daniel Yergin, author of *The Prize*, "By the summer of 1973, United States imports were 6.2 million barrels per day, compared to 3.2 million barrels per day in 1970 and 4.5 in 1972." At the same time, Saudi Arabia's "share of world exports had risen rapidly, from 13 percent in 1970 to 21 percent in 1973, and was continuing to rise." The Arabs concluded they could use their newfound power to leverage America against Israel.[23]

This proposition was put to the test in the early 1970s when Egypt, led by its new strongman, Anwar Sadat, sought to consolidate its stranglehold on the Suez Canal; at the time, the Israelis were firmly planted on the northern end of the canal. "Sadat aimed not so much for territorial gain but for a crisis that would alter the attitudes into which the parties were then frozen—and thereby open the way to negotiations," wrote Secretary of State Henry Kissinger. "The shock would enable both sides, including Egypt, to show a flexibility that was impossible while Israel considered itself militarily supreme and Egypt was paralyzed by humiliation. His purpose, in short, was psychological and diplomatic, much more than military."[24]

Sadat went to Saudi Arabia and gained the support of King Faisal for a war against Israel. Faisal had one demand: "We want to see a battle which goes on for [a] long enough time for world opinion to be mobilized," he reportedly insisted. By September 1973, with Middle Eastern tensions rising, the United States had begun pulling away from Israel. The Assistant Secretary of State stated on Israeli television, "While our interests in many respects are parallel to the interests of Israel, they are not synonymous with the state of Israel.... There is increasing concern in our country, for example, over the energy question, and I think it is foolhardy to believe that this is not a factor in the situation."[25]

In October, on the holiest day of the Jewish year, Israel was attacked by its Arab neighbors. The Jewish state was caught off guard as the Egyptian Air Force bombed Israeli positions in the Sinai in coordination with Syrian attacks from the north. Despite its earlier equivocations, the United States backed Israel in the conflict. Fearing Arab economic retaliation against the United States, U.S. oil executives opposed Nixon's pro-Israel position. "The whole position of the United States in the Middle East is on the way to being seriously impaired," the chairmen of Exxon, Mobil, Texaco, and Standard of California wrote to the president, "with Japanese, European, and perhaps Russian interests largely supplanting United States presence in the area, to the detriment of both our economy and our security."[26]

When the United States openly sent military supplies to Israel, OPEC withdrew from oil negotiations and began setting prices unilaterally. The cartel decided to cut oil production by 5 percent, vowing to enact additional 5 percent cuts each month until they forced Israeli concessions. When Nixon announced a $2.2 billion aid package to Israel—enough for Israel to maintain parity with the Arab states but not enough for it to win a decisive victory—the Saudis announced they would completely shut off the oil spigot to America, later extending the embargo to other nations. The next planned step, reportedly, was Arab nationalization of all U.S. oil interests in the Gulf.[27] The Europeans quickly came to heel as did Japan. In the end, so did the United States, which pressured the victorious Israelis to make some concessions and pull back some of their troops from Arab territory.

There is an important lesson in the 1973 oil embargo that America, unfortunately, failed to learn: when supplies of America's strategic resources, particularly oil, are not secure, America's enemies are encouraged to act—and they are unafraid to do so, even if their actions do short-term damage to their own economies.

GEORGE SOROS: FINANCIAL TERRORIST?

Nearly every part of George Soros' life has sparked controversy. This includes his childhood in Nazi-occupied Hungary, where the young Soros (originally named Schwartz) worked for the Nazi-established Jewish Council, which handled administrative issues affecting his fellow Jews, including deportations. After the war, Soros traveled to Britain, where he attended the London School of Economics and studied under the great philosopher Karl Popper. In 1970, he founded Soros Fund Management, and shortly thereafter he set up another hedge fund, taking in $12 million in investors. This became the famed Quantum Fund.

Soros quickly earned a reputation for being a brilliant and unscrupulous market operator. He made his bones shorting the living hell out of the British pound and bringing Britain to its knees. Soros conducted this legendary machination in 1992, when the pound faced serious problems due to an economic recession. Since 1979, the pound had been traded on the European Exchange Rate Mechanism (ERM); Britain had joined in an attempt to stabilize its currency and peg it to other European currencies, an arrangement that presaged the rise of the euro. Due to rising interest rates in Germany and a depreciating dollar, the pound began rapidly losing value, raising doubts about whether Britain could maintain the exchange rate necessary to stay in the ERM.

Recognizing the currency was already on the brink, British Prime Minister John Major refused to devalue the sterling. At that point Soros pounced, shorting $10 billion worth of pounds and forcing the sterling value down. As economic historian Dan Briody put it, "In essence, Soros was betting against Major and his ability to prop up the sagging pound. It has been called the highest stakes poker game in history. Currency speculators were either to believe in Major's ability to save the pound or Soros' intent to eviscerate it. Soros won."[28]

On September 16, 1992, the British government attempted to raise interest rates in order to increase the value of the pound. But their efforts were futile, as Soros' short selling prompted more and more traders to short as well. Soon there was a run on the pound, which lost value hand over fist. "On Black Wednesday," writes Briody, "the pound crashed, crippling the British economy and embarrassing the prime minister. Soros made a profit of $950 million."[29]

In light of Soros' ruthless attack on the British pound, other governments have suspected him of instigating the collapse of their currencies. In 1997, Malaysian Prime Minister Dr. Mahathir Mohamad blamed Soros for the collapse of the ringgit, whose value plunged 20 percent in the summer, taking the Malaysian stock market down with it. This had all the hallmarks of a Soros-style bear raid. Mahathir, a virulent critic of Israel, blamed the collapse on international Jewry in general and on Soros in particular (though ironically, Soros himself is a strident detractor of Israel and its American supporters). "We have definite information that [Soros] is involved," declared Mahathir. "He is not the only one but he started it. He has wiped out billions from our economy." While it's unclear whether Soros initially shorted the ringgit, we do know that he ended up *buying* the currency as it plunged, believing it was ready to hit rock bottom and reverse course. "[Mahatir] is using me as a scapegoat to cover up his own failure," Soros argued. "He is playing to a domestic audience, and couldn't get away with it if he and his ideas were subject to the discipline of an independent media inside Malaysia."[30]

Regardless of the role he may have played in the collapse of the ringgit, countries everywhere have reason to fear powerful traders like Soros. His activity even attracted the attention of at least two colonels in the Chinese Army, Qiao Liang and Wang Xiangsui. In *Unrestricted Warfare*, a seminal study of Chinese military strategy that recommends economic warfare as a primary means of attacking the United States, the two officers commented,

> During the 1990's… we began to get an inkling of a non-military type of war which is prosecuted by yet another type of non-professional warrior…. Perhaps he or she is a systems analyst or a software engineer, or a financier with a large amount of

mobile capital or a stock speculator.... His or her philosophy of life is different from that of certain blind and inhuman terrorists. Frequently, he or she has a firmly held philosophy of life and his or her faith is by no means inferior to Osama bin Laden's in terms of its fanaticism. Moreover, he or she does not lack the motivation or courage to enter a fight as necessary. Judging by this kind of standard, who can say that George Soros is not a financial terrorist?[31]

Whether a financial terrorist or not, Soros can launch powerful financial attacks that have far-reaching effects on entire nations. And as we will see, if Soros can do this, so can others—people who are motivated by something other than making money.

★ ★ ★

In the past, the main global threats to the United States were aggressive state actors such as Nazi Germany, Imperial Japan, and the Soviet Union. Now, however, the art of war has morphed and expanded. As Qiao Liang and Wang Xiangsui argued in *Unrestricted Warfare,*

Precisely in the same way that modern technology is changing weapons and the battlefield, it is also at the same time blurring the concept of who the war participants are. From now on, soldiers no longer have a monopoly on war. Global terrorist activity is one of the by-products of the globalization trend that has been ushered in by technological integration. Non-professional warriors and non-state organizations are posing a greater and greater threat to sovereign nations, making these warriors and organizations more and more serious adversaries.[32]

It should be clear that economics can be warfare by other means. Whether via blockades or embargoes, counterfeiting or short selling, America's enemies can and will find ways to strike us without using arms. It is one thing to kill thousands of American soldiers on the battlefield—that requires immense amounts of money, weapons, and manpower. But attacking America's economic infrastructure requires different resources: money and creativity. It doesn't require suicide bombers or standing armies or big arms caches. It requires only motive, means, and opportunity.

As we will see, our enemies had them all in September 2008. And they still have them today.

CHAPTER THREE

IT GETS PERSONAL

D espite all the storied history of economic warfare, I was fairly oblivious to the threat until a few years ago. During the bulk of my business career, the United States had been the economic king of the hill,
particularly in the investment markets. By October 2007, with the exception of the 9/11 attacks (from which we were recovering) and the dot-com
bubble (which was fast becoming a memory), we had experienced an
uninterrupted 30-year-long boom market. The Dow Jones Industrial Average surpassed the 14,000 mark—quite a surge from the 1,000 level where
it stood when I graduated from the University of Tulsa in 1983. Sure, the
market had crashed in 1987—but even at the lows of the crash, it was up
more than double over the preceding five years.

It was during the 1987 crash that I met my future employer, famed billionaire stock investor Sir John Templeton. The night before we met, Sir
John had been the featured guest on *Wall Street Week* with Louis Rukeyser,
where he delivered a simple message: people should buy stocks because
things were much better than they seemed. The crash had thrown Wall
Street into utter disarray; program trading had wiped 40 percent off share

prices in two months, with the bulk of the losses coming in a few hours. But Templeton was spreading hope, and he was right—the stock market increased 6-fold over the next dozen years.

There were, of course, the occasional investing bumps and bruises. When the dot-com bubble burst in 2000, it wasn't really a surprise to many traders; after all, start-ups with nothing more than an idea and a website shouldn't have multi-billion dollar valuations. Even the real tech companies such as Microsoft, Cisco, and Intel were significantly overpriced, selling at 70 times or even 100 times what they would earn in a good year. In other words, we were overdue for a serious bear market.

I went to work for Sir John in 1990 when he asked me to write a business plan for a new division targeting what he termed "the middle market." Starting from scratch, under the leadership of Jerry Ledzinski in Carmel, California, we built a $2.5 billion client base in less than a decade. We had a good track record, avoiding the high-flying, overpriced tech shares. After I left Templeton in early 2000, I was pleased to see that the strategy continued to perform well even as the Dow fell almost 20 percent between the start of 2000 and September 7, 2001, the last trading day before 9/11.

While the 9/11 attacks took a serious toll on the U.S. economy, we knew it would eventually recover. By 2006, the market was back to all-time highs. Granted, the economy was on steroids to a certain degree, as we will explain in chapter six. But all in all, stocks were not overpriced—with continued economic growth, it seemed everything would work out just fine. Some of the best economists were projecting a new global boom based on urbanization trends in emerging markets. Oil prices were down (falling to $50 per barrel by January 2007), unemployment was low, and the budget deficit was shrinking despite the expensive war in Iraq. This was the kind of environment in which good stock pickers make a lot of money for their clients. And I was just getting back into money management after taking a sabbatical to start a family.

As a Templeton disciple, I focused on finding good bargains for clients and then holding them long enough for the market to recognize their value.

With a decent economy and market, my strategy worked well. There was one exception, however: one stock I picked fell victim to short selling. In hindsight, the short sellers were probably right—the company was overly dependent on Chinese suppliers, and that created a vulnerability. Nonetheless, I was struck by the power short sellers had to drive down stock prices, and I began studying their tactics closely. What I discovered was unnerving. Over a few years, the number of traders who profited from declines in stock prices had grown dramatically. Once focused only on fraudulent companies or overpriced shares, short sellers had begun pummeling a vast array of stocks, some of which had solid fundamentals and would not normally have been vulnerable to this type of attack.

Other indicators made me nervous as well. Between January and July 2007, the price of oil jumped 50 percent to $75 per barrel. Moreover, the *Wall Street Journal* had published a report on new ways for sharia compliant funds—that is, financial institutions run according to Islamic law—to start short selling. I knew this would open up the big sovereign wealth funds—government-run investment funds popular in Middle Eastern petrol states—to join the growing list of financial players trying to profit from a market decline. Despite all this, the Dow Jones Industrial Average continued to climb, setting a new record above the 14,000 mark in October 2007.

Then things turned bad. Following the October peak, stock prices dropped 7 percent over the next two months. I pored over my research to determine if this was a minor correction or the start of a new bear market. I dug deep, company by company, to make sure my portfolios were well-positioned either way. I left for the Christmas holiday comfortable that my client holdings would do well in the new year. Little did I know what was to come.

In early 2008 the housing bubble began to pop and other structural problems began rippling through the economy, all magnified by credit default swaps, as explained in chapter five. As the economy weakened, oil prices rose rapidly, flirting with the $100-per-barrel level from November

2007 until February 2008. While many analysts attributed the surge in oil prices to strong global growth, I sensed that world markets were becoming unstable, an inkling that was confirmed by the collapse of Bear Stearns in early 2008; one of America's oldest investment banks fell victim to a short-selling blitzkrieg in just a few days. It was very rare for something of that size to disappear overnight. When I dug deeper, the story became even more unnerving—most of the selling appeared to be an illegal manipulation. Worse, no one seemed to care.

After Bear Stearns was "rescued" by a penny-on-the-dollar fire sale to JP Morgan Chase, the market seemed to recover. Sure, there had been a scare, but by May the Dow was back above 13,000. Meanwhile, oil prices continued rising, hitting $125 per barrel on their way to almost $150 in June. Once again, the conventional wisdom held that this reflected continuing global growth. If that was right, then the stock market would be fine even with a few ups and downs along the way.

But the short sellers were growing bolder. In early summer, mega-investment bank Lehman Brothers began to struggle. Its stock price fluctuated, moving with the market but occasionally dropping sharply on rumors. One of those rumors, later denied by all parties, was that Barclays was going to buy the firm. Normally, talk of a takeover would boost the share price, but that wasn't the case here due to the specifics of the rumor—namely, that Barclays would buy Lehman at a price 25 percent below its market value. If true, this would suggest Lehman was in really bad shape and desperate for a deal. There were other rumors of a Korean firm's interest. The truth was that regulators had begun to consider prospective suitors, including Barclays, just in case they were needed as they had been with Bear Stearns. Short sellers were either exploiting the breathless rumors or spreading them themselves in order to drive the stock price down.

By then, I knew more about short selling than I'd ever imagined I'd need to know. Historically, shorting occurred in the shadows of Wall Street. John Templeton never shorted stocks—he made plenty of money owning shares outright. Shorting requires planning for declines in share prices, something many managers viewed as akin to a vulture picking clean the bones of a dying animal. Hedge funds, though, made the practice more respectable. They tended to buy shares they thought would rise in value while shorting shares they expected to decline. That's why they are called "hedge" funds— they would use short positions to hedge against problems with their other holdings. That way, if the stock market declined, their gains on the shorts would more than offset the losses from the shares they owned (called "longs"). If the market went up, their longs should more than offset any losses from their shorts. The goal was to make money for clients in any market environment.

The problem I was seeing in mid-2008 was that the surge in short selling seemed to be much greater than mere hedge fund activity. As I heard more and more traders echo my suspicions, it became obvious to me that the rise in short selling threatened the whole stock market and thus the economy. By this point, the decline in housing and the inflationary pressures of high oil prices were pinching most Americans, and the Federal Reserve seemed to be either asleep at the switch or too conflicted to take action. In July, stocks entered bear market territory and never looked back.

In August, I attended a conference in Minneapolis that coincided with the Republican convention. I was warning everyone at the conference about the threat of unrestrained short selling. At a reception, I even sought out a Republican congresswoman I had met a few years earlier to alert her to the danger—Michele Bachmann from Minnesota. I had met Congresswoman Bachmann when she was a Minnesota state senator, long before she ran successfully for the 6th Congressional District seat; somehow, my wife Marnie and Michele were late to an event at the Capitol and ended up riding there together. Impressed with Michele's focused dedication and priorities, Marnie convinced me to donate a little money to her first campaign for the House. We later hosted a reception for Michele just after she claimed victory in the primary.

Now, I knew that Congresswoman Bachmann was a rising star in the Republican Party and was a member of the House Financial Services

Committee. I thought that if I could get Congress to pay attention to a growing problem, maybe we could fix it before it got out of control. I found the congresswoman and she remembered me. We chatted for a few minutes, and I explained some of the dangerous trends I perceived on the markets. I figured I'd give her a few hours to mull over my warnings and then find her again and press for a more formal meeting in D.C., where I could lay out my concerns in greater detail. That night, however, I received the devastating news that my mother was in an advanced stage of tongue cancer. I immediately dropped my incipient campaign to sound the alarm on stock manipulations. Rather than traveling to D.C., I made plans for regular trips to Tulsa, Oklahoma, to spend as much time with my mom as I could, hoping and praying for her to recover.

As we moved into September 2008, all hell broke loose on the markets. I watched from afar as Fannie Mae and Freddie Mac essentially collapsed. Shortly thereafter, Lehman Brothers went down without a whimper—the giant investment bank was open on Friday and being dismantled by Monday. That was about the time my mom's life expectancy shortened from years to weeks.

On September 29, 2008, the House of Representatives rejected the first incarnation of the bailout program eventually named the Troubled Asset Relief Program, or TARP. The market fell 7 percent on the news, one of the biggest single day declines in history. TARP, an attempt by Treasury Secretary Hank Paulson to stop the escalating financial crisis, was deeply unpopular—conservatives saw it as a government takeover of the banks, while Democrats condemned it as a bailout for the rich. The Bush administration, meanwhile, sold it as a necessary lifesaver for a drowning economy. Somehow, all of them were right.

On October 3, the House approved a new version of TARP that had already passed the Senate, and President Bush signed the bill into law a few hours later. That day, I was attending a board meeting of my alma mater, the University of Tulsa. I had already positioned my client portfolios using John Templeton principles, fully aware that it could be a volatile day for stocks. During a break at the morning meeting, I had a discussion with Michael Noland, one of Tulsa's successful wealth managers. We discussed how strangely the market had been acting. We had seen the sharp drop a few days earlier and wondered if the approval of TARP would spark a rally. The market did jump in anticipation of a positive vote on TARP but turned down in the afternoon.

Over the next week, the market plunged another 25 percent. The Friday after TARP passed, I sat with my mom in the chemotherapy room with the television on in the background, surrounded by families fighting for the lives of their loved ones. It was surreal to say the least. The Dow touched the 8,000 level that day before a violent afternoon rally took it back up 10 percent.

The crucial breakthrough came that same week, when I received a call from my good friend and former business partner Erik Davidson, a senior investment officer at Wells Fargo. Erik had called to see how I was doing and to pray for my mom. A frequent guest on CNBC and a financial analyst par extraordinaire, Erik knew that I had been focusing on short selling.

"Kevin," he said after our conversation turned to the market, "have you ever considered that short selling could be used as a tool for terrorists?"

He certainly had my attention. Erik had noticed a suspicious jump in short selling focused on Lehman and other financial services firms starting on September 11. Apparently originating in the Middle East and London, the trades focused on some of the companies hit hardest by the 9/11 attacks—the Wall Street firms housed in and around the World Trade Center. Erik explained that other Wall Street traders had noticed the same thing. I had been focused on the dangers of unbridled short selling, but the possibility of a terrorism element took the problem to a new level. Was this the plan long threatened by Osama bin Laden to destroy our economy?

The market stabilized at lower levels during October 2008. In November, the Dow greeted Barack Obama's election as president with better than a 300-pont gain, taking it back briefly near 10,000 before sinking by one-third over the ensuing four months.

GETTING THE BALL ROLLING

On November 17, 2008, I was invited to breakfast at the Four Seasons in Dallas with John Guandolo, former Marine and FBI Special Agent with a focus on counterterrorism, and Major Stephen Coughlin, an advisor to the Joint Chiefs of Staff in the Pentagon. They were in town giving national security briefings for a friend who thought I should connect with them to learn more about Islamic sharia law and groups seeking to implement it around the world. For my part, I wanted to see if anyone in the intelligence or defense community was investigating the possibility that we had fallen victim to a financial terrorism attack.

At breakfast, Agent Guandolo and Major Coughlin methodically laid out evidence showing how Islamists had quietly infiltrated government agencies and even the national defense establishment. The jihadists succeeded in these efforts largely thanks to a prevailing atmosphere of political correctness in which even obvious Islamic extremists are promoted through the ranks in the name of multiculturalism. The U.S. Senate would eventually expose this catastrophic security failure in a 2011 Senate committee report on the Fort Hood massacre. The searing report pronounced that the Fort Hood attack, in which jihadist Nidal Malik Hasan, a U.S. Army major, murdered thirteen Americans and wounded dozens more, was preventable. "Rather than discipline him or discharge him," declared the committee leaders, Senators Joseph Lieberman and Susan Collins, "Hasan's superiors sanitized his personnel evaluations so that evidence of his radicalization was praised as research on terrorism and Islam."[1]

Guandolo and Coughlin showed me court documents from the Holy Land Foundation terrorism funding case indicating that Islamists have conspired for years to infiltrate the United States. They also shared details of an Islamist plan to destabilize the Middle East—a scheme that matches quite well with the "Arab Spring" uprisings that have already helped to empower Islamists in Tunisia, with a similar result widely expected in Egypt and Libya. My interlocutors even warned me that U.S. Army bases were vulnerable to a jihadist attack from within our own armed forces; a year later, Hasan's shooting spree would prove them right. I was overwhelmed by the gravity of their message. Then, it was my turn.

I began explaining why it increasingly appeared that short selling and other machinations were throwing the markets into turmoil. While I had been concerned by their warnings, they seemed downright frightened by my story. It fit perfectly with everything they knew about terrorists, their plans, and their capabilities. They told me to start preparing a white paper to present to senior Pentagon decision-makers.

Several phone calls and a great deal of research later, I had my first contact with Rich Higgins at the Irregular Warfare Support Group housed in Special Operations/Low-Intensity Conflict (SOLIC) in the Department of Defense. Higgins shared with me a recently declassified letter from President Franklin Roosevelt to his Secretary of War authorizing the War Department to develop a plan for economic warfare. This was the same president who once declared, in reference to the short selling and other bear raids that helped bring down the stock market and usher in the Great Depression, "Unrestrained financial exploitations have been one of the great causes of our present tragic condition." FDR's economic warfare letter provided historical justification for a study of financial terrorism, and his quote hinted at where to start—looking into short selling and bear raids. Higgins wanted a white paper from me as soon as possible, so I got right on it. Ironically, I delivered the report the day after Bernie Madoff was arrested for running a Ponzi scheme whose scale was nearly unimaginable.

On January 5, 2009, I received word that my mom had slipped into a coma. We rushed to Tulsa and I spent the night and all the next day with her in the hospital. While I was there, Rich Higgins introduced me by email to Patrick Maloy, a former Wall Street type and Marine officer. We had a two-hour phone call the next morning beginning at 2:00 a.m. Maloy shared how he had been tracking financial terrorism for several years; he had first been alerted to the danger while in Iraq, and he had gathered additional evidence in North Africa and at other stops in the Middle East, sending in reports to the Defense Department, which eventually paired him with me.

On January 16, I received an email informing me that the President's Foreign Intelligence Advisory Board (PFIAB) had reviewed my white paper and was seeking additional information. I responded to some of their questions, and they replied, "Brilliant email. The PFIAB is about to start asking some hard questions." The board was concerned that the CIA and our intelligence apparatus were behind the curve on financial terrorism and needed to catch up quickly. On February 20, SOLIC gave me the green light to conduct a formal study of financial terrorism and its possible connection to the 2008 market crash. Less than a week later, on February 26, news outlets reported that potential "doomsday scenarios" were circulating in the D.C. intelligence community. These reports precisely matched my white paper.[2]

By March 6, the Dow reached a new low of 6,500—a decline of almost 55 percent that marked the worst bear market since the Great Depression. Two days later, I began writing the report with the insightful advice of Pat Maloy. On March 18, David Kotz issued a scathing report as Inspector General regarding the SEC's failure to investigate, let alone enforce, naked short selling abuses.[3] On March 23, George Soros penned an op-ed for the *Wall Street Journal* titled "One Way to Stop Bear Raids," which attributed the financial meltdown largely to short selling and credit default swaps.[4] The information flow reinforced our efforts. We kept researching and the data kept expanding. From March through May, we received tips from government contacts and private individuals around the globe.

On May 13, I made my first visit to the Pentagon. After participating in a high-level briefing, it seemed as if my concerns were being taken seriously, and the federal government was prepared to do whatever necessary to protect the American people. They recognized that Americans needed answers and objectivity, that people deserved to know why their 401(k) had suddenly shrunk into a 201(k). On May 16, I attended a national security briefing where I met Frank Gaffney, who heads the Center for Security Policy. When I shared my research with him, he offered full support. We seemed to be getting traction in addressing a serious problem. Our next step was to finalize the report and then disseminate it.

On June 26, 2009, I presented a formal copy of the report, "Economic Warfare, Risks and Responses; Analysis of Twenty-First Century Risks in Light of the Recent Market Collapse." In the next chapters, we will discuss the theory behind that report, detail the evidence, and lay out the case that financial terrorism not only decimated the U.S. economy in September 2008, but that it still threatens our economy today.

CHAPTER FOUR

THE MOTIVE

From the British during the Civil War to the Japanese and Germans during World War II, from the Soviets during the Cold War to communist China today, America has always had enemies with motive to do us harm. Today, the United States, as the world's hegemonic power, has become the primary target of those who oppose the world order; some nations seek to supplant us, some groups aim to bleed us, and some individuals seek to profit from our downfall. These various enemies are increasingly sophisticated and increasingly apt to resort to economic warfare or financial terrorism.

In order to understand how a network of our enemies perpetrated the greatest act of financial terrorism in American history, we first have to understand who these enemies are.

America's enemies can be grouped into three categories: terrorist groups, state terror sponsors, and individuals who want to see America's capitalist economy replaced with a more redistributive one. All three types of enemies stand to profit from America's downfall. Some of these groups are even ready to engage in the fiscal equivalent of a suicide bomb—willingly damaging themselves in order to harm us. In fact, some of them have already done so.

We will now discuss each of these types of enemies and show how they all share a common interest in sabotaging the U.S. economy.

TERRORIST GROUPS: "JIHAD WITH MONEY"

Often underestimated, al Qaeda has been a formidable foe to the United States for the last two decades. After the Islamic terror group pulled off the 1993 World Trade Center bombing, the United States treated the situation as a law enforcement investigation, failing to bring al Qaeda's foreign-based leadership to account. President Clinton, seemingly more concerned by a potential over-reaction among Americans than by the bombing itself, explained to an interviewer,

> I don't want the American people to overreact to this at this time. I can tell you, I have put the—I will reiterate—I have put the full resources of the Federal Government, every conceivable law enforcement information resource we could put to work on this we have. I'm very concerned about it. But I think it's also important that we not overreact to it. After all sometimes when an incident like this happens, people try to claim for it who didn't do it. Sometimes if folks like that can get you to stop doing what you're doing, they've won half the battle.[1]

Three years later, the coordinated bombings of the Khobar Towers in Saudi Arabia by al Qaeda-connected terrorists elicited tough talk from President Clinton. "The explosion appears to be the work of terrorists," he declared. "The cowards who committed this murderous act must not go unpunished."[2] But once again, al Qaeda did, in fact, go unpunished, and the terror group struck again in 1998 when it simultaneously bombed the U.S. embassies in

Tanzania and Kenya. President Clinton responded by ordering missile strikes in Afghanistan and Sudan, proclaiming, "Our mission was clear—to strike at the network of radical groups affiliated with and funded by Osama bin Laden, perhaps the preeminent organizer and financier of international terrorism in the world today."[3] Strangely, Clinton appeared to believe that firing a few missiles, with no additional follow-up, was enough to finish off the world's "preeminent organizer and financier of international terrorism."

Our string of weak responses to al Qaeda attacks strengthened Osama bin Laden's belief that the United States was a paper tiger. Emboldened, al Qaeda bombed the USS *Cole* in Yemen's Aden port in 2000.[4] Once again, Clinton reverted to the law enforcement approach, explaining, "If, as it now appears, it was an act of terrorism, it was a despicable and cowardly act. We will find out who was responsible, and hold them accountable. If their intention as to deter us from our mission of promoting peace and security in the Middle East, they will fail, utterly."[5]

The United States was caught off guard by all these attacks, as it was on 9/11. And today, we are still failing to imagine how our enemy can evolve and devise new tactics and strategies. Some politicians and analysts have downplayed the continuing threat posed by al Qaeda, arguing the group is only capable of limited terrorist strikes, not mass warfare. This is a fundamental misunderstanding of the situation, for al Qaeda doesn't need to take on U.S. Marines on the battlefield in order to do massive damage to the United States. In fact, they don't need any military capability at all—they can simply launch a financial terrorist attack. And with the deaths of bin Laden and Yemen-based al Qaeda chief Anwar al-Awlaki, the group's focus on non-traditional attacks will likely increase.

According to Charles Duelfer, former director of the Iraq Survey Group, and Jim Rickards, former general counsel to Long-Term Capital Management, "Al Qaeda has declared that damage to the American economy is its second most important goal after mass casualties. Presently, who would warn the White House if foreign entities made a concerted attack on our financial system? Who is charged with detecting such activity?"[6]

The answer: nobody. Professor Shawn O'Connell of St. Thomas University warns of the true danger we face: "If Islamic terrorists further pursue Economic Terrorism without an organized Western response, the impact upon [the] economy and tax-derived defense will be massive. Also, such attacks won't be isolated, but recurrent—given the small cost of assaults and massive potential reward.... Ultimately, as the poor and overmatched Islamic terrorists pursue their struggle against the West, they realize this is the best 'small war' strategy of all."[7]

Al Qaeda is not alone. Other terrorist groups with the financial wherewithal and the will to attack the U.S. economy include Hamas, the Palestinian wing of the Muslim Brotherhood; Hezbollah, the Iranian-backed terrorist group based in Lebanon; Abu Sayyaf of the Philippines; and countless other organizations along with their various branches and spin-offs. Terrorist groups across the world now recognize the power of targeting financial infrastructure. In July 2011, members of the Jama'atu Ahlis-Sunna Lidda'awati Wal Jihad, a Nigerian terror group, attacked several banks. Their spokesman announced, "We took the measure because the mode of operations of the banks was not based on Islamic tenets."[8]

Part of the problem is that the aims of al Qaeda and many other Islamic terror groups are widely misunderstood. They do not merely wish to convert the entire world to Islam—which alone would give them incentive to attack the U.S. economy. They also seek to force every country to adopt *sharia*, an all-encompassing system of Islamic law. While sharia's myriad penalties against Christians, Jews, and women are well known in the West, the system also includes specific financial stipulations that have attracted far less attention. These requirements are embodied in a collection of rules known as sharia compliant finance (SCF), which may be the fastest growing economic system on the planet.[9] In accordance with ancient Islamic teachings, SCF prohibits the taking of interest. However, it allows investment so long as the capital provider "is willing to share in the risks of a productive enterprise."[10] Never mind that lending at interest is itself investment, since the lender accepts the risk of default—SCF draws a false distinction between the two. SCF also rejects transactions involving gambling, speculation (*gharar*—a vague term subject to debate), and contracts that involve uncertainty or give rise to gharar. In order to solve the various economic problems these prohibitions create, Islamic scholars have devised clever interpretations and loopholes to create sharia-compliant investing methods that achieve the same ends as typical financial instruments.[11]

SCF may seem benign, but its framework was largely created over a century by the Middle East's Islamic extremists extraordinaire, the Muslim Brotherhood. According to scholars Rachel Ehrenfeld and Alyssa Lappen, the chief architect of modern SCF infrastructure, Muslim Brotherhood founder Hassan al Banna, "designed political, economic, and financial foundations to enable Muslims to fulfill a key form of *jihad* mandated by the *Qur'an*—financial *jihad*."[12]

Yusuf Qaradawi, an Egyptian Islamic theologian and host of *ash-Shariah wal-Hayat* ("Sharia and Life") on al Jazeera—a show with an audience of 60 million spanning the globe—is widely considered the world's foremost authority on financial jihad. A leading figure tied to the Muslim Brotherhood, he publicly endorses attacks on civilians, including suicide bombings—in his words, "Allah Almighty is just; through his infinite wisdom he has given the weak a weapon the strong do not have and that is their ability to turn their bodies into bombs as Palestinians do."[13] He also celebrates the Holocaust, stating, "Throughout history, Allah has imposed upon the Jews people who would punish them for their corruption.... The last punishment was carried out by Hitler. By means of all the things he did to them— even though they exaggerated this issue—he managed to put them in their place. This was divine punishment for them.... Allah willing, the next time will be at the hand of the believers." In case his call for genocide against the Jews was unclear, he expressly prays for it: "Oh Allah, count their numbers, and kill them, down to the very last one."[14]

Qaradawi reportedly believes Muslims have a religious obligation to do what they can to harm the U.S. economy, especially by boycotting the United States. He also insists that Muslims everywhere send "money for the *mujahideen,*" or Islamic fighters. These contributions are not gifts or charity, according to Qaradawi; they are a "duty necessitated by the sacrifices [the mujahideen] made for the Muslim nation." He leads an organization that helps direct this kind of financial activity—the seemingly misnamed "Union for Good," which comprises fifty Muslim Brotherhood groups including many openly affiliated with Hamas and al Qaeda. He is also on the advisory board and has been one of the largest shareholders of the al-Taqwa Bank, which the U.S. government designated as a terror funding operation for bin Laden.[15] "I like to call it Jihad with money, because God has ordered us to fight enemies with our lives and our money," Qaradawi told the BBC in July 2006.[16]

Qaradawi isn't alone in emphasizing financial jihad. According to Muslim Brotherhood spiritual leader Hamud bin Uqla al-Shuaibi, financial jihad is "more important ... than self-sacrificing." The goal of financial jihad, explains Dr. Hussein Shehata, professor at al-Azhar University in Cairo, is for Muslims to "purify the soul from stinginess"—and of course, to convert infidels to Islam. Dr. Abduallah Qadiri al-Ahdal, professor at al-Medina University, says that "financial jihad applies to all [Muslims] in accordance with each person's capability. No excuse can dismiss anyone from donating money to the *mujahideen* and their families." A favorite book of al Qaeda explains simply, "Money is the lifeline of jihad."[17]

What is the end goal of the financial jihad? Muslim Brotherhood founder Banna's goal was to "work towards establishing an Islamic rule on earth." To do that, Banna recommended creating a parallel economic structure to free Muslims from the supposed tyranny of the capitalist system. This is the same system preached by Osama bin Laden in his so-called "Letter to the American People":

> We call you to be a people of manners, principles, honour, and purity; to reject the immoral acts of fornication, homosexuality, intoxicants, gambling, and trading with interest.... You are the nation that permits Usury, which has been forbidden by all

religions. Yet you build your economy and investments on Usury.... You are a nation that permits gambling in its all forms. [*sic*] The companies practice this as well, resulting in the investments becoming active and the criminals becoming rich.[18]

To replace capitalism with SCF, capitalism must first be destroyed, as bin Laden understood. Immediately after 9/11, he explained how crucial it was to target the financial heart of the United States:

> I will talk briefly and concentrate on the need to continue the jihad action, militarily and economically, against the United States.... The economic bleeding is continuing to date, but it requires further strikes. The young people should make an effort to look for the key pillars of the US economy. The key pillars of the enemy should be struck, God willing. They shook America's throne and struck at the US economy in the heart.... This is a clear proof that this international usurious, damnable economy—which America uses along with its military power to impose infidelity and humiliation on weak people—can easily collapse. Thanks to Almighty God, those blessed attacks, as they themselves admitted, have inflicted on the New York and other markets more than a trillion dollars in losses.... It is very important to concentrate on hitting the US economy through all possible means.[19]

Bin Laden believed America's economic infrastructure was particularly vulnerable. Al Qaeda's supporters "know the cracks in the Western financial system like the lines on their own hands," he told a Pakistani journalist in 2001.[20]

Bin Laden's hatred of capitalism is characteristic of Islamic terrorists. Monin Khawaja, a Canadian citizen who attended Pakistani terror training camps and was later convicted of participating in a bomb plot in Great

Britain, wrote, "We have to come up with a way that we can drain their economy of all its resources, cripple their industries, and bankrupt their systems in place, all so that they are forced to withdraw their troops, so they cannot afford to go to war.... We need constant economic [jihad], blow after blow, until they cripple and fall, never to rise again."[21]

This anti-capitalist animus forms the basis of a natural alliance between Islamic terror groups and Marxists. Sayyib Qutb, Banna's successor as chief of the Muslim Brotherhood, merged the concept of financial jihad with basic Marxist principles. Qutb thought communism was "natural and logical" in fighting capitalism, since "the spirit of the West lacks the generous and human aspects of true human life." As shown in Andrew McCarthy's *The Grand Jihad*, Qutb often sounds like a militant leftist. For example, according to Qutb, rulers ought to have

> wide powers, which touch every aspect of life; and the establishment of social justice in all its aspects is a matter that is bound up with these powers. A ruler may, for example, go beyond the legal requirements in the matter of money; in addition to the *zakat*, he may introduce other taxes by which to encourage equality and justice; by these he may check malice and ill-feeling, and by these he may remove from the community the evils of luxury and penury, as well as that of artificially high prices, all of which evils are the product of the growth of excessive wealth.[22]

As NPR reported in 2003, "Qutb's writings would later provide the ideological impetus for many radical Islamic groups of today—including al Qaeda."[23] This ideological bedrock provides common ground for many of America's communist enemies and her Islamic enemies the world over.[24]

There is a reason why radical Muslims across the globe celebrated the disastrous events of September 2008 just as they had celebrated the 9/11 attacks—it's all part of the jihad against the West and especially against

America. A broad panoply of Muslim newspapers suggested that the collapse of the U.S. financial infrastructure stemmed from America's adherence to non-sharia finance. As Lahem al Nasser, head of The Islamic Solutions Center, a sharia finance organization, wrote in the world's premier pan-Arab daily newspaper, *Asharq Al-Awsat*, "The global financial crisis has shaken the foundation of capitalism all over the world, from the rich North to the poor South, from democratic regimes to dictatorial ones. Voices were raised everywhere; I am talking of course about the Muslim writers and intellectuals who predicted the collapse of capitalism, and the bankruptcy of capitalist countries, announcing that the Islamic financial system would soon prevail."[25]

ISLAMIC STATE SPONSORS OF FINANCIAL TERRORISM: ABOLISHING CAPITALIST "SLAVERY"

Muslim states have often rallied around the same set of anti-Western, anti-American, and Islamic supremacist values that are championed by al Qaeda and other Islamic terrorist groups. Saudi Arabia leads the way, pushing the SCF agenda more effectively than any other country. This is achieved in part simply through the Saudis' support of the Muslim Brotherhood. King Saud bin Abdulaziz provided the cash for the Brotherhood's creation of the Islamic University in Medina with the purpose of pushing the Brotherhood agenda—including SCF—abroad. Furthermore, according to Ehrenfeld and Lappen, "In 1962, the MB [Muslim Brotherhood] convinced the king to launch a global financial joint venture, which became the cornerstone and engine to spread Islam worldwide."[26] Finally, Saudi Arabia's Fiqh Academy in Jedda issues economic *fatwas*, or rulings on Islamic points, which correspond closely with the Muslim Brotherhood agenda.[27]

To Westerners, the Saudis portray SCF as an innocuous Islamic financial code. These soothing appeals have beguiled more than one representative of the U.S. government. For example, in November 2008, Frank Gaffney of the Center for Security Policy reported that Deputy Secretary of the

Treasury Robert Kimmitt seemed pleased to tell the Saudis that "the US government is currently studying the salient features of Islamic banking to ascertain how far it could be useful in fighting the ongoing world economic crisis."[28]

Saudi Arabia is hardly the only Muslim state to embrace SCF. In fact, the vast majority of Islamic states support SCF as well as the global sharia agenda. Dr. Mahathir Mohamad, as prime minister of Malaysia, founded the Islamic Financial Services Board (IFSB) in 2002 to develop a "universal Islamic banking system" with the purpose of abolishing the "slavery" of the Western international monetary system.[29] And Mahathir certainly understands the immense power of financial terrorism, having accused George Soros of wielding the finance weapon to take down the Malaysian economy.[30] In a PBS interview in July 2001, Mahathir observed, "In the old days you needed to conquer a country with military force, and then you could control that country. Today it's not necessary at all. You can destabilize a country, make it poor, and then make it request help. And [in exchange] for the help that is given, you gain control over the policies of the country, and when you gain control over the policies of a country, effectively you have colonized that country."[31]

Mahathir also demonstrated his familiarity with naked short selling, a particularly destabilizing form of short selling in which the trader shorts a stock without borrowing it first. As Mahathir noted, "As far as the stock market is concerned, we know that players in the stock market can also destroy the stock market simply by short selling. And to short sell you don't even need to have the shares." Interestingly, Mahathir and Soros met and ended their feud in late 2006, when Soros visited Malaysia to promote his book, *The Age of Fallibility*. In another example of the symmetry between the far left and anti-Western Muslims, Soros gushed, "We really did agree… our view of the world is really very similar."[32]

Iran is another global sharia advocate and SCF enthusiast, mandating that all its banking be SCF. In that country, sharia investments are generally overseen by mullahs and sheikhs, who ensure that certain profits get sent to terrorist groups. Iran's central bank is a member of the Islamic Finance Standards Board, alongside the central banks of Sudan, Syria, and the Palestinian Monetary Authority.[33] Iranian President Mahmoud Ahmadinejad, an ardent enemy of the United States and supporter of global terrorism, recently called the Iranian calendar year "The Year of Economic Jihad." His website stated that "economic jihad should be realized in every aspect of all Iranian's lives."[34] The regime is so committed to waging economic warfare against America that it refuses to conduct its oil trade in U.S. dollars even though global oil is priced in dollars.[35]

A similar commitment to SCF is evident throughout the Muslim world. Sudan is 100 percent SCF compliant, and Pakistan is largely compliant as well. Egypt, which has seen a resurgence of the Muslim Brotherhood since Hosni Mubarak was overthrown in the Arab Spring, will undoubtedly be drawn closer to sharia and the SCF agenda. In fact, during the Arab Spring, Yusuf Qaradawi returned to Egypt for the first time since 1981 and held a sermon for a massive crowd of 200,000 people in Egypt's Tahrir Square, a scene that the *Christian Science Monitor* called "a reminder that political Islam is likely to play a larger role in Egypt than it has for decades."[36] As Shadi Hamid, research director at the Brookings Institute's Doha Center in Qatar, explains, "Qaradawi is very much in the mainstream of Egyptian society, he's in the religious mainstream, he's not offering something that's particularly distinctive or radical in the context of Egypt. He's an Islamist and he's part of the Brotherhood school of thought."[37] Libya, too, will likely move toward sharia and SCF in light of the overthrow of Muammar Qaddafi, although under Qaddafi the country was already involved in SCF via the Libya Investment Authority.[38]

Many Islamic nations not only require their citizens to invest via sharia-compliant institutions, they also push SCF through the use of sovereign wealth funds (SWFs)—large pools of wealth invested by governments for their own purposes. According to the non-profit McCormick Foundation, SWFs have become the organization du jour for Muslim states. The state-owned Dubai International Financial Center—which houses nearly 1,000 firms, including many of the world's largest and most powerful asset managers with trillions of dollars under management—has become sharia compliant, creating "an Islamic hedge fund platform, an Islamic finance portal, a commodity exchange (*murabaha*), and Islamic finance institutes." The leaders of Qatar and other Islamic states are even handing over chairmanship of their banks to Qaradawi. In short, the Foundation says, "Given the explosive growth of SCF compared to conventional banking in the Gulf and the strong government support behind this trend, it is very likely that SCF and Gulf-based SWF are rapidly becoming one and the same phenomenon. This would mean that—at some point in the near future, if not already—SWF will become an instrument for promoting and legitimizing Shariah in the West."[39]

NON-ISLAMIC STATE SPONSORS OF ECONOMIC TERRORISM: "A NEW WORLD IS BEING BORN"

The threat of financial terrorism does not arise exclusively from the Islamic world. Many non-Islamic governments are direct competitors of America's capitalist system and seek to weaken American power, while other regimes are out to make a profit by taking the U.S. down a peg. All are willing to work with Islamic states—and sometimes even Islamic terror groups—in order to achieve their goals. Like the Islamic states, these governments often control sovereign wealth funds they can use to manipulate the market.

Communist China has traditionally seen the United States as a long-term enemy, if not its primary enemy. Michael Pillsbury, an expert on the Chinese government and military strategy, explains, "Beijing sees the U.S. as an inevitable foe, and is planning accordingly. We'd be remiss not to take that into account. We must acknowledge that we are facing in China what may become the largest challenge in our nation's history."[40] In one of the countless indications, both large and small, of Beijing's outlook, in May 2011, Britain's *Daily Mail* reported that the Chinese military was developing a first-person shooter game, "Glorious Revolution," with U.S. troops as the targets.[41] This is nothing new; back in 1999, columnist Robert Kagan observed in the *New York Times*, "China's leaders make no effort to conceal the fact they consider the United States an enemy—or, more precisely, the enemy."[42]

The Chinese economy is surging as the United States is mired in recession, encouraging Beijing to believe that America's dominance of world affairs can be brought to an end. "China's leaders are engaged in a war against America. They view us as a threat to their regime and way of life. Hence, they have embarked on a systematic, long-term program to surpass us militarily, economically and politically," says Brett Decker, co-author of *Bowing to Beijing*. "They are willing to do anything—purchase our national debt, steal our intellectual property, spend obscene amounts to buy influence in Washington, engage in extensive espionage in our government and large corporations, and sell sensitive missile and nuclear technology to our mortal enemies—to defeat us."[43]

As a communist regime, Beijing has an ideological interest in the downfall of the United States. It has a financial interest as well; while China, due to its hoarding of U.S. treasuries, would take a significant hit if the U.S. economy collapsed, it has repeatedly expressed interest in replacing the dollar as the global currency. China is beginning to offer yuan-based savings accounts and is negotiating with Russia to set up a non-dollar global currency.[44] Furthermore, as previously noted, in 1999 Chinese colonels Qiao Liang and Wang Xiangsui released an influential report, *Unrestricted Warfare*, which suggested economic warfare as a primary means of fighting America.[45] In *Bowing to Beijing*, Decker and his co-author Bill Triplett accurately note the myriad forms of economic warfare that China has waged against the United States over the past dozen years or so since the publication of *Unrestricted Warfare*, including unfair trading practices, currency manipulation, seizing control of U.S. energy supplies, industrial espionage, technology and intellectual property theft, and of course, using its massive holdings of U.S. debt as leverage to influence U.S. policy.[46] The communist leadership in Beijing has obviously embraced the approach—which includes covertly crashing our stock market.

North Korea's massive program for counterfeiting U.S. currency may also implicate China, since North Korea often serves as a wholly owned subsidiary of Beijing. The counterfeiting scheme is overseen by North Korean General O Kuk-ryol, who sits on the country's National Defense Commission and is tasked with creating a succession plan for the Kim family. David Asher, former State Department coordinator for tracking North Korean activities, said that such counterfeiting amounted to "hundreds of millions of dollars"—and that's just the cases the United States has uncovered. The front company for such counterfeiting is located in China. Asher openly identified the bank that launders the counterfeit cash, declaring, "Banco Delta Asia was washing massive amounts of money."[47]

After losing its superpower status with the downfall of the Soviet Union—an event Vladimir Putin has called the greatest geopolitical tragedy of the twentieth century—Russia is also looking to knock the United States down a notch. Russia harbors powerful criminal elements with substantial resources and ties to Iran, Venezuela, and various jihadist groups, while the Russian government itself provides vital support to Iran's nuclear program.[48] Like Iran and China, Russia chafes under a U.S.-dominated international system and strives to upend the world balance of power.

Despite his temporary demotion from president to prime minister, Putin remains the undisputed strongman of Russia, presiding over a regime that has largely quashed internal dissent and is widely accused of having murdered numerous journalists. In foreign affairs, Putin has consistently acted against U.S. interests everywhere, seeking to recreate a Russian-dominated sphere of influence over the former countries of the Soviet Union as a counterweight to NATO. He has undermined pro-Western forces in Ukraine and intervened militarily against a pro-Western government in Georgia. As previously mentioned, Russia is also looking to form a new reserve currency. It has traded its currency against the Chinese yuan in order to "promote bilateral trade between China and Russia, facilitate the cross-border trade settlement of [the yuan], and meet the needs of economic entities to reduce the conversion cost," according to a Chinese official. Putin was even blunter: "The ruble must become a more wide-spread means of international transactions."[49] In light of these actions—not to mention Putin's comparison of the United States to Nazi Germany—it's clear the Obama administration's vaunted attempt to hit the "reset button" on our relations with Russia has not worked as planned.

Anne Applebaum of the *Washington Post* suggests that the "reset button" language was utterly misconceived. She notes that Russian Foreign Minister Sergei Lavrov, to whom Secretary of State Hillary Clinton presented a symbolic reset button that was embarrassingly misspelled in Russian, believes in

> a vision of the world utterly unchanged by the [reset button]. Speaking to past and present policymakers—several of whom had helped dismember the Warsaw Pact and expand NATO in the 1990s—he offered his own version of those developments, as well as of some more current. Among other things, he said, or implied, that the West lied to Russia; that NATO remains a threat to Russia; that the Organization for Security and Coop-eration in Europe should replace NATO as the primary Western security organization; and that, by the way, Russia has plenty of potential clients for its gas in the Far East should its Western clients ever become problematic. As for Russia helping to pre-vent Iran from developing nuclear weapons—an Obama admin-istration suggestion—Lavrov's only comment was that "there is no proof that Iran even has decided to make a nuclear bomb."[50]

Notably, a recent case brought by Manhattan District Attorney Robert Morgenthau contains elements involving Russia, China, Iran, and the global banking system. Morgenthau suggests that in the Iranian drive to obtain nuclear weaponry, presumably from Russian sources, a Chinese individual helped to launder funds through global banks. Morgenthau reportedly warned Congress that he had already indicted a Chinese citizen and his company on charges relating to Iran's nuclear program. He argued that there is an enormous system of deceitful practices and fraud in place specifically designed to allow Iran to avoid U.S. and international sanctions. In a related British case, Lloyds Bank admitted it had created a "stripping" plan to hide Iran's fingerprints on more than $300 million in wire transfers.[51]

One of Russia's and China's close allies—and an effusive friend of Iran as well—is Venezuela. That nation is led by Hugo Chavez, an authoritarian socialist who became famous for his over-the-top denunciations of President George W. Bush; Chavez referred to Bush alternatively as "the Devil," "Bush-Hitler, the number one mass murderer and assassin there is on the planet," and as "a coward, a killer, a [perpetrator of] genocide, an alcoholic, a drunk, a liar, an immoral person…. A psychologically sick man."[52]

Iran has proven a willing partner in pursuing Chavez's oft-stated goal of curtailing American power. "Let's save the human race, let's finish off the U.S. empire," Chavez proclaimed in 2006 while accepting the Islamic Republic Medal in Iran. "This [task] must be assumed with strength by the majority of the peoples of the world."[53] According to Air Force General Douglas Fraser, commanding officer of the U.S. Southern Command, Iran and its proxy terrorist militia Hezbollah are working with Venezuela. "There are flights between Iran and Venezuela on a weekly basis and visas are not required for entrance into Venezuela or Bolivia or Nicaragua," Fraser notes. "So we don't have a lot of visibility in who's visiting and who isn't, and that's really where I see the concerns."[54] Ominously, Venezuelan defectors have reported that Chavez has been financing al Qaeda's activities, beginning with a $1 million donation in 2002. "Hugo Chavez would not admit it publicly, but in private, he was very impressed with Osama bin Laden's work," *Militares Democraticos* reported.[55]

Frequently expressing his abiding hatred of capitalism, Chavez declared during an April 2009 visit to Iran, "Capitalism needs to go down. It has to end. And we must take a transitional road to a new model that we call socialism." This is where the Islamist rubber meets the socialist road.[56] In conjunction with that speech, Chavez embarked on a world tour to Teheran,

Qatar (for a summit of Arab states), Beijing, and Moscow. In every case, his visit communicated the message that "capitalism must go down" and emphasized the need to foster economic ties in opposition to Wall Street. During a speech in Doha, Qatar, for example, he proposed an oil-backed currency to replace the dollar as the reserve currency. "A new world is being born," announced Chavez. "Empires fall. There is a world crisis of capitalism, it's shaking the planet."[57]

As of May 2009, Chavez had visited Iran no fewer than seven times, and he announced in that month that he would be forming a joint bank with Iran.[58] In light of Chavez's role as a leading advocate of an Islamist-socialist alliance to bring down world capitalism, it should come as no surprise that a Zogby poll found him to be the most popular leader in the Middle East.[59] George Soros was right when he recently named Venezuela, Russia, and Iran as "the enemies of the global world order."[60]

In sum, China, Russia, and Venezuela are the non-Muslim adjuncts in the worldwide Islamist campaign to upend international capitalism and strike down American power.

THE PIGGYBACKERS

As terror groups and hostile states continue attacking the U.S. economy, other players are seeking to profit from its vulnerabilities. In June 2009, according to the *Times of London*, two Japanese men were caught trying to move an enormous sum of fake U.S. Treasury bonds through a border crossing into Switzerland. The sum was so large that it would make these two counterfeiters the fourth biggest investors in U.S. debt, outranking Britain and following Russia. Each of the fake bonds was worth $500 million, plus ten Kennedy bonds with face values of $1 billion. Police reported that even if the bonds were forgeries, their existence indicated a counterfeiting racket "on an unprecedented scale." Police have since announced that the racket was run by the mafia—and oddly enough, the Japanese suspects were released. The Japanese government was utterly confused, announcing,

"We don't know where they are now." If this was a mafia scheme, they had help—the month prior to the arrests, Italian prosecutors announced they had broken open a $1 billion mafia-run bond con in coordination with—surprise, surprise!—officers in Venezuela's central bank.[61]

The astounding face value of the bonds takes this story out of the realm of the criminal and into the realm of financial terrorism and/or economic warfare, with enormous implications for U.S. national security. Ordinary criminals would never counterfeit such large denominations. It's also unlikely that a mafia group would undertake an operation like this if its sole aim was to profit off the fake bonds, because it would be impossible to pass bonds of that denomination. Rather, the most likely purpose of these bonds is to destabilize the U.S. economy and the currency by suddenly flooding the market with them during an economic crisis, when they might be deemed real for a short period. Alternatively, perhaps they could be placed on deposit and used as collateral for other efforts, including the concept of selling short against the box—if U.S. bonds were sold short in that quantity, it could cause a panic run on the dollar. After the damage was done, the sellers could deliver the counterfeit bonds and cash out. This would be a variation of naked shorting in which virtually counterfeit shares are created.

In such a scenario, the mafia could be acting in tandem with some larger entity. This would hardly be unprecedented—the mafia has been involved in market manipulations for years. For example, the whistleblower in the Bernie Madoff case, Harry Markopolos, testified before Congress that Madoff "had a lot of dirty money" obtained from the Russian mob and the Latin American drug cartels.[62] Long before that, in Operation Uptick in 2000, the FBI arrested 120 mobbed-up financiers who had cooked up a scheme to artificially inflate the price of nineteen public companies' stock and then short sell it. According to the FBI, "Twenty-one defendants are charged with participating in a RICO Enterprise consisting of members and associates of the Bonanno and Colombo Organized Crime Families of La Casa Nostra in the New York City area, that allegedly perpetrated massive securities fraud over a five-year period by forging corrupt alliances with members and associates of the remaining three New York City Organized Crime Families; controlling and infiltrating broker-dealers; conspiring with issuers of securities and individual stock brokers; ... The schemers used traditional boiler-room operations and current Internet techniques to carry out their alleged crimes."[63]

Radical labor unions such as the Service Employees International Union (SEIU)—America's second largest union—may also be willing to cooperate with financial terrorists in order to achieve their own economic ends. Director of SEIU Banking and Finance Campaign Stephen Lerner—a frequent visitor to the Obama White House—is involved in a campaign, according to the *Huffington Post*, to "partner with unions and groups in Europe, South America, and elsewhere to build a campaign to hold financial institutions accountable in a global economy."[64] Of course, holding Wall Street accountable is hardly objectionable. But Lerner's project goes well beyond that. Glenn Beck's *The Blaze* got hold of a tape of Lerner speaking at Pace University in March 2011. According to Lerner, he aimed to create a tremendous "strike" against the system of mortgage, student loan, and local government debt payments. Says BusinessInsider.com, this strategy would bring "the banks to the edge of insolvency and [force] them to renegotiate the terms of the loans. This destabilization and turmoil, Lerner hopes, will also crash the stock market, isolating the banking class and allowing for a transfer of power." The first step would be going after J. P. Morgan Chase. In Lerner's words, "We have a very simple strategy: How do we bring down the stock market? How do we bring down their bonuses? How do we interfere with their ability to be rich?"[65]

Leftist financiers like George Soros are likely to piggyback on attacks by financial terrorists. Soros thoroughly understands bear raids—a favorite tool of economic terrorists—and his Quantum Fund made $1.1 billion during the 2008 market meltdown at a time when he himself admits bear raids were triggering the collapse.[66] Soros may not have planned the attack, but once it began, he found a great opportunity to make a buck while contributing to the onslaught against the capitalist system he inexplicably despises.

Soros, in fact, has denounced capitalism again and again. He has written of capitalism, "The main failing of global capitalism is that it is too one-sided: it puts too much emphasis on the pursuit of profit and economic success and neglects social and political considerations."[67] Along the same lines, he has declared, "The system we have now has actually broken down, only we haven't quite recognized it and so you need to create a new one and this is the time to do it."[68] He told *Der Spiegel* in late 2008 that while he made piles of money speculating in currency, "I have the common interest at heart, not my personal interest," adding that European-style socialism "is exactly what we need now."[69] He wrote a piece for the Project Syndicate in 2009 arguing that "the system cannot survive in its present form.... Twenty years after the fall of the Berlin Wall and the collapse of communism, the world faces another stark choice between two fundamentally different forms of organization: international capitalism and state capitalism. The former, represented by the United States, has broken down, and the latter, represented by China, is on the rise." He has also stumped for a "grand bargain that rearranges the entire financial order."[70]

As shown by his ruthless attack on the British pound in 1992, Soros is not averse to sowing chaos in the financial markets for his own gain; and as demonstrated by his generous funding of a galaxy of far-left and anti-capitalist activist groups, he is not shy about pushing to usher in his vision of a new world order.[71]

★ ★ ★

Many entities have a vested interest in the collapse of America's economic infrastructure. Islamic terrorist groups top the list, recognizing that America's military might is based upon its financial might. Educated in economics and management, Osama bin Laden believed taking down the U.S. economy was the key to making America burn. His successors believe it, too.

Those successors need the help of Islamic states, which have the wherewithal to put financial terrorist plans into action. From Pakistan to Saudi

Arabia, from Iran to Dubai, Islamists are ready and willing to sacrifice their own financial fortunes to hurt the United States. Fortunately for them, they don't have to—through methods such as short selling, they can actually profit as they destroy our institutions.

They are aided in this attempt by their allies in rogue states like Venezuela and North Korea, as well as elements in Russia and China, who would love nothing better than to see American-style capitalism collapse. Each nation believes it will help fill the power vacuum created by America's demise.

Finally, there are the piggybackers who make money as the world burns. Like Slim Pickens at the end of *Dr. Strangelove*, they ride the bomb, whooping and waving the entire way down. Only when it is too late will they realize that their future will be a stark change from the luxurious life afforded to them by the capitalist system they have helped to destroy.

All these players had motive to initiate or participate in a financial terrorist attack on the United States. Not all were involved in the catastrophic events of September 2008—but many of them were. And many of them will undoubtedly take part in the next round of financial terrorism, which all indicators show will come soon. And when it does, it will likely dwarf the last attack by an order of magnitude.

CHAPTER FIVE

THE MEANS

As shown in the previous chapter, America's enemies have consistently proclaimed their intent to undermine our economy. In *Unrestricted Warfare*, Chinese colonels Qiao Liang and Wang Xiangsui argue,

> In this era of economic integration, if some economically powerful country wants to attack another country's economy while simultaneously attacking its defenses, it cannot rely completely on the use of ready-made means such as economic blockades and trade sanctions, or military threats and arms embargoes. Instead, it must adjust its own financial strategy, use currency revaluation or devaluation as primary, and combine means such as getting the upper hand in public opinion and changing the rules sufficiently to make financial turbulence and economic crisis appear in the targeted country or area, weakening its overall power, including its military strength.... Even a quasi-world power like China already has the power to jolt the world economy just by changing its own economic policies.[1]

The authors later specify that launching a financial attack doesn't even require a quasi-world power:

> Financial Warfare will undoubtedly be an entry in the 21st Century military jargon. The main protagonist in this section of the history book will not be a statesman or military strategist; rather it will be George Soros. As we see it, a single man-made stock market crash, a single computer virus invasion, or a single rumor or scandal that results in a fluctuation in the enemy country's exchange rates... can all be included in the ranks of new-concept weapons.[2]

Enemies like al Qaeda unquestionably know about such tactics. In fact, bin Laden himself had likely read the colonels' report, which has become an influential study of asymmetric warfare—a topic of crucial importance to a man who led a small band of followers to war against the world's superpower. Moreover, we know from video tapes captured in bin Laden's compound that the al Qaeda chief was obsessed with himself and with reports about his actions. Since *Unrestricted Warfare* mentions him early and often, the report probably did not escape his attention. The Chinese colonels, incidentally, dub bin Laden and George Soros "soldiers in the wars of tomorrow," arguing that combining bin Laden's passion with Soros' tactics would produce a "hyperstrategic" weapon.[3] All indications are that bin Laden took the book's message to heart, including its mention—two years before 9/11—of the World Trade Center as a potential target for another terrorist attack.

So, America's foreign enemies—including communist China, al Qaeda, and others—certainly are familiar with the concept of financial terrorism and have sought to put it into practice. Worryingly, over the past decade, exotic financial instruments have appeared that provide the means for these enemies to damage the U.S. economy while hiding their involvement in the onslaught. We will now discuss what these instruments are, and in later chapters, we will describe how they have been exploited to destabilize

American finance. Stick with us—some of these instruments are complex, which is the precise quality that made them useful to our enemies. In order to protect our markets in the future, we must first understand exactly how these markets work.

OIL MANIPULATION

Many theorists have speculated that the catalyst of the September 2008 financial crisis was not the real estate collapse of 2007, but the run-up in oil prices. Between 2007 and June 2008, oil-producing nations pulled in nearly $1 trillion in excess wealth, filling the coffers of their sovereign wealth funds, many of which subscribe to sharia-compliant finance. This spike in oil prices meant that the value of all OPEC oil in the ground was roughly $137 trillion, equal to the value of all other world financial assets combined, including every stock, bond, private company, government and corporate debt, and bank deposit.

High oil prices can have many causes, one of which is speculative bubbles. According to MIT Professor of Economics Richard Eckaus, "This is an idea that has some backing in financial circles, e.g. George Soros. The spiking price pattern would, itself, suggest it. It is very well known that hedge funds are very active in the oil market and their activity, along with other speculators, has raised the volume of oil transactions far above the volume warranted by ordinary commercial transactions."[4]

Speculation in oil, or so-called "paper oil," has grown exponentially in recent years. Volume increased "from $13 billion to $300 billion" in the five years leading to the 2008 price peak, when "27 barrels of crude were being traded every day on the New York Mercantile Exchange for every one barrel of oil that was actually being consumed in the United States."[5] At the time, there were no supply disruptions to justify the price increase, and demand was actually falling. In a 2009 interview on *60 Minutes*, Dan Gilligan, president of the Petroleum Marketers Association, explained what all this means: "Approximately 60 to 70 percent of the oil contracts in the futures markets are now held by speculative entities. Not by companies that need oil, not by the airlines, not by the oil companies. But by investors that are looking to make money from their speculative positions.... All they do is buy the paper, and hope that they can sell it for more than they paid for it, before they have to take delivery."[6]

When oil prices were spiking, some big Wall Street players unleashed a broad public disinformation campaign denying that price speculation was occurring. This was the gist of the testimony one J. P. Morgan executive gave to Congress. "We believe that high energy prices are fundamentally a result of supply and demand," the executive averred.[7] But according to *60 Minutes*, "Not even J.P. Morgan's chief global investment officer agreed.... The same day [the testimony was given], an e-mail went out to J. P. Morgan clients saying 'an enormous amount of speculation ran up the price' and '140 dollars in July was ridiculous.'"[8]

Strangely, the *60 Minutes* piece refers to testimony from Lawrence Eagles, Global Head of Commodities Research at J. P. Morgan, as does the Senate's website and a contemporaneous *New York Times* article.[9] A document on the Senate's website that is now labeled as Eagles' testimony, however, shows that the testimony was actually given by Blythe Masters, J. P. Morgan's Head of Global Commodities. Interestingly, Masters has been credited with helping to create credit default swaps, a "financial weapon of mass destruction" that seriously weakened the financial markets in the run-up to the 2008 collapse.[10] Regardless of which J. P. Morgan executive actually testified, the *60 Minutes* point is accurate: while at least one of J. P. Morgan's senior executives was telling Congress that oil prices simply reflected supply and demand, the firm was warning its clients that excessive oil speculation was making prices "ridiculous." Even the CEO of Exxon admitted in 2011 that speculation engineered by "high-frequency trading" and "quantitative hedge funds" explained why prices were over $100 per barrel when economic fundamentals would justify $60.[11] Likewise, OPEC has admitted that speculation plays a large factor in price moves.[12]

All the data—as well as plain old common sense—show that speculation plays a big role in oil prices, whether Wall Street admits it or not. The key question is whether such speculative activity could be used for manipulation.

Many people seem to think so but don't want to declare it openly. For example, according to *60 Minutes*,

> Asked if there is price manipulation going on, [Petroleum Marketers Association President] Dan Gilligan told [correspondent Steve] Kroft, "I can't say. And the reason I can't say it, is because nobody knows. Our federal regulators don't have access to the data. They don't know who holds what positions."
>
> "Why don't they know?' Kroft asked.
>
> "Because federal law doesn't give them the jurisdiction to find out," Gilligan said.
>
> It's impossible to tell exactly who was buying and selling all those oil contracts because most of the trading is now conducted in secret, with no public scrutiny or government oversight. Over time, the big Wall Street banks were allowed to buy and sell as many oil contracts as they wanted for their clients, circumventing regulations intended to limit speculation. And in 2000, Congress effectively deregulated the futures market, granting exemptions for complicated derivative investments called oil swaps, as well as electronic trading on private exchanges.[13]

Regardless of the denials on Wall Street and the reticence of others, it takes no particular courage or insight to speak the truth: oil price manipulation is a widespread and longstanding practice. Professor of Economics James Hamilton of the University of California at San Diego notes that ten of the last eleven U.S. recessions were caused by a run-up in oil prices—and most of those run-ups were purposeful contrivances by OPEC with the goal of affecting U.S. foreign policy.[14] As the U.S. State Department recounts,

> The Second Arab Oil Embargo, which lasted from October 1973 to March 1974, posed a major threat to the U.S. economy.... Implementation of the embargo, and the changing nature of oil

contracts, set off an upward spiral in oil prices that had global implications. The price of oil per barrel doubled, then quadrupled, leading to increased costs for consumers worldwide and to the potential for budgetary collapse in less stable economies.... The United States, which faced growing oil consumption and dwindling domestic reserves and was more reliant on imported oil than ever before, had to negotiate an end to the embargo from a weaker international position.[15]

Oil was also used as a weapon by Iran during the 1979 revolution and the ensuing hostage crisis, when oil prices reached a peak that would not be surpassed in inflation-adjusted terms for nearly three decades. In short, oil has frequently been used as an effective weapon since the mid-twentieth century, especially by the Muslim world. And with the relatively recent advent of "paper oil," it became a secret weapon that is extremely difficult to discover.

Islamic extremists today frequently advocate using oil as a weapon against the West. Muslim Brotherhood spiritual advisor and Islamic theologian Yusuf Qaradawi has often spoken of "the weapon of oil," or *Silah al Naft*. According to Walid Phares, former professor of Middle East Studies at Florida Atlantic University and Fox News analyst, "For years now, Salafist web sites and al Qaeda spokespersons have loudly called for an 'oil Jihad against infidel America and its lackeys.' Online material is still circulating. But more revealing are the official speeches by Osama Bin Laden and his deputy on the 'absolute necessity to use that weapon.'"[16]

And that's exactly how Islamic extremists view oil—as a weapon in their existential war against the West.

CURRENCY AND DEBT MANIPULATION

In 2008, Treasury Secretary Henry Paulson explained that the Russian government had made a "top-level approach" to the Chinese at the Summer

Olympics in Beijing, asking them to dump shares in Fannie Mae and Freddie Mac in order to press the U.S. government to bail out the mortgage companies. "The Chinese had declined to go along with the disruptive scheme," wrote Paulson, "but the report was deeply troubling."[17] While the Chinese rejected the Russian overture, the Russians did dump their own Fannie and Freddie holdings. In fact, they entered 2008 with $65.6 billion invested in those bonds and sold out completely during the year.[18]

The Chinese could have gotten away with it. Beijing can manipulate the U.S. currency through its control of huge amounts of U.S. debt, including half a trillion dollars of Fannie and Freddie debt.[19] If the Chinese had followed the Russians and dumped their holdings, it would have sown chaos on U.S. markets.

Echoing *Unrestricted Warfare*, an article in an official publication of the Chinese Communist Party recently warned, "What is the most powerful weapon China has today? It is our economic power, especially our foreign exchange reserves (USD 2.8 trillion)." The article went on to directly endorse economic warfare: "Of course, the most important condition is still that China must have enough courage to challenge the US currency. China can act in one of two ways. One is to sell US dollar reserves, and the second is not to buy US dollars for a certain period of time.... If China stops buying, other countries will pay close attention and are very likely to follow. Once the printed excess dollars cannot be sold, the depreciation of the dollar will accelerate and the impact on Americans [*sic*] wealth will be enormous. The US will not be able to withstand this pressure." This course of action would weaken the dollar tremendously while covering economic warfare with the patina of capitalist legitimacy. The article even boasted that such attacks would be "market-driven and it will not be able to easily blame China."[20]

This article, published in February 2011 in the *Qiushi Journal*, constituted a full endorsement of the *Unrestricted Warfare* doctrine. It admitted the existence of economic secret weapons and whole-heartedly advocated using them.

A direct economic attack on the U.S. Treasury and the U.S. dollar through the dumping of U.S. treasury bonds would send the American economy spiraling downward, possibly leading to a downgrade of U.S. debt. This could lead to rapidly rising interest rates and, conceivably, a collapse of the overall economy. In fact, finance ministers in major emerging market nations—including China, Russia, Iran, and the Arab states—have already discussed such a scenario both in international forums and within their respective countries.[21] In short, an attack against the U.S. monetary system remains an eminently feasible action widely contemplated by our enemies.

BEAR RAIDS

Many people assume that traders always profit when stock prices go up, but that is not always true. Some traders work hard to lower the price of a certain stock or even the entire market. The mechanism for this operation is usually a "bear raid," which is a particular type of short selling. Shorting a stock—that is, borrowing shares and then selling them with the intention of buying them back later at a lower price—is a legal practice that sometimes even improves market efficiency and liquidity. In contrast, bear raids are illegal actions in which a short seller or group of short sellers spread rumors or engage in other machinations in order to force down the price of a stock.

The bear raid has a long, nefarious history on Wall Street as shown in Edwin LeFever's classic book *Reminiscences of a Stock Operator,* which was first published in 1923. Detailing how bear raids operate, the book is widely believed to be the biography of stock market whiz Jesse Livermore, who reportedly made more than $100 million by participating in a series of bear raids in 1929 that crashed the stock market and ushered in the Great Depression. After the crash, widespread concern over market manipulation led to the creation of the Securities Exchange Commission, which almost immediately set out to curb manipulations like bear raids.

Although successful bear raids are a widely recognized phenomenon, some observers deny they are even possible. These arguments often rely on the efficient market hypothesis, which holds that the stock market does such a good job of pricing companies and securities that no one could mislead the market for long. In this view, if a trader began forcing down a stock price in a bear raid, then buyers would quickly step in to purchase the undervalued stocks. This theory, however, discounts the role emotion plays in investing and overstates the degree to which investors act rationally; panics break out in the market quite frequently, especially when brokers are playing with huge amounts of other people's money.

Another argument against the existence of bear raids is the false idea that all investors are guided purely by economic motives. In this view, there are no financial terrorists on the market, only rational economic actors. As previously discussed, however, sovereign wealth funds, sharia-compliant investors, and many others have myriad non-economic motivations, including, among some, the desire to harm the U.S. economy.

Of course, participants in bear raids don't typically discuss their activities in public. As noted by *Knowledge@Wharton*, the online journal for the Wharton Business School at the University of Pennsylvania, this is unsurprising: "No one openly admits to conducting a bear raid since deliberately manipulating stock prices is illegal. But, Wall Street has long believed bear raids can and do take place."[22]

And indeed they do. George Soros is a world leader in bear raids, having conducted the ultimate bear raid in 1992 when he forced Britain out of the exchange rate mechanism. As recounted by Sebastian Mallaby, Soros sold the sterling hand over fist, forcing the Bank of England to defend the currency by buying up millions' worth. "Every hour that went by, hedge funds and banks sold more sterling to the Bank of England, which was being forced to load up on a currency that seemed sure to be devalued. Britain was presiding over a vast financial transfer from its long-suffering taxpayers to a global army of traders."[23] Soros, who has supposedly reformed himself into a paragon of institutional investing, now says, "Up until the crash of 2008, the prevailing (academic) view—called the efficient market—was that the prices of financial instruments accurately reflect all the available information (i.e. the underlying reality). But this is not true."[24]

Of course it isn't true—Soros should know.

CREDIT DEFAULT SWAPS

Traders have developed substantially more sophisticated and efficient versions of the bear raid in the past few years. These weapons of financial destruction rely on complex derivative strategies that operate well ahead of the regulatory framework. They also exploit loopholes and regulatory lapses, making them ideal secret weapons.

One of those derivative strategies is the credit default swap (CDS). These are derivative instruments of the type Warren Buffett once described as "financial weapons of mass destruction carrying dangers that, while now latent, are potentially lethal."[25] CDSs were created by J. P. Morgan in 1994 as a mechanism for bond investors to insure their loans against default. This allowed the lender to free up capital reserves that would normally be held in case any loans went bad. More simply, if you were a lender and you were afraid that your debtor wasn't going to pay you back, you bought insurance against that risk in the form of a CDS.

Those seeking to insure their loans would buy the swaps, in essence paying a fee to another party in exchange for a promise to be compensated in the event of a default. As with most forms of insurance, the greater the risk of default, the higher the premium.[26] Conversely, this also suggests that the higher the premium, the more likely the default.

There are several problems with CDSs. First, they are totally unregulated, subject to neither traditional insurance regulations nor state laws.[27] This led to the second problem: it became possible essentially to buy insurance without an underlying interest in what was being insured. This is the equivalent of a man buying fire insurance on someone else's house; once he has bought it, he has a terrific incentive for setting that house aflame.

Because of that sort of conflict of interest, bucket shop laws were introduced after the 1907 financial crisis to prohibit betting on securities without some stake in the underlying asset. But credit default swaps allow traders to circumvent these restrictions. That's why George Soros called CDSs "instruments of destruction that ought to be outlawed." Soros explained that a CDS creates perverse incentives—when some bondholders own a CDS originated by others, they stand to gain more from the bankruptcy of the originator than by reorganization. Said Soros, "It is like buying life insurance on someone else's life and owning a license to kill him."[28]

The third problem with CDSs is that they have powerful ripple effects, because an unlimited amount of swaps could be written and bought on any issuer. In some cases, the notional value of outstanding CDS contracts was as high as ten times the value of the debt being insured. So if you had a contract for $1 million, you could buy insurance for $10 million. By the same token, there were no restrictions on buying or selling CDSs, so insurers themselves could buy them, thereby making someone else pay in the event of a default. This establishes a chain of buyers and sellers, creating a potential chain reaction through the industry in the event of a default. Due to the lack of transparency, it also becomes virtually impossible to know who owns what until or unless the swaps settle. Even then, because they are private transactions, there is little publicly available information on the settlement and even less available regarding who may have traded the instruments between origination and settlement. Just imagine if a $300,000 home were worth $3 million to strangers around the globe—but only if it caught fire. That's essentially the situation with CDSs.

Fourth, the risk/reward calculus of credit default swaps is asymmetrical. In other words, the cost of a CDS is limited to its purchase price, but the payout in the event of default is much greater. Since a debt can be insured at multiple times its actual value, the profit potential in the case of default becomes virtually unlimited. On the other hand, the sale of a CDS provides limited profit but virtually unlimited risks, thus encouraging speculation to support default.

The most insidious aspect of a CDS is that it is essentially a self-fulfilling prophesy. The mechanism is simple: strong buying interest is reflected in higher prices; the more demand there is for insurance, the higher the premiums. In turn, higher premiums suggest to the market that there must be a greater risk of default. Without ownership transparency, it is impossible to determine if the higher premiums are because of additional buying or greater risk. As a result, the market must conclude that the risk of default rose, which in turn raises CDS prices even higher.

That makes a CDS especially vulnerable to market manipulation. The *New York Times* reports the prescient words of one hedge fund manager: "That is the new template.... All you have to do is buy credit default swaps and spread rumors. No cost to borrow. No accountability." The reporter comments, "In fact, if you buy the credit default swaps and drive up their price, you don't even have to spread rumors. Other investors may conclude that the market knows something, and start selling shares. If you were already short the stock, there is plenty of profit to be made even if you did pay too much for the credit default swaps."[29] Soros seconds the motion: "What makes them toxic is that such speculation can be self-validating."[30]

CDSs have the power to determine the financial viability of virtually any company that depends on credit, regardless of size. For example, General Electric CEO Jeff Immelt once observed that "by spending 25 million bucks in a handful of transactions in an unregulated market," CDS traders could bring down major companies. "I just don't think we should treat credit default swaps as like the Delphic Oracle of any kind.... It's the most easily manipulated and broadly manipulated market that there is."[31]

Twenty-five million dollars to bring down GE, a corporation with a market cap exceeding $100 billion even at the worst of the 2008 crisis? That's a powerful secret weapon.

NAKED SHORT SELLING

In a typical short sale, a trader sells a security he has borrowed, typically from a broker-dealer or an institutional investor. The seller later goes to the open market to repurchase the shares, hopefully at a lower price, and uses these shares to repay the borrowed shares, a process known as "covering the short."

In order to understand naked short selling, it is first important to understand that stock prices are essentially set "at the margin." This means that the last trade, regardless of the volume, sets the price for the stock. As a result, a small number of trades at the margin can radically define the value of a company and ultimately the overall market and the whole economy. In other words, prices can be dramatically affected through the trading of a mere fraction of a company's outstanding shares.

Naked short selling occurs when a trader sells shares without first owning them or borrowing them. The practice is illegal, though a few exceptions are allowed in order to promote short-term liquidity. Unfortunately, regulatory authorities have not strongly enforced provisions against naked short selling in recent years, creating serious vulnerabilities in our financial markets.

Fordham University Professor of Finance John Finnerty explains that "naked short selling can increase the manipulator's profit. A short seller, who profits by buying the shares to cover her short position at lower prices than the selling prices, can drive the price of a stock lower by selling short a larger number of shares. Without enforceable restrictions requiring short sellers to borrow the shares before they can commit to sell, a short seller might destabilize the market for a particular stock through naked shorting."[32] In essence, naked short selling artificially drives up the supply of stock and drives down the price.

Naked short selling also undercuts investor confidence. Similar to the effect of high credit default swap rates, a large short position may reduce a company's ability to raise capital—after all, why buy newly issued stock when you can buy stock out of thin air? With a larger circulation of stock than there is actual stock, a company has trouble floating a secondary stock offering. The company's growth is constrained, a circumstance that can doom a firm to failure.

Using naked short selling, it is theoretically possible to target and attack key companies and industries. As we will see, compelling evidence suggests this is precisely what happened with major corporations like Bear Stearns and Lehman Brothers.

DOUBLE- AND TRIPLE-SHORT ETFS

According to the *Financial Times*, 40 percent of the New York Stock Exchange volume comprises exchange-traded funds, or ETFs—investment funds that are essentially traded and treated like stocks.[33] ETFs generally drive the movement in the stock market at the end of each trading day, when the funds consolidate their gains or losses by selling or buying huge blocks of stock.

Here's how they work: ETFs own enormous pools of stock that provide the basis for the value of the ETF. These stocks are divided into "creation units" that traders buy and sell. There are also short ETFs, which work the same way as normal ETFs except that short ETFs own futures contracts that replicate the short positions.

One problem is that creation units do not always perfectly reflect the price of the stock. So, for example, if the ETF owns two stocks, Stock A and Stock B, and each is worth five dollars, the ETF itself should be trading at $10—but in reality, that's often not the case. Let's say at the end of the trading day, the ETF should be $10, but it's actually trading at $10.10. In that case, traders will buy up Stock A and Stock B, trade them for creation units, and then sell the creation units at a profit over the value of Stock A and Stock B. This will continue until price comes into realignment in a process known as "arbitrage," which is conducted by or through market makers.

Because of the disparities between ETF prices and the underlying stock prices that commonly exist near the end of the trading day, there is a rush to buy and sell stock at that time. If investors pile into an ETF, the buying or selling of that ETF will be concentrated into the final trading hour. So, if investors want to go short, they will buy up shares of a short ETF, and that will be reflected in lots of selling at the end of the day.

"Leveraged" ETFs have also become popular on Wall Street. Here's how they work: ETFs will borrow money to double down on their stock owner-ship. "Double-short" ETFs borrow enough money to double the effects of the market—so, if you gain or lose 1 percent on a normal ETF, you'd gain or lose 2 percent on a double-short ETF. "Triple-short" ETFs do the same thing, only they're leveraged three times over.

According to Tom Lauricella, Susan Pulliam, and Diya Gullapalli in the *Wall Street Journal*, "On eight of the 10 worst days for the S&P 500 [between September 1, 2008 and December 1, 2008], 29% or more of the move took place in the final hour; on three days, more than half the selloff occurred after 3 p.m." The article further notes that "on many days, leveraged ETFs are now some of the most actively traded securities in the stock market."[34] Ananth Madhavan, head of trading research at Barclays Global Investors, "estimates that if a market index moves 15% in a day, leveraged ETFs could constitute 75% of all volume at the close of trading."[35]

This indicates that leveraged ETFs likely caused the end-of-day panic selling that characterized the 2008 market crash. Given all the ways to hide both trades and positions, it's possible to buy lots of shares of double- and triple-short ETFs in a way that creates massive end-of-day selling without having to openly sell short. Neither share borrowing nor extensive disclo-sure is required. With leverage, the market impact can be tremendous, both directly and in any ensuing panic.

The usual chorus of "see-no-evil" Wall Street types insist that short ETFs and even double-short or triple-short ETFs should have minimal market impact. No matter how you view these funds, however, they add dramati-cally to the selling pressure. At a minimum, the advent of these products exacerbated short selling trends in a down market. At worst, they served as another secret weapon to take down the market entirely.

SOVEREIGN WEALTH FUNDS

In the past few years, oil producing states and some other countries have created increasing numbers of sovereign wealth funds (SWF). According to the Sovereign Wealth Fund Institute, an SWF is a "state-owned investment fund composed of financial assets such as stocks, bonds, real estate, or other financial instruments funded by foreign exchange assets." Those assets include "balance of payment surpluses, official foreign currency operations, the proceeds of privatizations, fiscal surpluses, and/or receipts resulting from commodities exports." Mostly used to handle oil earnings, SWFs are essentially enormous slush funds owned and operated by the state. Forty-four percent of SWFs are located in the Middle East and 35 percent are in Asia.[36]

SWFs can be used to manipulate commodities and stock prices. The enormous amount of money they pour into the market enables them to define price movements. As Gal Luft, Executive Director of the Institute for the Analysis of Global Security, told the House Committee on Foreign Affairs, "In this context, we should view SWF as enablers of the new economic order. SWF are pouring billions into hedge funds, private equity funds, real estate, natural resources, and other nodes of the West's economy. No one knows precisely how much money is held by SWF but it is estimated that they currently own $3.5 trillion in assets and within one decade they could balloon to $10-15 trillion, equivalent to America's gross domestic product."[37]

Some observers argue that SWFs are benign or even beneficial for America, regardless of which government operates them, because they provide additional pools of wealth to which we can sell our debt or from which we can raise capital. This line of thinking assumes that SWFs are economic entities searching for the best possible returns. This case was made by Robert Kimmitt, Deputy Secretary of the U.S. Treasury, in a January 2008 article for *Foreign Affairs*.[38]

A more realistic viewpoint was articulated by Larry Summers, former Treasury Secretary, in an op-ed published in the *Financial Times*. Summers explained, "The logic of the capitalist system depends on shareholders causing companies to act so as to maximise the value of their shares. It is far from obvious that this will over time be the only motivation of governments as shareholders. They may want to see their national companies compete effectively, or to extract technology or to achieve influence.... Governments are very different from other economic actors. Their investments should be governed by rules designed with that reality very clearly in mind."[39] In other words, it *does* matter where the money comes from. As a servant of the government that operates it, an SWF is unlikely to be driven solely by the desire for better returns. In fact, the sovereign's interests may directly conflict with those of other investors.

According to the McCormick Foundation and the Center for Security Policy, SWFs routinely work with sharia-compliant financial institutions. "Given the explosive growth of SCF [sharia-compliant finance] compared to conventional banking in the Gulf and the strong government support behind this trend, it is very likely that SCF and Gulf-based SWF are rapidly becoming one and the same phenomenon. This would mean that—at some point in the near future, if not already—SWFs will become an instrument for promoting and legitimizing Shariah in the West."[40] Indeed, Sheikh Maktoum, owner of Dubai Holding and ruler of Dubai, embraces both SWFs and SCF. The two Islamic banks in Qatar are both owned by the ruling family and have Sheikh Qaradawi, the Muslim Brotherhood cleric, as chairman of their sharia advisory boards.[41]

There is a great deal of evidence indicating that sovereign wealth funds in Muslim nations are intimately connected to SCF. They are doubly dangerous because they use non-transparent methods including dark pools (described below) to funnel their money into U.S. markets. As Larry Summers observed, SWFs are powerful actors that may well be geared toward something other than earning a profit—they can be instruments of policy and potential secret weapons of warfare.

This is, according to James Rickards, "the dark side of SWF investments, how they could operate through what intelligence analysts call cut-outs, or front companies, such as trusts, managed accounts, private Swiss banks, and hedge funds. With these fronts in place, sovereign wealth funds could then be used to malign influence over target companies to steal technology, sabotage new projects, stifle competition, engage in bid rigging, recruit agents or manipulate markets.... Along with these specific threats... [there is] an even greater threat: a full-scale attack on Western capital markets to disable the engine of capitalist society."[42]

DARK MARKETS

Publicly traded markets are often heavily regulated. The same does not hold true of over-the-counter (OTC) markets, which are even more vulnerable to manipulation and insider trading. One such market is run by the Atlanta-based IntercontinentalExchange Inc., which has specialized in exotic instruments like credit default swaps.

Economic journalists Donna Block and Bill McConnell explain that traders can use such markets, especially their commodities listings, to impact all markets. "The hazy information about OTC trading volumes has prompted critics to label [such markets] 'dark markets,' susceptible to manipulation by anonymous investors. Lack of data about oil positions on... over-the-counter trading has prompted lawmakers to introduce roughly a half-dozen bills addressing 'speculation' in oil futures."[43]

In May 2008, such uncertainty provoked Senators Maria Cantwell and Olympia Snowe to send a letter to the Commodity Futures Trading Commission (CFTC) requesting that the commission "require greater scrutiny of foreign trading of U.S. delivered commodities." In an accompanying press release, the senators declared, "At a time when energy speculators are having substantial impact on the price at the pump it is essential that these markets are transparent and not subject to manipulation." Said Cantwell, "We must establish a clear, bright line to help protect consumers from any illegal activity that could be causing these out of control gas price hikes and burst the oil price bubble."[44]

The senators' letter was shocking. "Congress has received testimony from energy market experts, oil company executives, and major industrial energy consumers that the price of oil and gas can no longer be explained or predicted by normal market dynamics or their historic understanding of supply and demand fundamentals," the senators wrote. "Last month, an executive from Exxon Mobil testified under oath that the price of crude oil should be about $50 to $55 per barrel based on the supply and demand fundamentals he had observed. Yet current crude oil prices, and crude oil futures, are expected to remain well above $100 for the next several years with one prominent investment bank active in these markets predicting the price of crude could soon reach $200 a barrel."[45] Cantwell and Snowe were essentially asserting that speculation now rules the oil and gas market, thanks to the manipulation of dark markets.

As the senators further noted, the government looks the other way; the CFTC frequently sends out "no-action letters" designed to allow overseas energy trading platforms to be used to trade U.S.-based commodities. This dramatically impacts world commodities prices. Here's how it works: let's say a sovereign wealth fund wants to secretly inflate the price of oil. It simply goes on the unregulated OTC through an exchange like IntercontinentalExchange Inc. (ICE) and buys up all the futures in oil. This sends the price of oil through the roof as market actors assume that *somebody* knows *something*. If the price jumps on the OTC, that will be reflected on the New York Mercantile Exchange, too. As Cantwell and Snowe wrote,

> We believe that an informal Commission staff "no action" letter process is continuing to allow electronic exchanges located beyond our borders to trade U.S. based commodities, effectively free from direct U.S. regulation meant to prevent fraud, manipulation, and excessive speculation. In particular, one such "no action" letter permits trading of U.S.-based West Texas Intermediate (WTI) crude oil and related products such as home heating oil and gasoline upon ICE Futures Europe, a wholly

owned subsidiary of Atlanta based ICE. The WTI contract is trading in ICE Futures Europe in direct competition with the New York Mercantile Exchange's (NYMEX) signature oil futures contract, which is regulated by the CFTC.[46]

Michael Greenberger, a former CFTC employee and currently a law professor at the University of Maryland, wants Congress to close the so-called "Enron loophole," which allows energy commodities to be traded on unregulated exchanges. It was precisely that loophole that allowed Enron to move the market on energy and precipitated the California energy crisis that led to the recall of Governor Gray Davis. Many others agree. Michael Masters, managing member of Masters Capital Management LLC, says that "many physical commodity market participants are now losing faith in the futures price as a benchmark for their transactions." Masters cites stunning statistics: only a decade ago, farmers and producers who wanted to use the commodities they bought on the futures constituted almost 80 percent of the futures market while speculators comprised just 14 percent. Today, the plurality of futures traders—40 percent—are speculators, and another 26 percent are so-called "hedging counterparties," or third party insurers—folks who insure against the risk that futures contracts won't be delivered.[47]

Undoubtedly, the unregulated nature of the OTC market and exchanges like ICE provide a fertile ground for market manipulation by America's enemies. An oil price of $125 per barrel would produce something close to $1 trillion in a year for the sovereign wealth funds. If the SWFs were acting solely to maximize profits, they could invest a portion of their excess revenues in ways to positively speculate on increased oil prices—but they would pull back before prices became unsustainable. That's not what happened, however. To the contrary, in 2008 oil prices were driven so high that they collapsed, falling from nearly $150 per barrel in July to less than $40 per barrel by the end of the year. By driving oil prices well past sustainable levels, oil-based SWFs indicated they were not acting in their own economic interest. Instead, as we will show, they were generating a short-term pool of cash needed to conduct a financial attack.

DARK POOLS AND SPONSORED ACCESS

It is almost impossible these days to determine who is trading. Those who initiate trades are typically hidden behind brokerage firms, hedge funds, foundations, and other client pools. For example, look at the clients of Bernie Madoff's Ponzi scheme. The official client list, released to the public in February 2009, rambled for 162 pages and had over 13,500 entries, many of which appeared multiple times. In addition, all parties agreed that the list was nowhere near complete, and many questioned its overall accuracy. It may seem that simply listing the clients should have been straightforward enough—Madoff produced regular client statements with names and addresses. The complication is that his clients included hedge funds, funds of funds, offshore funds, and numerous other layers of intermediaries between the clients and the assets.

Now ask yourself this: if the investors were this hard to track down when they weren't trying to hide their identities, how hard would it be to identify traders who don't want to be discovered?

Participants in bear raids use every means at their disposal to protect their anonymity, creating layer upon layer of secrecy via foreign shell corporations, feeder funds (funds that pass cash to "master funds," or normal hedge funds), and numerous other pass-through entities. Historically, hedge funds have disclosed nothing to the government and very little to the public. Even for tax purposes, governments are incapable of tracking investment results back to most clients. Consider this: as of 2006, 85 percent of the hedge funds operating worldwide were registered in the Cayman Islands, which happen to offer hedge funds a 100-year exemption from taxation in addition to creating blankets of secrecy and preventing other governments from regulating them.[48] Unsurprisingly, the IRS has had little success in identifying U.S. citizens who hold hedge fund investments, let alone foreign entities. Feeder funds are not even required to collect information on their clients.

This lack of transparency makes hedge funds attractive for those who want anonymity. Says *Businessweek*, "When drug runners and terrorists want to park illicit cash, there may be no better haven than hedge funds.... As it stands, hedge funds have no responsibility to determine the source of investor funds or to analyze whether they're questionable."[49] In 2006, Senator Carl Levin characterized the Bush administration's "five-year failure to extend anti-money laundering controls to hedge funds with offshore money" as "inexplicable, ill-timed, and unwise."[50]

Complicating matters further, even if it were possible to identify a hedge fund's investors, it would be tough to find out where the hedge funds were invested. This is a second layer of secrecy, one that is staunchly defended by funds and even by the SEC in order to protect proprietary trading information. Despite a Transparency Act proposed by Senators Levin and Chuck Grassley, there is simply not much demand in Washington to force hedge funds to disclose either their trading activity or their customers. This lack of transparency was especially problematic in credit default swaps, which were unregistered, unregulated, and traded 15 to 20 times so that *nobody* knew who owned what or who would pay if there were a default.

Another tool hedge funds use to avoid transparency is dark pools. According to Anuj Gangahar, senior equity markets correspondent with the *Financial Times*, "Dark pools are private interbank or intrabank platforms that are widely used to trade stocks away from exchanges. They are used by clients such as hedge funds to buy and sell large blocks of shares in anonymity.... According to consultancy The Tabb Group, dark pools already accounted for 12 percent of US daily stock trading volume in 2009 and that percentage is rising."[51] Hong Kong Exchanges & Clearing Ltd. Chairman Ronald Arculli notes that dark pools provide a systemic risk. "The opaqueness has negative implications for corporate governance," says Arculli, adding that dark pools "increase price volatility and may add to surveillance difficulties."[52] Ralph Acampora, the New York Institute of Finance's director of technical analysis studies, agrees that dark pools increase market risks. "There's an ability to hide; people should be concerned about it," he explains. "You don't know where the (market) forces are coming from. In the past, you could identify it. Now it's a netherworld."[53]

At least forty active dark pools were operating in America during the 2008 crash, and fifty-two by the end of 2010, with another thirty-six in

Europe.[54] Each of these pools provides anonymity to its clients and hides trading activity, effectively eliminating oversight or regulation. James Brigagliano, co-acting director of the SEC's Division of Trading and Markets, said in 2009, "I'd like to give specific statistics on the trading volume, but there's very little reliable public information on dark-pool trading activity."[55]

Here's the bottom line: no one, not even the SEC, has access to accurate data on what happens in dark pools. But we do know that what happens in the dark pools strongly impacts normal exchange trading.[56] As the *Economist* observed, "Dark pools rely on anonymity. Their operators never reveal to users who is on the other side of their trades. No pre-trade data on order flow is published at all (although a few dark pools voluntarily publish data on unfilled orders, after a delay of days or weeks). Post-trade data is published some while after trades are completed, although in Europe even that is not compulsory under current rules. Regulators tolerate this opaque anomaly because they assume that giving pension funds and asset managers the ability to make big trades at good prices ultimately benefits their customers, the general public."[57] As with so many economic weapons, regulators *assume* that the intentions of dark pool participants are purely economic and largely beneficial to the market.

Another mechanism for hiding investor identity is "sponsored access." Nina Mehta, senior editor at *Traders* magazine, explains that sponsored access "refers to arrangements by broker-dealers that enable select market participants to fire off orders directly to exchanges . . . without passing through the broker's infrastructure."[58] Only registered broker-dealers have direct access to major trading exchanges, but by granting sponsored access, they can pass that privilege along to hedge funds and large clients. That means the buck stops with the sponsoring broker, who is responsible for the trades.

Monitoring and compliance, however, varies by broker, so hedge funds look for the most lenient ones. Differences in standards "expose the market to potential manipulation or operational exposure," says James Leman, head of markets at Westwater Corp, a New York-based advisory and consulting firm that often works with brokers. The Securities Industry and Financial

Markets Association (SIFMA) observes that these largely untraceable trades dramatically escalate market risk. "Under such a scenario," avers SIFMA, "were a significant amount of these trades to fail, the sponsoring exchanges and, by extension, the overall market, may be left with significant financial exposures that could adversely impact all trading activity in the market." As Brigagliano says, "These risks can affect many participants in the market structure.... Ultimately, the risks can affect the integrity of the market structure itself."[59]

By late 2010, the SEC recognized the extraordinary risks of a type of sponsored access called "naked sponsored access." As Bloomberg explained, "The U.S. Securities and Exchange Commission banned brokers from letting clients make unsupervised trades on stock exchanges amid concern that a rogue transaction could roil markets.... Naked access accounts for about 38 percent of U.S. equities trading, according to a December study by Aite Group LLC."[60]

In short, a huge portion of trading cannot be traced to its source. This clearly leaves room for a malevolent person or group to destabilize the markets without being identified.

ALGORITHMIC TRADING

One instrument that works hand-in-glove with both dark pools and naked sponsored access is high-frequency trading based on computer algorithms. Traders use sophisticated computer programs to profit from any price differentials between dark pools and the major exchanges, typically conducting these trades via sponsored access on the exchanges.[61] Thus, a price change in a dark pool can quickly be mirrored on the exchange and vice versa. This exacerbates the problems of anonymity, as it adds an additional layer of secrecy between the trader and the trade. It also exponentially increases market vulnerability.

Few people really know how trading algorithms operate, including their users. The complex algorithms are designed to profit from minuscule price differences and lightning fast trading. According to a Wharton Business School article,

> It sounds like science fiction—something from *I, Robot* or *The Terminator*, where the machines take over. But totally automated "high-frequency trading" is part of the stock market right now—a big part. According to some estimates, high-frequency trading by investment banks, hedge funds and other players accounts for 60% to 70% of all trades in U.S. stocks, explaining the enormous increase in trading volume over the past few years. Profits were estimated at between $8 billion and $21 billion in 2008.... Trading is so fast that some firms locate their server farms near the exchange's computers, to shorten the distance orders must travel through cables at light speed.[62]

While high-frequency trading may increase liquidity and help price discovery, there are also risks. For one, as nearly everyone knows from personal experience, computers can glitch. Another problem is that the trading speed creates the appearance of greater volatility, potentially scaring investors out of the market and reducing the amount of capital available to invest.

Another serious problem is that computers can be hacked and manipulated, as shown recently by the attempted theft at Goldman Sachs by Sergey Aleynikov. According to police reports, Aleynikov tried to walk out the door with a pocket flash drive containing Goldman's proprietary trading codes. According to an analysis by the Tabb Group,

> There's no doubt that Goldman Sachs, or any other proprietary trading firm, could indeed lose tens of millions of dollars from its proprietary trading if their strategies are stolen—and that is very serious. The competitors that obtain access to these trading secrets could (and would) use it to front run or trade against it,

ruining even the most well-planned tactics. This news story contains many very important sub-plots: trading espionage, the necessity for a trading firm to have sophisticated security systems built around its technology, the requirements for risk management, and even the potential for proprietary trading software to be targeted on a wider scale for terrorist activity; but more than anything else it highlights the critical role played by high frequency prop trading in this new market.[63]

The point is this: a relatively simple attack—such as an employee walking out the door with a computer flash drive—could potentially manipulate a major firm's trading programs even for the purposes of terrorist activity. Given the recent explosion in high-frequency trading, this must be considered another potential secret weapon.

ROGUE TRADERS

Manipulating algorithms is a high-tech form of economic warfare. Sending a spy in to retrieve them is an ancient art. As early as 2003, MSNBC reported that al Qaeda had a strategy to infiltrate financial institutions: "The Department of Homeland Security thinks al-Qaida terrorists might try to land jobs inside U.S. financial institutions, and from there launch attacks on the nation's economy, MSNBC.com has learned. An 'information bulletin' was sent out to the nation's financial firms late Friday night, warning of 'internal cyber threats.'"[64]

The report also discussed the broader topic: "Rogue employees and 'inside jobs' have long been the weak link in any corporate security system, particularly banks. It is hardly far-fetched to imagine organized criminals planting employees inside banks to facilitate economic crimes. In fact, a little over a year ago, the Treasury Department's Office of the Comptroller of the Currency issued a similar warning—in this case about bank teller employees who were actually working for organized crime rings."[65]

This is not a small risk. As reported in TheStreet.com, UBS disclosed in September 2011 "that a 31-year old trader, Kweku Adoboli, who worked in the bank's 'Delta One' trading desk, had been making unauthorized trades since 2008."[66] In 2008, Société Générale trader Jérôme Kerviel lost $7 billion trading almost $70 billion. The unwinding of his rogue trades riled the market and helped pave the way for the 2008 crash.[67]

Rogue employees clearly can impact the entire market, whether as traders or outright thieves. And we have reason to fear that al Qaeda might attempt to place such employees at major banks. There is a clear risk that a rogue employee with access to data or systems could crash the market. Despite the warnings from Homeland Security as early as 2003, however, the government has exerted little effort to address the risks of terrorists infiltrating our financial markets.

ARBOON

All this begs an overarching question: Can Islamic groups carry out financial machinations using the weaponry described in this chapter? One would think they'd certainly like to try; after all, if Islamic extremists could engineer the wholesale collapse of interest-based banking institutions, that would boost their efforts to replace global capitalism with sharia. On the other hand, sharia has historically prohibited Muslims from selling what they do not own. This would seem to remove a fundamental tool of financial terrorism—short selling—from the Islamic arsenal. Thus, advocates of sharia seemingly have the motivation to attack America's economy but lack the primary means to carry it out.

The advent of *arboon* solves this problem. Sheikh Yusuf Talal DeLorenzo, working with Barclays Bank and New York-based Shariah Capital, adapted the Arboon contract to facilitate an Islamic version of short selling. "DeLorenzo," reported the *Wall Street Journal*, "a Massachusetts-born convert to Islam, [was] on a mission to meld centuries-old Islamic law with modern finance in the U.S." His solution was elegant: holding currencies instead of futures, and buying non-debt heavy S&P 500 stocks to avoid interest problems.[68] For its part, Barclays had a strong interest in becoming involved in sharia compliant finance, since such activities gave it a leg up in courting big investments from Gulf-based sharia-compliant sovereign wealth funds.[69]

Essentially, arboon is the Islamic substitute for short selling—like short selling, it is meant to generate a profit through the decline in value of a security. What shares would make ideal arboon targets? At the top of the list are interest-earning banks, which are proscribed by sharia and have long been a target of jihadists. Thus, arboon gives jihadists an Islamic-sanctioned means to attack infidel finance and to make a profit doing so.

It's important to understand that Islamic figures now own huge stakes in America's major financial institutions. Saudi Prince Alwaleed bin Talal bin Abdulaziz manages a royal fund and has been one of the largest holders of Citigroup shares for nearly two decades.[70] The Abu Dhabi government bought a 4.9 percent stake in Citigroup for $7.5 billion in December 2007.[71] By the end of 2008, Abu Dhabi and Qatar held a third of Barclays with clauses to take majority control if the bank needed to seek other capital.[72]

At first glance, such ownership stakes might appear to preclude any possible short sale of financial companies. But such large stakes might create a need to resort to short selling as a hedge against long holdings; if you own lots of stock in Citigroup, you're going to want to short sell on occasion in order to offset your holdings, just in case they drop. Using hedge funds and dark pools, it would be possible to take substantial short positions to offset the exposure. There is likely also a tipping point at which the profits from short selling would exceed the losses from long holdings.

This is exactly what we saw during the fourth quarter of 2008. In that quarter, Prince bin Talal's Kingdom Holding fund claimed a loss of over $8 billion.[73] However, when the accountants for the Kingdom Holding Company published a local report, they claimed a fourth-quarter *gain* of $73.6 million.[74] There may be legitimate explanations for how an $8.3 billion loss converts to a $73.6 million profit—and one of them is that the fund could have been hedged with short positions. Unfortunately, like most giant funds based in the Middle East, Kingdom Holding traditionally operates in secrecy.

The U.S. government denies that sharia involvement in U.S. markets presents any danger. When Borse Dubai, the stock exchange for the United Arab Emirates, attempted to buy 20 percent of the NASDAQ in 2007, Democratic Congressman Barney Frank cavalierly dismissed the national security implications of the proposed sale. This echoed the blasé reaction many Bush administration officials had shown in 2006 to the proposed sale of a U.S. port management company to Dubai's state-owned company DP World—until public outrage forced Congress to block the deal. Frank remarked, "In the ports deal, the concern was smuggling something or someone dangerous. What are we talking about here—smuggling someone onto a stock exchange?"[75]

Like Frank, many U.S. leaders fail to understand that a sharia-driven investor, by definition, elevates long-term considerations above short-term profits, a circumstance that allows the investor to accept strategic short-term losses to accomplish greater purposes—and those purposes may have nothing to do with earning a profit.

★　★　★

Some of the tools our enemies use against us are longstanding weapons of economic warfare—oil and gold are not difficult to manipulate, especially when they are in short supply. But these weapons can hurt the wielders nearly as much as the intended victims.

Over the past two decades, various new financial instruments have arisen. Many of them grew out of selective deregulation, a process that paved the way for new forms of investment that entail less transparency, more risk, and the possibility of being used for financial terrorism. Financial terrorists may be willing to sacrifice their own economic interests to their ideological agenda. But new finance tools mitigate downside risk for potential financial terrorists, meaning that they themselves could actually profit by attacking the U.S. economy. Tools like credit default swaps, naked short selling, and leveraged ETFs can be used to attack us while the perpetrators hide their identities in dark markets and dark pools or behind computer trading with rogue traders. And they can even work around their own religious objections with manipulations like arboon.

When the 9/11 Commission ruled out market manipulation as part of the terror attacks, it relied on the assumption that market transparency would flush out any nefarious activity. But since it published its study, transparency has all but disappeared, and the weapons of financial warfare have become increasingly sophisticated.

Our enemies have the motive. They have the means. All they need is the opportunity.

CHAPTER SIX

THE OPPORTUNITY

Someone with the motive and means to carry out an act of financial terrorism needs one other vital element to succeed: opportunity. Tragically, the failures of American governance over the past two decades created the perfect opportunity for financial terrorists to attack us in September 2008.

Throughout the 1990s and 2000s, selective deregulation of the financial markets, failures of government oversight, and deficiencies in the overall regulatory regime created glaring vulnerabilities in the U.S. economy. These problems were magnified by the greed and hubris of the U.S. real estate and banking communities, as well as by misguided government policies ostensibly meant to help the poor. All this made America ripe for the picking.

THE UPTICK RULE

In 1938, Congress passed the so-called "uptick rule," which essentially stipulated that a stock could only be sold short following a trade in which the stock had sold up in price. So, say you wanted to short sell a Citigroup stock priced at $40 per share. According to the uptick rule, you could not short the stock if the last trade was at $39 7/8 (at the time, stocks were priced in one-eighths rather than cents), but you could short it if the last trade was at $40 1/8. The rule was meant to prevent a short seller from selling over and over, flooding the market with stock and driving down the price. Instead, the market would be given time to pause and breathe, so to speak. According to the Securities and Exchange Commission (SEC), the uptick rule was also designed to prevent "short sellers from accelerating a declining market by exhausting all remaining bids at one price level, causing successively lower prices to be established by long sellers."[1]

The rule was adopted after the market crash of 1937–1938, in which the Dow dropped nearly 50 percent in about thirteen months. According to Charles M. Jones, Robert W. Lear Professor of Finance and Economics at Columbia Business School, the SEC investigated the crash and found that "short sales were a small part of total sales during the decline, but there was concentrated shorting by a small number of Exchange members in certain stocks in certain times.... On October 5 [1937], when prices were stabilizing after a sharp intraday decline, floor trades arrived with orders to short 2,700 shares of US Steel, about 20% of the stock's average daily volume. The Commission was concerned that 'public support of US Steel at this level could not withstand this concerted assault.'"[2]

Experts today disagree whether these short sellers were, in fact, conducting bear raids, though few doubted it at the time. Regardless, the crash eroded public confidence in the market and hampered an economic recovery that had begun in 1932; as of 1936, the stock market had regained two-thirds of the losses suffered in the 1929 crash.

After the uptick rule was implemented, the market never again fell below the 1937 lows. But in 2007, the SEC cancelled the rule, announcing, "Today's markets are characterized by high levels of transparency and regulatory surveillance. These characteristics greatly reduce the risk of abusive or manipulative short selling going undetected if we were to remove price test restrictions, and permit regulators to monitor the types of activities that Rule 10a-1 and other price tests are designed to prevent. The general anti-fraud and anti-manipulation provisions of the federal securities laws would also continue to prohibit activity that improperly influences the price of a security."[3] Notably, the uptick rule was adopted close to the market's bottom in 1937 and was rescinded seventy years later close to its peak.

There is a fierce debate in academic circles about whether a spike in short selling that occurred in August 2007 was due to the abolition of the uptick rule the previous month. Critics of the rule point to a six-month SEC study based on a 2005 pilot program that compared 943 randomly selected stocks from the Russell 3000 (a broad-based index of U.S. stocks) to the remaining 2,067 in the index. The 943 were not subject to the uptick rule. Over that six-month period, the SEC found that the stocks not subject to the uptick rule had 2 percent lower returns than those subject to the rule, a result the SEC considered statistically irrelevant.

Proponents of the uptick rule, however, believe the study had several key flaws. In a November 2008 *Wall Street Journal* op-ed defending the uptick rule, Robert Pozen, chairman of MFS Investment Management, and Yaneer Bar-Yam, president of the New England Complex Systems Institute, criticized the six-month study for being too brief to determine the rule's efficacy. They further argued that the study took place during a calm period in the market that squashed any "bear raids" effect, and that the 2 percent differential was inordinately small because outliers in the statistical sample were not factored out.

Anecdotally, Pozen and Bar-Yam pointed out a "marked increase in the number of NYSE-listed stocks with price drops of over 40% in a day—a rough proxy for a bear raid." By comparison, the twelve months following the 2007 market peak (after the uptick rule was eliminated) had roughly twice as many stocks drop 40 percent in a day than in the twelve months after the market peaked in 2000, when the uptick rule was in place. Yet the period overall had similar market declines and high volatility.[4]

A significant group of analysts opposed the SEC's decision to cancel the uptick rule. Reacting to its demise, Muriel Siebert of Siebert Financial Corporation complained to the *New York Times*, "I don't think we know the effect of it. The SEC took away the short-sale rule and when the markets were falling, institutional investors just pounded stocks because they didn't need an uptick. We have to look at that and say, 'Did that influence and add to the volatility?'"[5] MSNBC analyst Jim Cramer—for what it's worth—also supported reinstating the uptick rule. In July 2008, Congressman Gary Ackerman and six other members of Congress even co-sponsored a bill to bring back the rule.[6] Corporate America seemed to support the congressmen's efforts; an October 2008 study by the New York Stock Exchange of 438 corporate executives found that 85 percent favored restoring the uptick rule and 82 percent believed it would instill investor confidence.[7]

The SEC, it seems, soon regretted its actions. In July 2008, it issued an emergency order barring traditional short sales for certain equity securities on specific financial institutions; in September 2008, with the stock market in free fall, the SEC issued an emergency order prohibiting short selling in publicly traded securities for other financial institutions.[8] In October, Erik Sirri, director of the SEC's Division of Trading and Markets, said the SEC would discuss whether to restore the uptick rule. "We've [had] a lot of calls to bring it back," he said. "It's something we have talked about and it may be something that we in fact do."[9]

At the end of 2010, the SEC adopted what it termed the "alternative uptick rule." It applies only to stocks that have fallen 10 percent in a single trading session. When that is triggered, the stock may be sold only on an uptick for the rest of that trading session and for the next one. Containing exemptions for "bona fide" arbitrage transactions,[10] the new rule is a small step in the right direction, but it's riddled with loopholes; even when properly working and applied, the rule would still allow naked short sellers to hit stocks with impunity for 10 percent declines every other trading day. In addition, the exemptions are easy to meet through a variety of existing tools.

Note that even these flimsy safeguards did not exist in September 2008, when the cancellation of the uptick rule the previous year gave our enemies a prime opportunity to launch a financial attack.

THE HOUSING BUBBLE

As recently as late 2007, many experts were proclaiming that the world had entered an unprecedented era of prosperity. Experts generally expected annual global GDP growth of around 3.5 percent, rising as high as 6 percent by 2050. The April 2007 IMF forecast was for 4.9 percent annual growth, with their best economists estimating a mere 20 percent chance that global growth would fall below 4 percent in 2008.[11] These optimistic forecasts assumed that globalization and the spread of democratic opportunity would allow a rapid uplift "of all metrics of human development."[12]

In the United States, the real estate sector was booming and home prices were skyrocketing in the decade leading up to the crash of September 2008. The median sales price of new U.S. homes sold at the beginning of 2001 was just over $200,000; by the beginning of 2007, it was around $325,000. From 1997 to 2005, U.S. housing prices jumped 73 percent. They rose 12.5 percent just between 2004 and 2005, with prices in California, Florida, Nevada, Hawaii, Maryland, and Washington, D.C. shooting up more than 20 percent. Apparently caught up in the exuberance, Federal Reserve Chairman Alan Greenspan declared in 2004 that "a national severe price distortion" in real estate was "most unlikely"; a year later, he insisted that home prices "largely reflect strong economic fundamentals."[13] The *Economist*, however, had a sobering take on the situation; by 2005 it was already labeling the global rise in housing prices "the biggest bubble in history." The magazine presciently warned, "Prepare for the economic pain when it pops."[14]

The housing boom indeed was a bubble. It largely arose from the Fed's loose monetary policy, which depressed interest rates on mortgages while propping up materials prices. These trends encouraged speculation and fed the bubble. During the nineteen years in which Greenspan served as chairman of the Federal Reserve (1987–2006), he famously kept interest rates low. During that period, the currency in circulation rose from $248 billion to $802 billion, a growth rate much faster than the overall economy, with much of the cash going abroad. As the Cato Institute points out, "In a period when debit cards and possibly ATMs were reducing currency demand, analysts were aware that all this new cash was not bulging in the wallets and purses of the average America. It was going abroad, as a stable dollar evolved into an international currency." This kept inflation under control, but it also drove up real estate and commodity prices as those dollars were used on American resources.[15]

With more dollars in circulation, home prices escalated. The cost to produce housing increased with higher raw materials prices and rising labor costs. But thanks to the low interest rates, people could still afford to buy homes. This pushed home prices even higher and made the existing home supply more valuable. That, in turn, allowed lenders to offer Home Equity Lines of Credit (HELOCs), adding further to the available money supply, since individuals could borrow against their homes. The lenders faced no risk, since if a borrower couldn't pay the mortgage, the house could still be sold at a profit—the rising tide lifted all boats.

As housing became one of the best performing investments, the spending cycle continued and the bubble grew. Investors, looking for a solid place to store their money, began buying much more housing than they needed for personal use. This meant bigger and more expensive homes as well as multiple investment properties. The housing boom also further increased the cost of raw materials. In some cases, speculators would buy and sell prospective condominiums even before construction had begun. This created a housing glut that still plagues the market today.

As *Forbes* pointed out, there was another major element in the brewing crisis. "The low interest rates of the early 2000s may explain the growth of the housing bubble, but they don't explain the poor quality of these mortgages."[16] After all, good mortgagers continue to pay the mortgage even when their house goes underwater. Only bad mortgagers don't.

That element was the federal government's commitment to expanding home ownership for the poor, especially poor minorities. This policy led to the so-called subprime crisis. The government encouraged banks to expand subprime loans to poor applicants who otherwise would not qualify for a mortgage. The problem was, subprime borrowers were unqualified for a reason—they were generally low-income applicants with weak credit scores. The typical subprime head of family was in his or her early thirties and had $37,000 of disposable income after taxes. Notes Professor Herman Schwartz of the University of Virginia, "As late housing market entrants, these families, on average, paid a high price relative to their incomes— borrowing $200,000 on average—because housing prices rose well ahead of incomes." Because they were putting little money down and couldn't carry their mortgages in typical fashion, subprime borrowers generally took out adjustable-rate mortgages—that is, mortgages with interest rates that change over time. During the bubble, writes Schwartz, "The share of subprime and Alt-A [non-traditional, more risky] mortgage originations jumped from 2 percent in 2002 to 20 percent in 2006, and 92 percent of these were ARMs." Meanwhile, HELOCs grew exponentially—about a quarter of homeowners had one, and all in all, that debt totaled more than $1 trillion, "over 10 percent of total mortgage debt."[17]

Why would lenders undertake such risky loans? After all, these companies were led by some of the nation's highest paid experts on the housing industry. They should have known that the market was becoming oversupplied. The good times couldn't go on forever—or could they?

When the federal government gets involved in a market, it takes away that market's natural ups-and-downs and encourages private actors to take more risks. This is evident in what happened—and continues to happen— in the U.S. housing market, where Fannie Mae and Freddie Mac, two government-sponsored entities, backstop most mortgages. In 1991, Jim Johnson, a former aide to Senator Walter Mondale, became CEO of Fannie Mae. Soon after, the Boston Fed released a deeply flawed study alleging widespread racial discrimination in bank-mortgage lending. According to Gretchen Morgensen of the *New York Times* and Joshua Rosner, Managing

Director at research consulting firm Graham Fisher & Co., Johnson recognized that "lending to minorities could help his company's expansion efforts, as well as its image," and soon he began "fanning the flames lit by the Fed's report."[18]

In 1992, Congress instructed Fannie and Freddie to focus on affordable housing and then had the Department of Housing and Urban Development write up the regulations to make it happen. For his part, Johnson forced through a "trillion-dollar commitment" to affordable housing. Meanwhile, new regulations under the Community Reinvestment Act forced banks to show they were lending to "underserved communities"—namely, subprime clientele. As Forbes noted, "Shortly after these new mandates went into effect, the nation's homeownership rate—which had remained at about 64% since 1982—began to rise, increasing 3.3% from 64.2% in 1994 to 67.5% in 2000 under President Clinton, and an additional 1.7% during the Bush administration.... There is no reasonable explanation for this sudden spurt, other than a major change in the standards for granting a mortgage or a large increase in the amount of low-cost funding available for mortgages. The data suggest that it was both."[19]

Fannie and Freddie subsidized this whole deal—between 1994 and 2003, the two firms increased their ownership of mortgage originations from 37 percent of the market to 57 percent, "effectively cornering the conventional conforming market."[20] By 2002, private-sector involvement was only 4 percent of the nonconventional mortgage market. In 2008, bad mortgage-backed securities owned by private companies comprised less than one-third of all subprime loans in the market. The rest were held by Fannie, Freddie, and other government agencies.[21]

The key element waived by Fannie and Freddie for subprime borrowers was the traditional 20 percent down payment on any mortgage. Bear Stearns, among other firms, tried to tell investors in mortgage-backed securities that 5 percent down from a poor family was just as good as 20 percent from a rich family—a counterintuitive and absurd statement that turns the concept of risk on its head in the interests of political correctness. Nevertheless, by 2001, Fannie and Freddie were offering mortgages with no down payments.

Between 2003 and 2008, Fannie picked up almost a trillion dollars in mortgage-backed securities.[22]

Because they were backed by the government, these mortgages became highly valuable. Meanwhile, credit derivatives became more common and increasingly complex. Leverage ratios were huge—banks began trading these securities, slicing and dicing them in a form of financial alchemy. Taking sub-prime loans and repackaging them to get Triple-A ratings was creative and profitable, even if it masked the underlying risks.[23] Unfortunately, the bond rating agencies blessed the efforts, leaving banks and investors with a false sense of security that the repackaged mortgages were "safe."[24]

The ensuing profits encouraged increasing leverage. From 2004 to 2007, the leverage ratios for Merrill Lynch increased from 16:1 to 31:1, Morgan Stanley rose from 23:1 to 33:1, and Bear Stearns grew from 26:1 to 33:1. According to the Financial Crisis Inquiry Commission, "From 1978 to 2007, the amount of debt held by the financial sector soared from $3 trillion to $36 trillion, more than doubling as a share of gross domestic product. The very nature of many Wall Street firms changed—from relatively staid private partnerships to publicly traded corporations taking greater and more diverse kinds of risks. By 2005, the 10 largest U.S. commercial banks held 55% of the industry's assets, more than double the level held in 1990. On the eve of the crisis in 2006, financial sector profits constituted 27% of all corporate profits in the United States, up from 15% in 1980."[25]

In 2007, the bubble popped. As Bloomberg reported that June, "The share of all mortgages entering foreclosure rose to 0.58 percent [in the first quarter of 2007] from 0.54 percent in the fourth quarter [of 2006], the Mortgage Bankers Association said in a report today. Subprime loans entering foreclosure rose to a five-year high of 2.43 percent, up from 2 percent, and prime loans rose to a record 0.25 percent." Bloomberg further noted that the trend was "led by subprime borrowers pinched in an economy that grew at the slowest pace in four years."[26]

Later, a congressional investigation would blame the housing crisis largely on Wall Street firms that speculated in housing debt. Investment banks like Goldman Sachs, said Democratic Senator Carl Levin, "contaminated" the market with "toxic mortgages." Similarly, Republican Senator Tom Coburn condemned Wall Street for allowing "greed [to] run wild." The senators had a point. As explained by Washington Mutual's chief credit officer, "Any attempts to enforce a more disciplined underwriting approach were continuously thwarted by an aggressive, and often times abusive, group of sales employees within the organization."[27]

Greed was part of the reason for the crisis, but not the only one. The federal government deserves a good share of the blame. The congressional report acknowledged this to a small extent, for example, by noting that the Office of Thrift Supervision didn't tell Washington Mutual to stop these practices, and in fact, tried to prevent the Federal Deposit Insurance Corporation from taking action.[28]

With hindsight, we can confidently identify four causes of the housing crisis: Wall Street greed, a failure of the ratings agencies, the federal government's sponsorship of the real estate bubble, and lax regulatory enforcement. The bursting of the housing bubble would inevitably be harmful, but it should not have brought down the whole economy. While non-performing loans exceeded the bank loan loss reserves during the crisis, the situation was far from unprecedented. In fact, reserves at the end of 2008 were significantly higher relative to loan non-performance than in 1984 and roughly in line with the 1984–1994 average, a period of general economic prosperity.

As it turns out, there was more happening on the markets than met the eye. The housing crisis had created vulnerabilities that were being exploited by our foreign enemies.

NATIONAL DEBT

Aside from the housing crisis, high levels of debt throughout the U.S. economy were another source of strategic vulnerability. This debt was a major structural problem, but it should not have been as destructive as it turned out to be. Alarmists note that the ratio of non-financial debt (debt held not by financial institutions but by households, businesses, and the government) to GDP was the highest in history. In rough numbers, the ratio as of 2009 was around 2.3 times nominal GDP, up from 1.4 times in 1980.

Some economists argue that the Fed's easy money policy, especially following the technology bubble and the 9/11 attacks, helped to create the debt problem just as it helped stoke the housing crisis. In their view, interest rates were kept too low for too long, encouraging excessive debt-driven speculation. The idea was that if interest rates were low, it was easy to borrow money, make a higher return, and then pay back the money and take a profit.

This argument has some merit, but it's far from complete. The primary issue is that the ratio compares total debt to annual income. It ignores the term of the debt and the value of the assets behind it. Not all debt is created equal.

Consider your personal balance sheet. Term is significant because longer maturity debt typically has less impact due to smaller required payments. For example, a $50,000 car loan with a 3-year term would require nearly $1,400 in monthly principal payments (not including interest) while a 30-year mortgage would have average monthly principal payments of less than $140. According to research from Alliance Bernstein, around 70 percent of outstanding debt today is considered "long term," compared to 55 percent in 1980.[29] While such long-term debt can be disastrous for the country, it is disastrous in the *long term*.

The second problem with basic debt-to-GDP analysis is that it ignores the asset levels supporting the debt. Using the previous example, a car loan of $50,000 has a greater negative wealth effect than a $50,000 mortgage if the car is expected to depreciate while the home has the potential to appreciate over time. In addition, a higher level of assets supports a greater level of debt even if income lags.

In this case, the more important ratio is the comparison of debts to assets. Looking at Federal Reserve data, this ratio, while rising, has been reasonably stable over time. The seemingly dramatic jump in 2008 is explained, in part, by the dramatic short-term drop in assets such as home prices and stock portfolios. Without these sharp declines, the 2007 ratio is not far from the ratios that prevailed between 1980 and 2000.[30] Therefore, on its own, private sector debt was insufficient to cause the economic crisis of 2008. But it was more than enough to create vulnerabilities that our enemies could, and did, exploit.

THE REPEAL OF GLASS-STEAGALL

Another factor in the 2008 market crash was ineffective and unenforced regulations. A vast regulatory framework was created in the 1930s in an attempt to prevent a repeat of the Great Depression. In the decade leading up to the 2008 crash, much of this framework was dismantled, including a partial repeal of the Glass-Steagall Act in 1999. That annulment eliminated some safeguards that prevented commercial banks from becoming over-leveraged as investment banks. It ultimately allowed consumer banking functions such as deposits and consumer loans to be tied to investment banking leverage.

Let's begin with the basics. There are two types of banks: commercial and investment. Commercial banks are the types where you open a checking or savings account, rent a safety deposit box, or get a mortgage loan. By contrast, investment banks arrange financing for corporations and governments, handle mergers and acquisitions, invest on behalf of clients, and engage in asset management.

Foreseeing rising values of stocks and bonds, commercial banks in the 1920s wanted to become involved in investing. Since they couldn't involve themselves in investment banking, they opened holding companies to buy and sell securities. But these holding companies were not properly capitalized, so they used their depositor dollars to invest. So long as the economy remained strong, all was well. But as with the 2008 real estate collapse, when the underlying assets were called in, or when those investments went south, people lost a lot of money.

In reviewing the market collapse of 1929, the Senate Banking and Currency Committee held the so-called Pecora Hearings. According to Wall Street Watch, "The Pecora hearings concluded that common ownership of commercial banks and investment banks created several distinct problems, among them: 1) jeopardizing depositors by investing their funds in the stock market; 2) loss of the public's confidence in the banks, which led to panic withdrawals; 3) the making of unsound loans; and 4) an inability to provide honest investment advice to depositors because banks were conflicted by their underwriting relationship with companies."

In 1933, Congress passed the Glass-Steagall Act, designed to separate commercial banks from investment banks. This had two main ramifications: it made it more difficult to get a loan, since banks weren't making as much money from their investments, but it also protected bank deposits because it made banks focus on serving depositors rather than taking risks in the financial markets.

Over time, Glass-Steagall earned vociferous opposition from the banking community, which chafed at its perception that foreign firms were capitalizing on their integration of commercial and investment banking. Consequently, financial regulators began to loosen Glass-Steagall's restrictions. In 1986, the Fed restricted enforcement of the investment banking provisions so that 5 percent of a bank's gross revenues could spring from investment banking; the following year, the Fed allowed traditional banks to start working with commercial paper and mortgage-backed securities. Alan Greenspan, a proponent of these changes, soon replaced Fed Chairman Paul Volcker, an opponent of them. In 1989, the Fed again revised enforcement so that 10 percent of a commercial bank's gross revenues could come from the investment banking side. This was raised to 25 percent in December 1996.[31]

In 1999, President Clinton signed a formal repeal of Glass-Steagall under the Financial Services Modernization Act. Treasury Secretary Robert Rubin had fought for the move, declaring, "The banking industry is fundamentally different from what it was two decades ago, let alone in

1933."[32] Rubin's successor, Lawrence Summers, cheered as the bill was passed, "Today, Congress voted to update the rules that have governed financial services since the Great Depression and replace them with a system for the 21st century. This historic legislation will better enable American companies to compete in the new economy."[33]

Even before the act was cancelled, companies anticipated its repeal and began acting accordingly. For example, in what one commentator described as a "form of corporate civil disobedience," in 1998 Citibank merged with Travelers Group, a massive insurance company. That merger was illegal, but the government had weakened its enforcement of Glass-Steagall prior to its repeal.[34] Citigroup quickly began using its newfound leeway to create new instruments like mortgage-backed securities.

The nonpartisan public policy and research organization Demos blamed the 2008 financial crisis largely on the repeal of Glass-Steagall, stating, "Commercial banks played a crucial role as buyers and sellers of mortgage-backed securities, credit-default swaps and other explosive financial derivatives. Without the watering down and ultimate repeal of Glass-Steagall, the banks would have been barred from most of these activities. The market and appetite for derivatives would then have been far smaller, and Washington might not have felt a need to rescue the institutional victims."[35]

At the very least, repealing Glass-Steagall set the stage for a mass bailout of the banking industry. If commercial banks had not been allowed to partake in investment banking, they would not have been nearly as vulnerable to loss; at the same time, if they did not have the covert guarantee of the Federal Deposit Insurance Corporation and the federal government backing them up, they would have been more careful with the money.

Specifically, the end of Glass-Steagall coincided with the dramatic rise in mortgage-backed securities and credit default swaps. This is no coincidence. Whereas before, banks had to ensure that their loans would pay off, now they could simply pass those loans on to others via securitization. The toxic assets poisoned everyone but gave the impression they weren't poisoning the originators. Nobel Prize winning economist Joseph Stiglitz ably sums up the problem:

> The most important consequence of the repeal of Glass-Steagall was indirect—it lay in the way repeal changed an entire culture. Commercial banks are not supposed to be high-risk ventures; they are supposed to manage other people's money very conservatively. It is with this understanding that the government agrees to pick up the tab should they fail. Investment banks, on the other hand, have traditionally managed rich people's money—people who can take bigger risks in order to get bigger returns. When repeal of Glass-Steagall brought investment and commercial banks together, the investment-bank culture came out on top. There was a demand for the kind of high returns that could be obtained only through high leverage and big risk taking.[36]

The weakening of the regulatory environment didn't end with the repeal of Glass-Steagall. For many years, the SEC's governing philosophy held that broker-dealers could not borrow money more than twelve times the amount of their assets if they wanted to work in the stock market. But in 2004, the SEC abolished the rule, instead adopting a voluntary system that allowed investment banks to determine the risk they could handle based on their own computer modeling. The five biggest banks participating in the new program were Bear Stearns, Goldman Sachs, Morgan Stanley, Merrill Lynch, and Lehman Brothers, all of which suffered immensely in the 2008 meltdown and all of which leveraged themselves at ratios far surpassing 12:1. According to the SEC's Inspector General, the SEC didn't even bother to monitor these firms, especially Bear.

By the end of the 2008 crisis, all five of those firms were either bankrupt, absorbed by another firm, or received a government bailout subject to Federal Reserve regulatory authority.[37]

UNREGULATED DERIVATIVES

Although Glass-Steagall proved to be a vital regulation, most observers agree that by the time it was repealed, the overall regulatory system designed for a 1930s economy had become outmoded. For example, modern financial instruments such as credit default swaps, hedge funds, and exchange traded funds that have grown substantially over the past decade were largely left out of the regulatory structure. Even those entities and instruments that were subject to regulation could operate in a variety of gray areas with multiple regulators. The primary impact of this was to make the system less transparent and more vulnerable.

Take the controversial credit derivatives as an example. Credit default swaps played an integral role in the 2008 financial collapse. The fact that the CDS market reached $62 trillion in notional value at the end of 2007 (nearly five times U.S. annual GDP) according to the International Swaps and Derivative Association, up from less than $1 trillion in 2001, demonstrates how important these formerly obscure instruments have become relative to the overall economy. Despite the huge marketplace for CDSs, however, a lack of transparency and regulation led to a situation that made the overall system vulnerable to manipulation.

Despite their significance to the marketplace, the CDS market was "regulated by no one" according to SEC Chairman Christopher Cox's testimony before the U.S. Senate on September 23, 2008. Cox also testified that "neither the SEC nor any regulator has authority over the CDS market, even to require minimal disclosure to the market." This is tantamount to saying that this enormous market was completely unregulated. But it was even worse: not only did regulators lack the authority to reign in the market, they weren't even allowed to monitor what was happening. This is why Cox concluded that "the (CDS) market is ripe for fraud and manipulation."[38]

Jurisdiction over the regulation of CDSs, like that of all other derivatives, would naturally fall in the domain of the Commodity Futures Trading Commission (CFTC). Unfortunately, the CFTC was not called upon to properly exercise that authority. Clinton Treasury Secretary Robert Rubin—

who you will recall supported the repeal of Glass-Steagall—along with Fed Chairman Greenspan and SEC Chair Arthur Levitt, stood shoulder to shoulder against regulation of derivatives.

CFTC chair Brooksley Born, by contrast, advocated myriad new regulations. She proposed that derivates be forced onto regulated exchanges rather than OTC exchanges; that people be required to meet financial requirements to trade in derivatives, to ensure that they wouldn't come up short on their liabilities; and that derivatives issuers be required to disclose the risks. Once Larry Summers became Treasury Secretary, he fretted that these proposals "cast the shadow of regulatory uncertainty over an otherwise thriving market." Greenspan seconded the motion. "Regulation of derivatives transactions that are privately negotiated by professionals is unnecessary," he said. "Regulation that serves no useful purpose hinders the efficiency of markets to enlarge standards of living."[39]

When, in 1998, the derivatives-centric hedge fund Long Term Capital went belly up, requiring the New York Fed to bail it out with a $3.6 billion investment, Congress responded not by cracking down on derivatives trading, but by mandating that the CFTC back off. In the end, the President's Working Group decided that "government regulation should serve to supplement, rather than substitute for, private market discipline. In general, private counterparty credit risk management has been employed effectively by both regulated and unregulated dealers of OTC derivatives, and the tools required by federal regulators already exist."[40]

Congress followed up that beautifully stated idiocy with some of its own. Under the Commodity Futures Modernization Act, Congress and Clinton exempted financial derivatives, including CDSs, from regulation and governmental oversight. While Phil Gramm, one of the moving forces behind the bill, says that he doesn't regret having supported it, former SEC Commissioner Harvey Goldschmid admitted, "In hindsight, there's no question that we would have been better off if we had been regulating derivatives."[41]

Famed economist Hernando De Soto goes even further. "These derivatives are the root of the credit crunch," he wrote in the *Wall Street Journal*.

"Why? Unlike all other property paper, derivatives are not required by law to be recorded, continually tracked and tied to the assets they represent. Nobody knows precisely how many there are, where they are, and who is finally accountable for them. Thus, there is widespread fear that potential borrowers and recipients of capital with too many nonperforming derivatives will be unable to repay their loans. As trust in property paper breaks down it sets off a chain reaction, paralyzing credit and investment, which shrinks transactions and leads to a catastrophic drop in employment and in the value of everyone's property."[42]

FREEDOM TO GET NAKED

Now let's look at naked short selling. With sufficient capital and no restriction on the amount of shares that can be shorted, it is theoretically possible to target and attack key companies and industries. That becomes even easier when the government refuses to enforce rules against naked shorting.

Here's how naked short selling works: sometimes those who sell shares they don't own can't deliver on them—such situations are known as "fail-to-delivers." In such instances, the rules should require that the broker buy the shares back for delivery and charge the short seller. What mostly happens, however, is that the broker creates an "IOU" that looks and feels like a real share. The buyer doesn't know the difference. The problem is that this activity increases the supply of shares in the market. Meanwhile, the selling can spook other investors and reduce demand. According to basic economic law, if you increase the supply and reduce the demand, the price will fall. This makes naked short selling a self-reinforcing mechanism.

The fact that 33 million shares of Lehman Brothers were sold and not delivered to buyers on time (a 57-fold increase over the peak in the prior year) during a global financial meltdown cannot be overlooked. Trade settlement expert Dr. Susan Trimbath estimated that failed trades from naked short sales accounted for between 30 percent and 70 percent of the decline in share values for Bear Stearns and Lehman. Former SEC Chairman Harvey Pitt stated, "We had another word for this in Brooklyn. The word was 'fraud.'" According to Senator Ted Kaufman, "Abusive short selling amounts to gasoline on the fire for distressed stocks and distressed markets."[43]

A report by the SEC Office of the Inspector General found that the SEC received many complaints alleging that "Enforcement has failed to take sufficient action regarding naked short selling. Many of these complaints asserted that investors and companies lost billions of dollars because Enforcement has not taken sufficient action against naked short selling practices. These complaints further indicated a lack of confidence on the part of some members of the public in Enforcement's ability to protect investors." It wasn't merely investor complaints, though—there were good reasons to suspect nonfeasance on the part of the SEC. According to the report, "Our audit disclosed that despite the tremendous amount of attention the practice of naked short selling has generated in recent years. Enforcement has brought very few enforcement actions based on conduct involving abusive or manipulative naked short selling.... Of approximately 5,000 naked short selling complaints received in the ECC between January 1, 2007 and June 1, 2008, only 123 (approximately 2.5 percent) were forwarded for further investigation.... None of the forwarded complaints resulted in enforcement actions."[44]

Many of these complaints were likely frivolous, but a good number were surely real. The audit "determined that Enforcement's existing complaint receipt and processing procedures hinder Enforcement's ability to respond effectively to naked short selling complaints and referrals." One of the problems is that the SEC's system only forwarded the complaints if the offender at issue was already under investigation. No supervisory review was performed of the initial review. The system could hardly have been worse. As Pitt put it, the "agency must make it extremely clear that any naked short selling is illegal and it has to remove the ambiguities so the rules are very clear."[45]

In 2008, the SEC launched a probe into "possible market manipulation" and later banned short sales in financial stocks. According to Trimbath, the daily average value of fail-to-deliver trades multiplied by almost an order of magnitude from 1995 to 2007—from $838 million to $7.4 billion worth of fails per day. Those fails-to-deliver, says Trimbath, are a direct result of naked short selling. "You can't have millions of shares fail to deliver and say, 'Oops, my dog ate my certificates,'" she affirmed. And that was *before* the great collapse of 2008 in which naked short selling reached astronomical proportions. As former Lehman Brothers CEO Richard Fuld observed, "The naked shorts and rumor mongers succeeded in bringing down Bear Stearns."[46]

There is little question that naked short selling occurs frequently and that rules against it are lightly enforced. Dr. Leslie Boni, who served as a visiting financial economist at the SEC, published a paper in September 2005 in which she found there was a "pervasiveness of delivery failures.... Market makers strategically fail to deliver shares when borrowing costs are high.... Many of the firms that allow others to fail to deliver to them are themselves responsible for fails-to-deliver in other stocks. Our findings suggest that many firms allow others to fail strategically simply because they are unwilling to earn a reputation for forcing delivery and hope to receive quid pro quo for their own strategic fails."[47]

Dr. Trimbath agrees. She told *Investment News*, "The most important part of the 'naked shorting' problem is that broker-dealers are allowed to fail to deliver shares at settlement...until something is done to strictly enforce settlement, this problem will persist. Ignoring the source of the problem is no way to find a solution."[48]

Dr. Trimbath has the education, training, and experience to understand this issue in detail. She is a former manager of depository trust and clearing corporation in San Francisco and New York and a senior advisor on a capital markets project to create trade clearing and settlement in Russia. She also holds a Ph.D. in economics from New York University. On August 29, 2006, Trimbath wrote a 14-page letter to the SEC, urging enforcement of naked short sale rules by demanding settlement of all failures to deliver. She made an articulate case, describing how fails-to-deliver "disrupt market efficiency" and cheat investors "of ownership rights and privileges." Trimbath also noted that by the SEC's own admission, "not only do the broker-dealers not know whose shares are bought, sold and lent; they can't even tell if a selling customer has delivered shares. I am highly confident that they can keep track of whose money has been received; there is no excuse for not extending the same level of fiduciary care and diligence to the securities side of transactions."[49]

Similar regulatory failures were noted in an academic study entitled, "Failure is an Option: Impediments to Short Selling and Options Pricing." The report's abstract read, "Regulations allow market makers to short sell without borrowing stock, and the transactions of a major options market maker show that in most hard-to-borrow situations, it chooses not to borrow and instead fails to deliver stock to its buyers." To clarify, any stock can be "hard to borrow" if all shares available to borrow have already been sold short. This means that in a massive bear raid, market makers can and will go naked short. One of the more interesting findings is that in a two-year study of a market maker, "86 of the 69,063 failing positions, or 0.12% were bought in over the 2-year period." In other words, there was virtually no effort to force buy-in on failures to deliver.[50] This is essentially saying that counterfeit shares entered the market.

Pathetically, the SEC has not attempted to force compliance. Inspector General of the SEC Kotz said the SEC's enforcement arm "is reluctant to expend additional resources to investigate" complaints.[51] The SEC does not require public disclosure of naked short sale data. It is ironic, therefore, that it would justify its inaction by citing the lack of a data-driven study showing the harm of naked short selling. Beyond that, the data that the SEC and Depository Trust & Clearing Corporation have released—all geared at downplaying the potential harm of short selling—have been called statistically poor at best and outright misleading at worst. Dr. Timbrath commented,

"The Commission specifically asks commentors to 'provide analysis and data to support their views.' This is exceedingly difficult to do since the DTCC is obfuscating the real magnitude of the problem by using poor metrics and biased statistics."[52]

The SEC's attempts to downplay the risks of naked short selling have borne poisonous fruit. In 2006, *Forbes* reported, "Suspicious trading last year in shares of Global Links, a small Nevada real estate holding company, was far more intense than previously thought. New data... reveals trade settlement fails to early February 2005 that were 27 times greater than the total number of shares Global Links had issued at the time."[53] This is an astonishing number. How is it possible for the number of shares traded to surpass the number of shares issued by a factor of 27? Naked shorting made up the difference. And how many of those shares were delivered? Certainly there is no way it came close to the total number traded.

In fact, one individual, Robert Simpson, bought 100 percent of the existing outstanding shares, and all failed to deliver. He bought 126,986 shares more than the 1,158,064 shares that were officially issued at the time. Mr. Simpson filed with the SEC as 100 percent owner of Global Links. Then, over the next two trading days, approximately 60 million shares changed hands even though Mr. Simpson did not trade a single share.[54]

While Global Links was a penny stock of arguably dubious value, the real question relates to the overall system that allows such clear manipulation. A further question asks why the SEC was not at the forefront of enforcing rules even in regard to a penny stock.

And Global Links wasn't alone. A RICO-based lawsuit was filed regarding a company called TASER, maker of the famed stun-gun. Among other things, the complaint charged that the defendant had flooded the market with counterfeit shares. "For example," the complaint alleged, "at the time of TASER's 2005 annual vote, TASER had approximately 61.1 million shares outstanding. Yet approximately 82 million shares voted, an additional over-vote of approximately 20 million shares." The day of the vote, about

17.2 million shares of TASER stock were shorted. This means at least 3.7 million shares were counterfeit.[55] The scale of the problem was made clear in a 2005 Securities Transfer Association review of 341 shareholder votes that found evidence of over-voting in each and every case.[56] That indicates false shares were being sold at record rates.

So, we have traders who can short sell shares without borrowing them, creating counterfeit shares and depressing prices. Then we have a failure to investigate naked shorting, and even when investigated a failure to enforce the rules. We haven't even kept track of which shares are short and from whom. All of this provided plenty of opportunity for financial terrorists.

THE MADOFF EXEMPTION

Long before he was convicted of defrauding the American public of some $50 billion through a Ponzi scheme, Bernie Madoff was Chairman of the National Association of Securities Dealers (NASD). In that capacity, he appeared regularly at the SEC and served on agency panels. "When it came to Bernie, people paid more attention," said Georgetown University Law School Professor Donald Langevoort, who worked on an SEC panel with Madoff. "This was a guy who really knew how markets worked. He was the grown-up in the room. If there was confusion or a question or two people on opposite sides going at each other, Bernie would speak up and explain what the deal was. I'm sure in some way that may have thrown even the commission off their guard."[57]

One of Madoff's key accomplishments at the SEC was to get a rule approved—the so-called "Madoff Exemption"—that allowed market-makers to naked short sell. Market-makers are broker-dealer firms that gain fees by holding shares of securities in order to help grease the wheels of trading; if someone buys stock in a company, it is the market-makers who sell the stock and then find an offsetting order. This keeps the markets flowing smoothly. In the case of short selling, if the market-maker has no inventory of the shares sold, the firm is allowed to create an "IOU" for the shares. This is a form of naked short selling legalized by the Madoff Exemption.

Harry Markopolos, the fraud investigator who uncovered Madoff's Ponzi scheme, said that the SEC "roars like a lion and bites like a flea," and "is busy protecting the big financial predators from investors." Markopolos understandably feared Madoff—as he told the House financial panel, Madoff "had a lot of dirty money" from the Russian mafia and Latin American drug cartels.[58]

While the Madoff Exemption did not create as big a strategic vulnerability as some other regulatory changes did, it demonstrates the deep problems with the SEC. Even SEC Chairman Christopher Cox seemed to acknowledge something was fundamentally wrong; Reuters reported that Cox declared he was "'deeply concerned' by the agency's apparent multiple failures to thoroughly investigate almost a decade of credible allegations of wrongdoing at Madoff's brokerage firm."[59]

The Madoff affair proves three important points: that self-regulatory organizations can be corrupted; that a lack of enforcement by the SEC does not necessarily indicate a lack of wrongdoing; and that market-makers' actions can be self-serving, as exemplified, perhaps, by the Madoff Exemption.

ACCOUNTING TRICKERY

Since the collapse of Enron, Americans have been sensitive to allegations that companies are cooking the books. Unfortunately, the government seems far less concerned. For years, commercial banks have moved securities mortgage loans off their balance sheets. When things get ugly, however, these toxic assets begin to infect everything else at the bank. According to the Consumer Education Foundation, off-balance sheet assets amounted to almost sixteen times the amounts *on* balance sheets in 2007. From 1992 to 2007, off-balance sheet assets grew seven times faster than on-balance sheet assets. One former SEC official called this practice "nothing more than just a scam."

Here's how it works: lenders can sell their mortgages to Qualified Special Purpose Entities (QSPEs), which are also owned by the lenders. If the lenders sell to another company owned by the lender, they don't have to show the assets on their normal balance sheets. Typically, this makes sense—if I own a car and then sell it to my LLC, my LLC is responsible for the car and I am not. The same is not true for mortgages—the lender may carry the liability for mortgage defaults.

The Enron example is relevant here. The energy giant created spin-off companies designed to incur debt on behalf of the company. Thanks to this little arrangement, credit ratings firms routinely scored Enron close to perfect. After Enron imploded, the government tried to close the loophole, but they left it open in one area: securitized assets, which are the precise assets at issue with QSPEs. The Financial Accounting Standards Board Chairman, Robert Herz, relates that such accounting tricks were a huge problem. "Unfortunately, it seems that some folks used [QSPEs] like a punch bowl to get off-balance sheet treatment while spiking the punch. That has led us to conclude that now it's time to take away the punch bowl."[60]

Another one of the most scrutinized accounting methods is mark-to-market accounting. Until the last twenty years or so, historical cost accounting was the accepted method of determining asset value. This method took the original value of the asset and accepted that as good until there was some sort of re-transmission of the asset. So, for example, if you bought a house for $300,000, that house would be listed on your asset sheet as $300,000 until the next sale.

With mark-to-market, that isn't the case. Under that system, the house would be reassessed continually, as per the current market value. That value is determined by looking at similar assets sold in the market, meaning you could be forced to take a write-down on your books.

During the Great Depression, mark-to-market accounting was used routinely. It caused the failure of many banks, which had to continually call in cash to keep their balances within legal limits as their assets depreciated. As Brian Wesbury and Robert Stein of *Forbes* write, "Franklin Roosevelt suspended it in 1938, and between then and 2007 there were no panics or depressions. But when FASB 157, a statement from the Federal Accounting Standards Board, went into effect in 2007, reintroducing mark-to-market accounting, look what happened." [61]

Mark-to-market may give a more accurate picture of what assets are worth in normal times, but it also accelerates declines during a panic. It forces banks to write off losses before they actually occur—in the housing example above, you aren't selling your $300,000 house for $250,000, but you're forced to realize the $50,000 loss anyway. Stein and Wesbury point out, "By wiping out capital, so-called 'fair value' accounting rules undermine the banking system, increase the odds of asset fire sales and make markets even less liquid. As this happened in 2008, investment banks failed, and the government proposed bailouts. This drove prices down even further, which hurt the economy. And now as growth suffers, bad loans multiply. It's a vicious downward spiral."[62]

During the 2008 panic, prices were marked ridiculously low. A perfect example can be seen in the fire-sale of Lehman assets that occurred right after the firm's bankruptcy announcement. Barclays bank stepped in immediately and paid just $1.75 billion for real estate and various profitable operations worth well over $5 billion at the time. Ironically, just two months later, Barclays was forced to "mark up" its former Lehman holdings by $5 billion.[63]

It's important to understand that mark-to-market rules could force other institutions with similar assets to drop their valuation to the fire-sale level. Clearly, the daily marking of asset prices can produce serious volatility. If the temporary markdown is large enough, it could even put an otherwise profitable company out of business by forcing a downward spiral of asset sales into a panicked market. Worse still, those aware of the mark-to-market rules could use them as a tool of manipulation to push firms over the cliff.

THE NMS REGULATION

SEC reforms undertaken in 1975 made the market even more vulnerable to bear raids. Those reforms, titled the National Market System initiative, were supposed to make trading speedier and more efficient, make pricing more transparent, and ensure that buyers and sellers were not ripping off one another.

The NMS largely achieved these goals. But there was a downside: NMS prevents initial public offerings (IPOs) from gaining steam and exposes our market to tremendous instability.

Investment bankers used to make a fortune helping to broker IPOs. That's because "block dealers"—stock dealers who trade huge blocks of stock at uniform prices—have been made obsolete by the myriad markets at which you can buy stock at uniform prices. Large trades became many smaller trades. Electronic markets took over for manual ones.

This sounds great, but there are drawbacks. The New York Stock Exchange and NASDAQ were constantly raising new buyers for the companies that traded on them. That's not the case anymore. As Steve Wunsch, inventor of the ISE Stock Exchange and the Arizona Stock Exchange, writes, "Investment banks and bankers were transformed from socially useful capital raisers to socially harmful, too-big-to-fail problems for the US taxpayer." They shifted their focus from raising capital for good projects to speculating on the markets.[64]

Eventually, the additional speed allowed by NMS worked against both transparency and liquidity, the two features it was designed to improve. That's because it aided the spread of high-frequency computerized trading, in which trades happen in milliseconds without any human judgment involved. Trades are based instead on complex computer algorithms. Firms tend to move such orders to the "dark markets" where there is even less transparency. In addition, high-frequency traders regularly place and cancel orders that can affect markets and cause volatility. The volatility, in turn, reduces big-picture liquidity by driving more traditional longer-term investors from the market. The bottom line is that NMS changed Wall Street dramatically and opened the door for market manipulation by computer algorithms.[65]

OPENING THE DOOR TO FINANCIAL JIHAD

Since 9/11, the U.S. government has cracked down hard on funders of Islamic terrorism. As usual, it was late to the game. According to the 9/11 Commission Report, bin Laden and company only needed between $400,000 and $500,000 to carry out the attack. Said the commission, "The plotters' tradecraft was not especially sophisticated, but it was good enough. They moved, stored, and spent their money in ordinary ways, easily defeating the detection mechanisms in place at the time."[66]

It took much more than that to finance the entire al Qaeda operation—something like $30 million per year. Bin Laden didn't finance the organization personally. Instead, he used corrupt charities as fronts for collecting zakat—Islamic-mandated charitable donations. Since the Saudis run many of these charities, the commission tried to determine how involved the Saudis are in terror financing. It eventually discounted direct Saudi involvement in the terror funding system, although it admitted it could not "exclude the likelihood that charities with significant Saudi government sponsorship diverted funds to al Qaeda."[67]

Though the 9/11 Commission gave the federal government failing grades for its post-9/11 security reforms, the commission *did* issue an A- for the government's "vigorous efforts against terrorist financing."[68] The government did not deserve that grade, however, because it has largely tracked money only going one way—from financial institutions to terrorists. It has not tracked, and has not adopted mechanisms to track, investment by terrorist-affiliated groups in the U.S. economy.

Since 9/11, the Islamic world has used sharia-compliant finance to disguise its money manipulation. To distract attention from SCF itself, Muslims have re-christened (no pun intended) the system as "ethical investing," and Muslim financiers are increasingly insisting that all banks include the option. Attorney David Yerushalmi detailed the problem in *National Review*: "The financial jihadists built their strategy upon both sovereign wealth and the cravenness and fecklessness of the Western facilitators who would sell their own well-being and physical security for a place among the *Fortune* 500. Led by the Saudis but also joined by the other oil-soaked Persian Gulf regimes, the Shariah-inspired jihadists learned quickly that Western financial institutions and their professional lackeys in the legal and accounting fields would do anything for that next billion-dollar transaction."[69]

Terrorists and terrorist sponsors can now use legitimate means of investment to promote their own ends. Deposed Libyan dictator Muammar Qaddafi, for example, had tens of billions of dollars in assets invested in U.S. markets and as much as $200 billion worldwide.[70] He had $55 million of it stashed with Allen Stanford, an accused Ponzi schemer second only to Bernie Madoff. Interestingly, Qaddafi got enough information to withdraw his cash before the scheme collapsed. Stanford traveled to Tripoli and met with the Libyan authorities in January 2009, and the Libyans withdrew $12.6 million. Just a few weeks later, the SEC sued Stanford. "[I]t is clear the Libyan Defendants had access to Mr. Stanford that was substantially superior to other investors," said the court filing, "and the Libyan defendants were aware of the impending demise of the Stanford investment scheme well before the Receivership was imposed on the Stanford parties."[71]

The point here is simple: Libya was more aware of what was happening at Stanford than was the SEC or 28,000 other investors. This shows that the Islamic world—even a regime led by a bizarre dictator of questionable sanity—has the ability to play at high levels in the game of American finance. As a side note, Stanford also had major dealings in Venezuela, with as much as one-quarter of his assets coming from Hugo Chavez's workers' paradise.[72]

Recall that MSNBC reported that the Department of Homeland Security feared al Qaeda terrorists would "try to land jobs inside US financial institutions, and from there launch attacks on the nation's economy." Commander David Wray, spokesman for the department, said, "There is new intelligence that indicated specific interest in financial services and indirect indication...that led us to believe we should provide additional awareness that threats could come from within as well as without."[73]

That advice hasn't been heeded. For example, in 2003, Abdurahman Alamoudi, a designer of the U.S. military chaplain program, was arrested while attempting to smuggle $340,000 to terrorist groups in Syria. He received that money from Libya's Qaddafi, which is a story unto itself. Despite the fact that Alamoudi supported Islamic terror groups like Hamas and Hezbollah, he had been granted access to "senior US government officials to create the Islamic chaplain program, and also founded a group to recommend young Muslims to serve as clerics." Meanwhile, both the accrediting organizations that recommended Muslim chaplains for the military—the Graduate School of Islamic and Social Sciences and the American Muslim Foundation—have been tied to terrorist organizations.[74] One of Alamoudi's reported associates through the Fiqh Council of North America, Sheikh DeLorenzo, was granted permission to sponsor a trading platform called the Al Safi Trust with Shariah Capital and Barclays Bank, which was designed to allow Muslim traders and hedge funds to participate in short selling as well as to invest (or to speculate) in commodities.[75]

This is just scratching the surface. As already described, Islamic finance has expanded dramatically since 2001, and so have sovereign wealth funds. Furthermore, dark markets, dark pools, and other opaque practices have enabled foreign money to enter the United States undetected. Remember, it was precisely transparency that the 9/11 Commission cited as our main defense against financial terrorism. As this chapter has demonstrated, however, what transparency we had has virtually disappeared.

★   ★   ★

Over the past two decades, the gates were opened wide for a financial attack on the U.S. markets. Our enemies had the motive, they had the means, and thanks to government failings like poor regulatory oversight, politically correct policies that distorted the market, backstopping of bad risks, and old-fashioned corruption, they now had the opportunity.

Some argue that many of these problems hardly contributed to the crash of September 2008. In that view, the repeal of Glass-Steagall was not really a problem, nor was the lax regulation of short selling. A larger number of analysts admit that credit default swaps and weak banking oversight were serious problems. But nearly everyone believes that the crisis of September 2008 was brought on by domestic forces. The opportunities laid forth in this chapter, in this view, came to fruition by themselves.

They did no such thing. They were triggered by forces beyond our borders—and those forces are well prepared to attack us again.

CHAPTER SEVEN

HOW THEY DID IT

Few people predicted the September 2008 crash of the U.S. financial markets. A year after the meltdown, liberal economist Paul Krugman commented, "During the golden years, financial economists came to believe that markets were inherently stable—indeed, that stocks and other assets were always priced just right. There was nothing in the prevailing models suggesting the possibility of the kind of collapse that happened last year."[1] Robert Samuelson, a contributing editor to the *Washington Post* and *Newsweek*, agreed. "If you de-emphasize financial markets and financial markets are decisive, you're out to lunch," he wrote. "A study by the International Monetary Fund, called Initial Lessons of the Crisis, admits there was an under-appreciation of systemic risks coming from financial sector feedbacks into the real economy. That's an understatement."[2]

The reason so few economists foresaw the crash is because hardly any of them were paying attention to global market participants and their motives. Warren Buffett hit close to the mark when he called the initial market plunge an "economic Pearl Harbor."[3] He had no idea how right he was. Just as with Pearl Harbor, America had fallen victim to a sneak attack.

This time, however, the battlefield was the economy and we have yet to galvanize our defenses.

To quickly sum up, there were two phases to the collapse. The first phase, lasting from 2007 through June 2008, was a speculative run-up in oil prices that generated trillions of dollars of excess wealth for oil-producing nations, enriching their sharia-compliant sovereign wealth funds. Undoubtedly, this spectacular rise in oil prices stemmed from market manipulation. There is no other reasonable explanation why prices tripled over eighteen months even as the world entered a recession and as the supply-demand picture argued for lower prices. This manipulation was enabled by the spread of oil speculation over the previous five years, to the point that prices were effectively being set on the futures markets. This chapter will explain how that happened and who was behind it.

The second phase was an unprecedented manipulation of the stock market and credit markets. The goal was to bring down the U.S. economy by killing off the financial industry—the same goal held by the 9/11 plotters. This phase began in early 2008 with a series of bear raids targeting significant U.S. financial services firms. An initial bear raid against Bear Stearns brought the firm to near bankruptcy, but the danger was briefly averted when the bank was acquired by J. P. Morgan Chase. Similar bear raids were conducted against various other firms during the summer, each ending in an acquisition. The attacks culminated with the collapse of Lehman Brothers in mid-September. This created a system-wide crisis, completely froze the credit markets, and nearly brought down the global financial system.

The bear raids were perpetrated by naked short selling and manipulation of credit default swaps, both of which were virtually unregulated. The short selling was enabled by recent regulatory changes, including the repeal of the uptick rule, loopholes such as "the Madoff Exemption," and other reforms described in chapter six.

To this day, the source of the bear raids has not been identified due to transparency gaps for hedge funds, trading pools, sponsored access, and sovereign wealth funds. What *can* be demonstrated, however, is that two relatively small broker-dealers emerged virtually overnight to trade "trillions of dollars worth of U.S. blue chip companies. They were the number one traders in all financial companies that collapsed or are now financially supported by the U.S. government. Trading by these two firms has grown exponentially while the markets have lost trillions of dollars in value."[4]

Various Wall Street players may have had the knowledge and resources to pull off the attack. But who would do it? Wall Street traders don't want the economy to collapse. Besides, they would be risking prison time as well as being wiped out if the market turned against them during their attack.

As this chapter will show, the 2008 meltdown stemmed from a willful act of economic destruction. The naked short selling volume was so large that it could not have been coincidental. And whoever did it used every trick in the book to avoid detection. But the perpetrators still left some clues and tell-tale signs that few people have noticed because hardly anyone has looked for them.

Some people believe the 2008 collapse was a natural result of corporate greed or incompetent regulators or bad government policy. These all certainly played a role, but they are also used as a smokescreen to hide the identities of our attackers. This is in line with the doctrine outlined in *Unrestricted Warfare*, in which the Chinese authors discuss how a financial terrorist could cause a stock market crash and then conceal himself "in the forests of free economics."[5]

Despite the hurdles, we have discovered where the attacks were focused, how they took place, and which trading firms were used. Possessing the motive, means, and opportunity to launch a financial attack on the U.S. economy, our enemies merely had to carry it out.

PHASE ONE: THE OIL RUN-UP

The initial danger sign in the rosy-looking economy of 2007–2008 was the rapid rise in oil prices. Starting from a low in January 2007 near $50 per barrel, oil prices rose steadily to almost $150 a barrel by June 2008. This tripling of prices occurred even as economic growth appeared to be leveling and oil drilling activity increased. At the time, analysts debated whether speculation was causing the price spike or if it was due to natural supply and demand. The former view was convincingly argued in research by MIT Professor of Economics Emeritus Richard S. Eckaus, who wrote,

> The oil price really is a speculative bubble. Yet only recently has the U.S. Congress, for example, showed recognition that this might even be a possibility. In general there seems to be a prefer-ence for the claim that the price increases are the result of basic economic forces: rapid growth in consumption, pushed par-ticularly by the oil appetites of China and India, the depreciation of the U.S. dollar, real supply limitations, current and prospective and the risks of supply disruption, especially in the Middle East.

Eckaus continued,

> Since there is no reason based on current and expected supply and demand that justifies the current price of oil, what is left? The oil price is a speculative bubble. This is an idea that has some backing in financial circles, e.g. George Soros. The spiking price pattern would, itself, suggest it. It is well known that hedge funds are very active in the oil market and their activity, along with other speculators, has raised the volume of oil transactions far above the volume warranted by ordinary commercial transactions.[6]

Unlike the housing bubble, which had some short-term benefits for the domestic economy, the oil price spike had a largely negative effect. It reduced household income, crowding out spending for other items. As prices peaked in June 2008, consumers began to panic.

The most likely suspects in an oil price shock are those who benefit most from higher prices. While it's possible hedge funds undertook such speculation solely for profit, the sheer size of the oil shock indicates otherwise—previous large-scale oil shocks invariably stemmed from deliberate acts by oil producing states meant to influence U.S. foreign policy.

When oil producers were not targeting America, they kept prices remarkably stable. Even during the 1991 Gulf War, oil prices were maintained at reasonable levels despite lost production in both Kuwait and Iraq. Thus, from the Iranian revolution of 1980 until 2004, hedge funds and other traders refrained from trying to drive oil prices higher through speculation, believing their efforts would fail in light of the massive market power of oil producing states.

But around 2004 something changed: Islamic oil-producing states, which had kept oil prices stable for some time, were angered by the U.S. occupation of Iraq. In light of the fierce denunciations of our Iraq policy that echoed throughout the Middle East, it's reasonable to suspect oil producers abandoned their commitment to reasonable oil prices and began trying to maximize their profits. If they wanted to do this without being punished by the United States, they could have acted secretly through over-the-counter markets and hedge funds, using speculative tools to push prices up.

The price spike was big money for the Middle East; at the peak price of nearly $150 per barrel, the world would be paying $3 trillion per year more for energy than it did at $50 per barrel, earning OPEC an additional $1 trillion. Even taking into account the drop in prices at the end of 2008, it is reasonable to assume that the price spike earned hundreds of billions of dollars for Middle Eastern sovereign wealth funds.

Dr. Walid Phares, a Fox News analyst and teacher of Global Strategies at the National Defense University, identifies the geopolitical forces behind the rise in oil prices: "Combined Salafist-Wahabi and Muslim Brotherhood circles in the Gulf with consent from the Iranian side on this particular issue, used the escalating pricing of oil over the past year to push the financial crisis in the US over the cliff.... The 'oil-push' put the market out of balance, hitting back at Wall Street. Basically, there was certainly a crisis in misman-agement domestically... but the possible OPEC economic 'offensive' crumbled the defenses of US economy in a few months."[7]

Of course, oil prices don't rise in a vacuum. Yes, OPEC is a cartel dom-inated by Islamic states and other problematic regimes such as Venezuela. And yes, the cartel has shown the ability to set the price over the short term both through political means and by increasing or decreasing supply. But what happened in 2007–2008 was something different—oil prices tripled largely due to the financial markets. As previously discussed, in 2008 "paper oil" traded at a daily volume 27 times greater in New York than all of Amer-ica used in an average day.[8] And that is just the U.S. NYMEX trading of paper oil based on West Texas Intermediate Crude. A relatively new phe-nomenon, trading in paper oil grew 2,300 percent in the five years leading to the peak, the vast majority of which was not hedging but rather specula-tive efforts to profit from higher prices.[9] The paper oil market also operates in Europe, in the Middle East, and in dark markets, with serious price implications. Conveniently for OPEC, neither the United States nor anyone else could pressure or threaten the cartel over high oil prices, since blame fell at the feet of anonymous speculators.

So who was buying all this paper oil? There is no way to definitively say due to the dark markets, unregulated derivatives, and other impediments to transparency. But threading together the strains of evidence suggests a jihadist purpose. Obviously, oil producers have an economic interest in achieving the highest sustainable price for oil. But what if their interests go beyond simple economics? We have already seen that OPEC nations have repeatedly used oil as a political weapon, and we have also established that their sovereign wealth funds serve a geopolitical purpose. Finally, we have documented that serious global players including Venezuela, Iran, and various Islamist groups favor once again wielding higher oil prices as a weapon against the West.[10]

So, how did they do it? Dr. Gal Luft, Executive Director of the Institute for the Analysis of Global Security (IAGS), explained to the House Committee on Foreign Affairs how sovereign wealth funds can be used for this kind of speculative activity:

> One of the dangers here is that through their investments SWF can shape market conditions in sectors where their governments have economic and/or political interests or where they enjoy comparative advantage. In recent months, for example, commodity futures have increased dramatically largely due to astronomical growth in speculation and bidding up of prices while actual deliveries are far behind. Commodity markets are easily manipulated and the impact of such manipulations could often reverberate throughout the world as the current food crisis shows. While U.S. companies are not allowed to buy their own products and create shortage to increase revenues, foreign governments with economic interest in a particular commodity face no similar restrictions bidding on it, via their proxies, in the commodity market. Under the current system, oil countries can, via their SWF as well as other investment vehicles that receive investment from SWF, long future contracts and commodity derivatives and hence affect oil futures in a way that benefits them.[11]

And indeed, in the lead-up to September 2008, there was intense and focused investment in the commodity markets both directly and via proxies coming from oil producers and sovereign wealth funds.[12] There was a spike in trading of the leveraged oil ETFs, a jump in sharia-compliant oil buying, and a rush into oil futures and commodity derivatives. Much of this can be traced to those we have identified with motive.

While paper oil speculation pushed prices ever higher, the producers enjoyed the benefit. Prices were pushed so far beyond levels that could be justified by supply and demand, however, that prices ultimately collapsed, plunging from the peak of nearly $150 per barrel to below $40 per barrel by year's end. It's hard to believe oil producing states would be so foolish as to engineer this outcome if their goal was simply to maximize their long-term oil income. But that wasn't the only goal. For some, the purpose of the oil run-up was to weaken the capitalist economy while generating the funds needed to carry out the coming financial attacks.

PHASE TWO: THE BEAR RAIDS

If Americans were scared by rising oil prices in early 2008, they were panicked by the March collapse of Bear Stearns. Bear was, until recently, the fifth largest U.S. investment bank. It had survived the Great Depression, World War II, the 1987 market crash, and the terrorist attacks of 9/11. On January 12, 2007, the firm's stock traded at $171 per share. A little more than a year later, on March 16, 2008, J. P. Morgan agreed to buy Bear for just $2 per share (the tender offer was later raised to $10 per share), with government help to make it happen.

SEC Chairman Christopher Cox later attributed the collapse of Bear Stearns to self-fulfilling "market rumors" about the firm's liquidity. These rumors spread even though Bear Stearns' capital exceeded regulatory standards, with its liquidity pool topping $18 billion at the time of its collapse. Clearly, the rapid downfall of Bear Stearns hurt the market and economy overall and was considered a sufficient threat for the Federal Reserve to seek a buyer for the firm.

What exactly happened? According to *Rolling Stone*'s Matt Taibbi, on March 11, 2008, an unnamed person or entity "made one of the craziest bets Wall Street has ever seen. The mystery figure spent $1.7 million on a series of options, gambling that shares in the venerable investment bank Bear Stearns would lose more than half their value in nine days or less. It was madness." In order for the gambler to win, "Bear would have to fall harder and faster than any Wall Street brokerage in history. The very next day, March 12th, Bear went into free fall." That $1.7 million investment turned into $270 million virtually overnight.[13]

Taibbi says this was clearly a case of insider manipulation. He isn't alone. Thomas Haugh, general partner of PTI Securities & Futures LP with eighteen years experience as an options market maker, expressed the majority view on Wall Street: "Even if I was the most bearish man on earth, I can't imagine buying puts 50 percent below the strike price with just over a week to expiration. It's not even on the page of rational behavior, *unless you know something*"[14] (emphasis added). Another trader compared the trade to buying $1.7 million worth of lottery tickets, all with the same number.

Naked short sellers moved in almost immediately after the mysterious $1.7 million trade was made. Prior to March 11, there wasn't any problem with Bear stock being sold but not delivered—the hallmark of naked short selling. According to Taibbi, however, on March 12, "the number of counterfeit shares in Bear skyrocketed.... On March 11, there were 201,768 shares of Bear that had failed to deliver. The very next day, the number of phantom shares leaped to 1.2 million. By the close of trading that Friday, the number passed 2 million—and when the market reopened the following Monday, it soared to 13.7 million." This was, Taibbi says, "one of the most blatant cases of stock manipulation in Wall Street history."[15] Experts believe all this likely started with activity by just 10 to 15 people—that's all it took to draw sufficient blood and attract sharks.

It's clear something criminal happened, yet authorities could not trace it. Senator Christopher Dodd, chairman of the Senate Banking Committee, asked SEC Chairman Cox whether he was "looking at this," suggesting that there must have been "some sort of bells and whistles at the SEC. This goes beyond rumors."[16] Despite Dodd's pressure and the feds' access to the trading record, however, there have been no convictions for insider trading or for illegally spreading rumors in connection with the Bear collapse. We know why. It was financial terrorism and was designed to be untraceable.

Six months later, as Taibbi explains, the same thing happened again at Lehman Brothers.[17] George Soros then wrote an op-ed for the *Wall Street*

Journal explaining what was really going on. According to Soros, "It's clear that AIG, Bear Stearns, Lehman Brothers and others were destroyed by bear raids in which the shorting of stocks and buying CDS mutually amplified and reinforced each other. The unlimited shorting of stocks was made possible by the abolition of the uptick rule, which would have hindered bear raids by allowing short selling only when prices were rising. The unlimited shorting of bonds was facilitated by the CDS market. The two made a lethal combination."[18]

Even the SEC eventually seemed to agree, as evidenced by its Emergency Order dated July 15, 2008. The order stated, "False rumors can lead to a loss of confidence in our markets. Such loss of confidence can lead to panic selling, which may be further exacerbated by 'naked' short selling. As a result, the prices of securities may artificially and unnecessarily decline well below the price level that would have resulted from the normal price discovery process. If significant financial institutions are involved, this chain of events can threaten disruption of our markets."[19]

Another major event in the market meltdown was the destruction of mortgage giants Fannie Mae and Freddie Mac. During the summer of 2008, short sellers began attacking the two government sponsored entities (GSEs), which were overextended in the housing bubble. Fannie stock, which exceeded $60 in late 2007, plunged below $1 per share by September 2008. Freddie stock followed a similar pattern, provoking the Treasury to inject tens of billions of dollars to prop up the ailing companies.

The collapse in Fannie and Freddie's stock price was accompanied by a massive rise in the cost to insure their debt. This hampered their ability to raise capital, creating a situation of near chaos and exacerbating the housing market's woes. The situation was dire—together, the GSEs held loans of $5 trillion, the "largest debt ever held by any private company in history… larger than any other country's debt, with the exception of that of the United States," NPR reported. "Allowing Fannie Mae and Freddie Mac to collapse would have been akin to letting Japan or the United Kingdom go bankrupt. Global economic leaders say even those unimaginable scenarios would have paled beside the fallout from a Fannie/Freddie implosion." Domenico Siniscalco, former finance minister of Italy, said that Fannie and Freddie's bankruptcy "would have meant Armageddon. Meltdown of the financial system, the global financial system."[20] Unsurprisingly, the federal government bailed out both institutions at enormous expense to the taxpayers.

In his memoirs, former Treasury Secretary Henry Paulson reveals some key details about the Russians' attempts to carry out a "disruptive scheme" against Fannie and Freddie by encouraging the Chinese to join them in dumping their holdings in the GSEs. Their intent, according to Paulson, was to force our government into a costly bailout that would have harmed our economy.[21] This was a textbook case of economic warfare.

Paulson claims the Chinese told him they turned the Russians down, although the Russians seem to have liquidated their own shares anyway. So did the Russians ultimately act alone, or were they coordinating their actions with financial terrorists? Credible, independent sources have confirmed to me that the Russians knew all about the financial attacks that were taking place. As far as we can tell, they were not organizing the onslaught but rather "piggybacking" on the attacks of others.

Once the government saved Fannie and Freddie, short sellers moved on to other targets. Beginning on September 11, 2008, in rapid-fire fashion, financial firms once again came under attack. This was six months to the day after Bear Stearns was attacked and on the seventh anniversary of the 9/11 attack. Lehman Brothers was first on the list. The FBI received an early tip that something suspicious was going on from Erik Davidson, now Deputy Chief Investment Officer at Wells Fargo. I've known Erik for a long time. We worked together at Templeton and were business partners in a start-up a decade ago. He is not someone given to conspiracy theories or panic. But he was so concerned by the huge spike in short selling on Lehman Brothers that occurred on September 11 that he notified the authorities. As the attack on Lehman gained pace, Wall Street panicked—even the best hedge funds were shocked. The credit markets collapsed.

As with Bear Stearns, the move against Lehman was a full bear raid using naked short selling, rumor spreading, and the manipulation of credit default swaps. According to a Bloomberg report by Gary Matsumoto, 23 percent of the trading in Lehman on September 17, 2008 comprised failed trades, a strong sign of naked short selling. The Bloomberg report maintained, "The biggest bankruptcy in history might have been avoided if Wall Street had been prevented from practicing one of its darkest arts."[22]

The bear raid on Lehman came on the heels of two false rumors that hurt the firm that summer. In both cases, naked short selling spiked as the rumors circulated. On June 27, naked shorting jumped 23-fold. The next trading day, June 30, a rumor circulated that Barclays would buy Lehman at a price 25 percent below the market price. The stock fell 11 percent despite adamant denials by both Lehman and Barclays. Over the next six trading days, the number of failed-to-deliver trades—indicative of naked short sales—occurred at a rate forty-six times greater than the level of June 26. Then on July 10, another rumor began spreading that two significant clients had stopped trading with the firm. Despite denials by all parties, Lehman's stock dropped an additional 27 percent.[23]

On September 15, Lehman Brothers collapsed. That same day, Congressman Paul Kanjorski made a shocking announcement—more than a half trillion dollars had vanished from U.S. money market accounts:

> At 11 in the morning the Federal Reserve noticed a tremendous draw-down of money market accounts in the United States, to the tune of $550 billion was being drawn out in the matter of an hour or two. The Treasury opened up its window to help and pumped a $105 billion in the system and quickly realized that they could not stem the tide. We were having an electronic run on the banks. They decided to close the operation, close down the money accounts and announce a guarantee of $250,000 per account so there wouldn't be further panic out there.... If they had not done that, their estimation was that by 2 o'clock that

afternoon, $5.5 trillion would have been drawn out of the money market system of the United States, would have collapsed the entire economy of the United States, and within 24 hours the world economy would have collapsed.... It would have been the end of our economic system and our political system as we know it.[24]

By the time Lehman failed, false rumors and naked short selling had driven its stock price to nearly zero. The amount of naked short selling was more than 1,600 times greater than the amount just three months earlier. As with Bear Stearns, Lehman had sufficient capital to meet regulatory standards almost until its final collapse. In testimony to Congress, Lehman CEO Richard Fuld noted that Lehman's leverage had been reduced to a remarkable 10.5, one of the lowest ratios on Wall Street at the time and well below levels most analysts typically viewed as dangerous.[25] The constant rumors, prohibitively high credit default swap rates, and the stock decline combined to destroy the firm's ability to access capital or conduct business. Without the rumors, Lehman likely could have continued operating or at least found a business partner and retained some shareholder value. This, in turn would probably have eliminated the need for the TARP bailout and avoided much of the ensuing turmoil. Instead, in the course of a week, a 158-year-old firm disappeared.

Former hedge fund manager Andy Kessler wrote in the *Wall Street Journal* that this was all a "bear-raid extraordinaire." He explained,

In a typical bear raid, traders short a target stock—i.e., borrow shares and then sell them, hoping to cover or replace them at a cheaper price. Once short, traders then spread bad news, amplify it, and even make it up if they have to, to get a stock to drop so they can cover their short. This bear raid was different. Wall Street is short-term financed, mostly through overnight and repurchasing agreements, which was fine when banks were just doing IPOs and trading stocks. But as they began to own things for their own account (mortgage-backed securities, collateralized debt obligations) there emerged a huge mismatch between the duration of their holdings (10- and 30-year mortgages and the derivatives based on them) and their overnight funding. When this happens a bear can ride in, undercut a bank's short-term funding, and force it to sell a long-term holding.[26]

Now, these banks did have insurance for their long-term debt. Unfortunately, that insurance was in the form of credit default swaps, mostly issued by AIG, itself a target of bear raids. Those CDSs were empty vessels—there was no money to back them up in case they had to pay out. And they were sliced and diced so much that nobody really knew who would have to pay up if insurance was invoked. Kessler compared the CDS market to "buying insurance from the captain of the Titanic, who put the premiums in the ship's safe and collected a tidy bonus for his efforts."[27]

The banks bought the insurance and then stuck it in their vault, as if it made their risky debt acquisition safer. But the price of that insurance impacted the value of the other bank-owned assets. When insurance prices went up, for example, the value of collateralized debt obligations (CDOs) and mortgage backed securities (MBSs) went down, since the insurance prices would only rise if CDOs and MBSs were found to be risky. Because of mark-to-market rules, if the price in the general market rose for the insurance, the banks would have to write off a loss on CDOs and MBSs. Then they'd need more money in order to replace the lost cash on their balance sheet. That meant, said Kessler, that "Wall Street got stuck holding the hot potato making them vulnerable to a bear raid."[28]

As Kessler further noted, GE CEO Jeff Immelt worried that "by spending 25 million bucks in a handful of transactions in an unregulated market," traders in CDSs could destroy the market. "I just don't think we should treat credit default swaps as like the Delphic Oracle of any kind. It's the most easily manipulated and broadly manipulated market that there is," Immelt averred. Kessler wryly observed, "Complain all you want, it worked."[29]

Aggressive buying of credit default swaps was itself a secret weapon, unregulated and virtually undetectable, but with catastrophic consequences. As Immelt noted, this weapon didn't require much in the way of resources. In conjunction with naked short selling, CDSs were dangerous weapons that a few people could launch in secret.

The reality is that both Bear Stearns and Lehman Brothers fell victim to a modern form of bear raid. Government intervention reduced the overall impact of the attack on Bear, but in the case of Lehman, the government declined to act, and that triggered economic chaos.

After Lehman failed, the SEC appeared to get religion. On September 18, 2008, the commission issued another emergency order, this time banning all short selling in nearly every financial services firm in America.[30] The initial ban, covering 799 stocks, was quickly increased to nearly 1,000. The ban was slated to last until October 2, but was extended until a bailout package could be put in place. In making the ruling, the SEC announced,

> In our recent publication of an emergency order under Section 12(k) of the Exchange Act (the "Act"), for example, we were concerned about the possible unnecessary or artificial price movements based on unfounded rumors regarding the stability of financial institutions and other issuers exacerbated by "naked" short selling. Our concerns, however, are no longer limited to just the financial institutions that were the subject of the July Emergency Order.... Given the importance of confidence in our financial markets as a whole, we have become concerned about recent sudden declines in the prices of a wide range of securities. Such price declines can give rise to questions about the underlying financial condition of an issuer, which in turn can create a crisis of confidence, without a fundamental underlying basis.[31]

That last sentence is significant, affirming the self-reinforcing nature of bear raids. In fact, the whole ban is significant, as the SEC acknowledged that short selling was the trigger. The problem is that the weapon had already been fired. Once the bear raid had begun via abusive naked short selling and credit default swaps, panic spread quickly—a ban on short selling could no longer contain it. In fact, even with a ban, synthetic short selling occurred with similar detrimental effects.

Lehman's collapse precipitated a domino effect, with panic spreading to virtually every financial firm including Merrill Lynch and Washington Mutual (which were eventually merged into other banks), Citigroup, Bank of America, and even Goldman Sachs. All of this, in turn, put AIG on the brink. Norway immediately lost almost $1 billion from its pension fund. Books around the globe were weighed down by billions' worth of uncollectable debts for hedge funds and banks where Lehman was the counterparty. LIBOR—the intra-bank lending rate—realized the sharpest spike in its history, blowing up from 1 percent before Lehman's failure to 6.44 percent afterward. The Reserve Primary Fund, which held Lehman debt, "broke the buck," the first time a money fund fell below $1 per share in fourteen years—and that was once considered a solid fund.

As firms encountered trouble, they were forced to sell assets to raise capital. Each sale brought a lower "market" markdown as required under mark-to-market rules. The markdowns forced the firms to raise additional capital at even lower sale prices, creating a death spiral in the pricing of virtually all financial assets.

This led to a virtual shutdown of the credit system, making it difficult for consumers to get loans to buy big-ticket items and for businesses to get capital needed for operations and expansion. This, in turn, severely impacted economic activity, causing a direct downturn in GDP, sparking depression and deflation fears.

The stock market plunged more than 50 percent from its peak by early 2009. The government undertook various rescue measures including the $700 billion TARP program and a total of $12.8 trillion in rescue packages plus fiscal/monetary stimulus through mid-2009 alone. The ultimate impact went far beyond Wall Street, with historic failures such as General

Motors and major retailers. Unemployment skyrocketed from historic lows to levels unseen since the early 1980s. Tax collections dropped sharply, and government debt rose dramatically.

Economists, analysts, and leaders across the political spectrum in both the United States and in Europe agreed Lehman's collapse was the catalyst of the chaos. Economist Paul Krugman declared, "The collapse of Lehman Brothers almost destroyed the world financial system."[32] James Surowiecki called the Lehman failure "the first, and crucial, moment in [the 2008] market panic."[33] French Economy Minister (now IMF head) Christine Lagarde said that Lehman's failure threatened "the equilibrium of the world financial system." Federal Reserve Bank of San Francisco President Janet Yellen called Lehman's failure "devastating," adding, "That's when this crisis took a quantum leap in terms of seriousness."[34] The consensus view was summed up in the title of an October 2008 *Insurance Journal* article: "The Lehman Failure Seen as Straw that Broke the Credit Market."[35]

George Soros also agreed. He explained, "The financial system as we know it actually collapsed. After the bankruptcy of Lehman Brothers on September 15, the financial system really ceased to function. It had to be put on artificial life support. At the same time, the financial shock had a tremendous effect on the real economy, and the real economy went into a free fall, and that was global."[36] Soros blamed the situation on wild short selling enabled by the abolition of the uptick rule and the infected CDS market.[37]

Many people view Soros' expressions of concern for the market as hypocritical. At a minimum he was a piggybacker on the attacks, raking in $1.1 billion as the markets collapsed.[38] Others theorize, without sufficient evidence, that Soros was a driving force behind the market collapse, noting that the meltdown occurred just before the 2008 presidential election. Soros clearly favored Barack Obama, and John McCain was leading 54–44 in the polls of likely voters as late as September 7, just prior to the attack on Lehman. McCain's lead rapidly vanished amidst the ensuing economic turmoil.[39]

WHODUNNIT?

So who carried out the bear raids? Based on a review of NASDAQ market participant reports, an anonymous author submitted a paper titled "Red Flags of Market Manipulation Causing a Collapse of the U.S. Economy" to various law enforcement agencies, members of Congress, and regulators. The report contains some startling statistics that seem to support the notion that the market collapse was the work of financial terrorists. In fact, the author contacted me following the release of my initial work to confirm that I was on the right track. He supplied me with page after page of analyzed trading reports, each of which was supportive of my theory.

The "Red Flags" report opens by stating,

> This report discusses extensive research that shows significant "red flags" of danger to the world's economy from what appears to be market manipulation in the global financial markets, which includes trading in common stock, options, futures, commodities, currencies, oil and bonds. Two companies...are at the heart of this trading and they consistently work in concert. These firms became, virtually overnight, the largest traders in the U.S. financial markets. These companies provide a one-stop-shop for trade execution, back office clearing and bookkeeping that cater to hedge funds and small broker dealers. To give perspective, the amount of trading executed by these two firms in October 2008 exceeded the trading of securities firms Goldman Sachs, JP Morgan and Merrill Lynch combined in the NASDAQ market participant reports.[40]

This implies a shocking centralization of market action that could conceivably be used to take down the entire market. The report states that those two firms traded trillions of dollars' worth of U.S. blue chip companies; they were the top traders in all financial companies that collapsed or are now financially supported by the government. Trading by these two companies grew exponentially while the markets have lost trillions of dollars in value. The report also states that the firms owned almost no shares in the companies in which they traded, implying that their market maker status was used to facilitate naked short selling under the Madoff Exemption.

According to "Red Flags," the firms had a combined seventy-six different symbols under which they acted as market maker. (Citigroup, by contrast, had just six.) Both firms offer naked sponsored access—allowing unknown parties to invest at breakneck speed—as well as access to dark pools. From June through September 2008, the two firms appeared to concentrate on Lehman Brothers, trading 1.04 billion shares as the stock price collapsed from $33.83 to $0.21 on September 15. This pattern seemed evident in every other major financial stock. According to the report, the two firms completed as many as 641,000 trades per hour in October 2008 (based on market participation statistics and average trade size from the last available data). Total trading volume by month in the financial sector listed for these two firms grew from around 350,000 shares (less than 1 percent of all market participant trading) in September 2006 to roughly 600,000 shares in the sector (about 6 percent of all market participant trading) in September 2007, to over 8 billion shares in the sector (about 19 percent of all market participant trading) by September 2008—a total increase of 2.4 million percent in two years.

During the period when stocks were collapsing (generally September or October 2008, but earlier for Bear Stearns), the two firms seemingly dominated trading. That was true for trading in AIG, American Express, Bank of America, Bank of New York Mellon, Bear Stearns, Citigroup, Countrywide, Comerica, Capital One, Discover, Fannie Mae, Freddie Mac, JP Morgan Chase, Lehman Brothers, Moody's, M&T Corp., Nat City, Provident, PNC, Regions, Royal Bank of Canada, Sovereign Bancorp, Suntrust, State Street, Toronto Dominion, UBS, Wachovia, Wells Fargo, and Washington Mutual. In short, it was true for all the big financials that collapsed or nearly collapsed.[41]

"Red Flags" further notes that the firms appeared to work in concert. Combined, they traded 203 billion shares, mostly concentrated in major financial services companies. This compares to a total of 427 billion shares outstanding of all issues on the New York Stock Exchange. From July 2008 through September 2008, the two firms "traded more shares of Fannie and Freddie than were issued," even as the share prices were collapsing. They were also the largest traders in the UltraShort leveraged ETF during that period.[42] The UltraShort is among the leveraged ETFs blamed for much of the volatile trading in recent years.[43]

The names of the two firms were withheld from my original report for several reasons, though all the underlying data was provided to law enforcement and intelligence agencies. I had hoped that a covert investigation could be undertaken to determine precisely who was behind the activity and why. I was also afraid that naming the firms might cause the authorities to launch a showpiece raid on the companies. That is what appears to have happened with Ponzi scheme operative Allen Stanford, as the SEC and the FBI made a big show of arresting him after they were stung by criticism for taking so long to discover Bernie Madoff's crimes.[44] We now know that Stanford was connected to both Qaddafi and Hugo Chavez, and his splashy arrest and very public "perp walk" tipped off all his associates that they needed to get rid of any evidence connecting them to Stanford's illegal activities. Chavez even nationalized the Stanford bank, depriving authorities of any insight into whatever nefarious activities were occurring there.[45] While in jail, Stanford was beaten so badly he was declared unfit for trial. He also developed a chemical dependency and suffered from delirium, according to reports.[46] By withholding the names initially, I was planning to gather interest from the trading data first and then formulate a strategy to investigate further.

I had to change my strategy when my research was made public. But in every interview, I still declined to name the two firms identified in the "Red Flags" report, hoping to give authorities just a little more time to quietly investigate. Today, however, the story is out, and those who were trading there have no doubt withdrawn back to the shadows. Before naming the firms, it is important to understand that trades placed through a company, especially under the sponsored access rules at the time, do not by themselves indicate any wrongdoing by the company, even if the traders had malicious intentions. But there is compelling evidence showing that these two firms were used as a conduit for orders placed by others.

Due to a lack of transparency, it is impossible to trace all the orders and determine with certainty who was pulling the trigger at the time. The data suggest that most of the naked short selling was conducted in hidden ways such as through naked sponsored access (also called "unfiltered access"). That being the case, the two brokerage firms did not initiate the massive flow of trades that went through them. In other words, they seem to have been unwitting tools of financial terrorists. Only after the collapse did the SEC realize the risk of allowing unidentified parties to execute unfiltered trading activity through other firms. "Unfiltered access is similar to giving your car keys to a friend who doesn't have a license and letting him drive unaccompanied," SEC Chairman Mary L. Schapiro said later as the agency proposed new regulations to curb the practice. "Today's proposal would require that if a broker-dealer is going to loan his keys, he must not only remain in the car, but he must also see to it that the person driving observes the rules before the car is ever put into drive."[47]

Actually, the situation in 2008 was far worse than that. Naked sponsored access can be as bad as allowing your drunk friend to loan your keys to total strangers or to sell them to the highest bidder. Until the recent SEC ban, naked sponsored access accounted for 38 percent of all trading in 2009 (up from just 9 percent in 2005) and likely much more during the market collapse.[48]

The growth of naked sponsored access coincides closely with the rapid growth of the two firms identified in the "Red Flags" report: Penson Financial Services, Inc. of Dallas, Texas, and Wedbush Morgan Securities, Inc. of Los Angeles.[49] These two firms were both pioneers in developing naked sponsored access prior to the 2008 crash, and both lobbied heavily to keep the practice legal.[50] That's a key point: before the 2008 crash, naked sponsored access was completely legal, meaning there is no real way to track who was ultimately behind the trading given "cutouts, or front companies, such as trusts, managed accounts, private Swiss banks, and hedge funds" as well as many other forms of obscurity available to sophisticated investors.[51] In other words, there's no way to demonstrate that specific trades were placed by Osama bin Laden or any other terrorist through a particular broker.

There have been reports of unusual "associations" for Penson and Wedbush by the website "Deep Capture," considered by some to be a leading source of information on the dark art of naked short selling. Others detest the site and accuse it of all sorts of misreporting. Interestingly, the Deep Capture website, founded by Overstock's Patrick Byrne, was shut down by an order from a Canadian court at the request of Vancouver stock promoter Altaf Nazerali, who reportedly did not appreciate the way the site portrayed him or his associations.[52] That was not the first attack on Deep Capture or on Patrick Byrne, who has been fiercely criticized for his denunciations of naked short selling. He is clearly controversial and has made many enemies on Wall Street.[53] However, several of his warnings have proven true and some have been echoed in the *Economist*.[54] As Chairman of the Board for Milton Friedman's Freidman Foundation for Educational Choice, he is a serious man who deserves a hearing.[55] At any rate, the stakes of financial terrorism are too high to dismiss compelling evidence based on one's opinion about Patrick Byrne.

Deep Capture published a 20-installment series that used Penson and Wedbush as the subject of the "Kevin Bacon" game (aka, the "degrees of separation"). The Deep Capture reports suggested links between one or both of the trading firms and other companies connected to the May 2010 "flash crash" that were accused by the NYSE of allowing large volumes of erroneous orders to flow to the market. The reports further suggested the firms had connections to a wide range of suspicious individuals, including individuals identified by authorities as "Specially Designated Global Terrorists" as well as al Qaeda financiers, an investment manager once accused by the

FBI of handling an account for Osama bin Laden (with advance knowledge of the 9/11 attacks), Hamas financiers, the Russian mafia, Chinese traders, and various jihadist foundations. Connections were also identified with B.C.C.I. (called "the dirtiest bank of all" by *Time* magazine), Refco (a financial services company that collapsed in 2005 amidst a fraud scandal), and the "Golden Chain" (thought to be a group of billionaires funding al Qaeda).[56]

Of course, we can't pronounce guilt exclusively by reports of association. What we can say is that naked sponsored access made nefarious trading possible and impossible to trace. It was a mechanism seemingly tailor-made for exploitation by financial terrorists. As noted by "Red Flags," Penson and Wedbush were among the largest traders of the specific securities under financial attack. They also were huge players in the naked sponsored access world, even lobbying for its continuance. While we can't definitely verify the associations cited by Deep Capture, I believe something untoward was happening, though the two trading firms undoubtedly did not know who was ultimately trading through them. They were just legally filling orders according to the naked sponsored access rules in place at the time.

NOT BUSINESS AS USUAL

Overall, the market takedown was a complex operation. Naked short selling was supported by naked sponsored access and force multiplied by naked credit default swaps. All these were tools of hedge funds and could be used by sharia-compliant sovereign wealth funds thanks to the newly approved Islamic version of short selling—arboon. These new SCF tools were created just prior to the market collapse and allowed synthetic short selling and synthetic commodity speculation. Interestingly, the Al Safi Trust helped develop arboon precisely because short selling—in particular, the borrowing of shares—violates sharia. And notably, the short selling that drove the 2008 market meltdown was largely naked short selling, meaning shares were not being borrowed. This begs a key question: did the arboon continue even after the SEC banned short selling in mid-September? And if so, does this at least partly explain why the market continued to fall even after the ban was in place?

Another major factor in the crash was the hedge fund industry. For the most part, however, it wasn't the usual suspects at work. This was documented at the time by Barry Ritholtz. The title of his September 19, 2008 column, which appeared just after the SEC banned short selling, was "Terror Attack on US Financials?" In that article, Ritholtz explained,

> I have been trying to contextualize this, and I keep coming back to what seemed like a wild theory yesterday that seems a whole lot less wild today. During the day, I had an interesting phone conversation with Joe Besecker of Emerald Asset Management.... None of the many hedgies he knew were pressing their bets recently. The bear raids on the banks and brokers were NOT a case of piling on by US based hedge funds. And from what he was seeing and hearing about in terms of order flow, the vast majority of the financial short selling the past week or so were being done overseas. It appears that the lion's share of shorting was coming out of overseas bourses such as London and Dubai. It may not be a coincidence that the financial short selling ban is both here and in London. Then there is another coincidence: The huge increase in shorting of the financials occurred on the anniversary of 9/11. And on top of that, the same institutions attacked on 9/11/01 were the ones suffering in recent days. Joe asked the question: Is anyone investigating whether this is a case of financial terrorism?[57]

Ritholtz is no novice. He's a respected journalist and market strategist who is well-connected on Wall Street and was named one of the "15 Most Important Economic Journalists in 2010." And he was right: it was not the traditional hedge funds that were furiously selling U.S. financials. Unsurprisingly, much of the trading did come from London and Dubai and appeared, even to a seasoned pro, to be financial terrorism.

Ritholtz concluded his column by noting, "If you want to know who to blame for the past five years of naked shorting, you only have two places to look: The Financial brokers themselves, and the nonfeasance of a feckless SEC." Once again Ritholtz nailed it; the SEC—and indeed the whole of Wall Street—had been blind to the possibility of naked short selling being used as a weapon.

Jim Cramer of CNBC fame also commented on the theory of financial terrorism as noted by the National Terror Alert in October 2008:

> Cramer suggests the damage being done to stocks through short selling, where Wall Street's most legendary institutions are losing value at alarming rates, could be the work of financial terrorism.
>
> Cramer's been talking to the short sellers he knows, and that's the theory they've been putting forward. His sources said that it's doubtful that the market's traditional short sellers are behind the negative action we've seen lately. So there is the possibility that someone else has been trying to wreak havoc in the markets rather than just profit from the problems of Goldman Sachs.
>
> Cramer, who was merely relaying what he heard, did say that, given the fact that the U.S. is in a "financial nationally emergency," [sic] the "financial terrorism thing, to me, has to be put on the table just because the regular short sellers are not doing this."[58]

This again illustrates that the short selling mania of late 2008 was not the work of normal short sellers or typical hedge funds.

Even with all this, Lehman and the broader economy still might have been saved, as was the case six months earlier when Bear Stearns was sold to J. P. Morgan Chase. But Lehman instead went down thanks to a decision made by British-based Barclays, a bank that, at the time, was heavily dependent on capital from the Middle East and China.

Barclay's contribution to the collapse of 2008 is largely unknown, but the story can be pieced together from a few key sources. In his book *On the Brink*, former Treasury Secretary Henry Paulson recounts the collapse of Lehman. Apparently, many of the world's major banks had acquiesced to the American proposal that Barclays buy up Lehman while dumping its $52 billion pile of bad assets. The result would have devastated Lehman shareholders but kept the firm operational and prevented further economic contagion. But in a fateful phone call, British Finance Minister Alistair Darling told Paulson, "without a hint of apology in his voice, that there was no way Barclays would buy Lehman. He offered no specifics, other than to say that we were asking the British government to take on too big a risk, and he was not willing to have us unload our problems on the British taxpayer."[59]

Darling's authoritative decision is odd considering the British government did not own Barclays. In 2008, two sovereign wealth funds, from Abu Dhabi and Qatar, invested billions in Barclays, ultimately owning enough stock and warrants to take controlling interest under certain conditions. This explains why Barclays was the only major bank in either the United States or the United Kingdom allowed to reject government bailout funds—the bank's agreements with the SWFs required it.[60]

If the SWFs had this much leverage in the bank, they were probably strong enough to force the bank to refrain from rescuing Lehman. Barclays, in fact, had already stated that it would be advised by the Qatar Investment Authority. Furthermore, Barclays had other investors who were unlikely to favor rescuing the U.S. economy. These included Challenger, a company owned by Sheikh Jamad Bin Jassim Bin Jabr Al-Thani, prime minister of Qatar and chairman of Qatar holding, and the China Development Bank.[61] This is the same Barclays, of course, that helped develop arboon as a means for sharia-compliant short selling.

The meltdown caught most of the traditional hedge fund community off guard. In fact, the hedge fund industry as a whole lost a record 21.44 percent in 2008, with the vast majority of established funds losing money.[62] Interestingly, the hedge funds that performed best during the carnage were new, large ones. Under normal circumstances, this would seem bizarre, since smaller firms are typically more nimble. However, given the theory under consideration—namely, that one or more entities invested in such a way as to deliberately harm the U.S. economy—it does make sense that larger and newer funds would outperform. That's because larger funds would be required to have the market impact, and newer funds would be more eager for cash. For a fund to be both large and new would require a serious recent investment. Large influxes of secret cash into new enterprises are seldom innocent, and they were not here. It is reasonable to conclude that a large amount of money moved into newer, lesser known, offshore hedge funds focused on shorting the market.[63] From there, the money could have been funneled through Penson and Wedbush as decribed in the "Red Flags" report.

This fits perfectly with analyses of how a financial terrorist attack would operate. According to Jim Rickards, "If terrorists or countries wanted to send US financial markets into a tailspin, they would not need an explosion. Several financial doomsday scenarios have circulated in intelligence and financial circles. One goes like this: A foreign government or a terrorist group with substantial financial backing sets up several overseas hedge funds. Acting together, they dump US stocks, perhaps by short-selling a major financial index or by targeting key US companies. The attack begins slowly, picking up speed over several hours as it creates panic and confusion in the market."[64] The key point is that "weaponized" hedge funds would tend to be new, offshore, and presumably large.

★ ★ ★

Our enemies picked the right target and the right time. They precipitated an old-fashioned bear raid using naked short selling and credit default swaps—both instruments in which you can make a profit without having to own anything. These are the instruments Warren Buffett called "financial weapons of mass destruction." State sponsors of Islamic terrorism, jihadists, and their Chinese benefactors learned well, and they used these instruments just as Buffett had feared. By shorting the market, our enemies shouted "fire" in a crowded theater, prompting market actors to all "de-risk" at once. They were piggybacked by a few market traders like George Soros, who made a bundle. And the entire U.S. economy paid the price.

Due to the presence of dark pools, dark markets, sponsored access, and leveraged ETFs, the identification of the perpetrators is difficult to prove definitively. As Taibbi writes in *Rolling Stone*, "Without a bust by the SEC, all that's left is means and motive."[65] He's right. But as we've shown, the means and motive belong to America's enemies. A mountain of evidence points to them even if absolute proof is elusive. Although some observers have pinned the blame on Goldman Sachs, noting various ways the firm positioned itself to profit from the meltdown, the financial giant in fact saw its shares collapse near the end of 2008, dropping to a price of $53 on November 21, 2008 from a previous high of $233 in October 2007. Even as of late 2011, when Goldman has supposedly recovered, the share price is well below $100. Although Goldman is often rightfully denounced by both the Left and the Right for assorted corporate sins, it was much more a target of the 2008 financial attack than a perpetrator.

Who were the real beneficiaries? Certainly our enemies have gained in terms of global power and prestige. After cheering the collapse of the U.S. financial system, they now stand in a commanding position over the U.S. economy, with their boot on our neck.

CHAPTER EIGHT

NO SOLUTION IN SIGHT

Since the crisis of September 2008, our defenses against economic warfare and financial terrorism have not improved much. In fact, in many ways, we're *worse* off, as the vulnerabilities that the attackers exploited have grown even more dire.

First off, oil prices can still be manipulated. Yes, in small ways federal regulators have begun to crack down on manipulation. For example, in May 2011, the Commodities Futures Trading Commission (CFTC) sued traders James Dyer of Oklahoma's Parnon Energy and Nick Wildgoose of European company Arcadia Energy. Dyer and Wildgoose bought large quantities of physical oil to create the impression that oil supplies were tight. Later, after prices rose, they shorted oil and then dumped their own crude onto the market to drive prices down and profit from their shorts. "Defendants conducted a manipulative cycle, driving the price of [crude] to artificial highs and then back down, to make unlawful profits," according to the lawsuit. The two traders allegedly reeled in $50 million in excess profits. Senator Maria Cantwell cheered the lawsuit, stating, "This is exactly what we expect the CFTC to be doing.... I expect the CFTC to be aggressive in policing these markets and standing up for consumers who are getting gouged at the pump."[1]

This relatively minor crackdown, however, is offset by the CFTC's continuing softness on commodities speculation. In September 2011, the *New York Times* reported that the CFTC's rules on ownership of commodities contracts actually *help* speculators. According to Senator Bill Nelson, "Despite a clear directive from Congress to rein in excessive speculation, regulators still are listening too much to Wall Street and not acting quickly enough to protect American consumers." Nelson cited statistics showing that speculators add between $21 and $27 to each barrel of oil.[2]

Keep in mind, these are just the piggybackers. When it comes to true oil price manipulation, the OPEC nations are still kings of the hill. Able to control prices by adjusting supply levels or by using back channel markets, the cartel could easily squeeze America as it has in the past, throwing our economy back into recession or even into a full-blown depression.

Likewise, credit default swaps are still a problem, while the regulation of derivatives generally remains ineffective. Under the Dodd-Frank Wall Street Reform and Consumer Protection Act, signed into law by President Obama in July 2010, twenty different regulatory agencies were charged with creating 387 different rules. But we can't expect much improvement under Dodd-Frank because the powerful ten-member Financial Stability Oversight Council is made up of the same regulators who failed in 2008. Dodd-Frank was supposed to crack down on non-transparent derivatives trading, forcing them onto the visible markets, but Treasury Secretary Tim Geithner wants foreign exchange derivatives to be "exempted from the requirement that derivatives trade on exchanges." Senators Chuck Schumer and Kirsten Gillibrand have also tried to stop the regulation. So has the SEC.[3]

Just as important, Dodd-Frank has done nothing to end "too big to fail," the policy by which the federal government bails out large firms that have taken on too much debt. To the contrary, Dodd-Frank creates "orderly liquidation," i.e., the government-managed seizure of financial institutions.

There is no judicial review of this process. By the same token, the bailout authority provides additional moral hazard for firms that want to risk their clients' money. Meanwhile, due to Dodd-Frank regulations that force banks to keep a certain cash reserve, banks have been pocketing government cash to shore up their accounts rather than lending it out to spur the economy.

The housing bubble also remains a problem. The Obama administration's efforts to keep the housing market from bottoming out have prevented the market from clearing effectively, meaning bad assets remain as a potential cancer on bank balance sheets. This keeps potential buyers on the sidelines waiting out the deflation. In essence, says Mike Larson of Weiss Research, "You are making a bet with taxpayer money that house prices are going to rebound [and] that if that person goes from [an interest rate of] 6.5 percent to 6 percent, they are never going to default and that everything will be hunky-dory. That's a big bet to be making with taxpayer dollars, considering Fannie and Freddie are in conservatorship."[4]

The Obama administration has further destabilized the market by trying to secure the judicial power to modify loans retroactively in bankruptcy settlements. Says Richard Moody, chief economist at Mission Residential, "Anyone who is going to be either lending or investing under these conditions is going to demand more protection in the form of higher fees or higher interest rates."[5] Mortgage rates have come down but only due to extraordinary Federal Reserve activity that will have unintended consequences. And despite the Fed's activism, those who need the lower rates the most have been unable to access them.

Meanwhile, Fannie and Freddie continue to bleed money while the government continues to prop them up. Since the 2008 government takeover of the companies, taxpayers have eaten a $160 million bill just for legal fees to protect the heads of Fannie and Freddie from fraud lawsuits. The total losses from the takeover to January 2011 are estimated at $150 billion.[6]

Glass-Steagall isn't being reinstated, either. Under Dodd-Frank, banks are still allowed to invest up to 3 percent of their cash in private equity and hedge funds.[7] The so-called Volcker Rule, a part of the Dodd-Frank bill endorsed by President Obama, is essentially a far weaker version of Glass-Steagall. But a new proposal to reform the Volcker Rule would render it completely toothless. Now being debated by regulators, the rule would allow banks to hedge their risk on a "portfolio basis," which includes the "aggregate risk of one or more trading desks." In other words, banks can trade. "If you can do portfolio hedging, that gives you a license to do pretty much anything," says Robert Litan, a former Clinton administration official.[8]

As Nouriel Roubini, the so-called doomsayer of the current down market, said, "The Volcker Rule goes in the right direction, but in my view, the model of the financial supermarket where within one institution you have commercial banking, investment banking, underwriting of securities, market-making and dealing, proprietary trading, hedge fund activity, private equity activity, asset management, insurance—this model has been a disaster. The institution becomes too big to fail and too big to manage. It also creates massive conflicts of interest."[9]

As for reforms that would crack down on accounting trickery, those too have gone by the wayside. Off-balance sheet assets are only to be calculated with regard to maintaining capital requirements—otherwise, they need not show up on the balance sheets.[10] Mark-to-market still prevails in the marketplace, although the SEC can suspend it by authority the agency received under the Emergency Economic Stabilization Act of 2008. But in December 2008, the SEC specifically recommended that Congress *not* suspend mark-to-market. According to the commission's press release, "The report notes that investors generally believe fair value accounting increases financial reporting transparency and facilitates better investment decision-making. The report also observes that fair value accounting did not appear to play a meaningful role in the bank failures that occurred in 2008."[11]

A few months later, Fed Chairman Ben Bernanke endorsed mark-to-market as well, declaring he "would not support any suspension of mark-to-market" even as he admitted that when the markets are stressed, "the numbers that come out can be misleading or not very informative."[12] But that's precisely the problem; mark-to-market works fine until markets are under duress. In the case of a financial attack, terrorists can exploit the otherwise helpful rule to force a downward spiral.

Bear raids remain an enormous threat, too. The uptick rule really has not been re-instituted even though the SEC may claim it has. The new rule allows individual stocks to fall 10 percent before a weakened rule kicks in. But by that point, the fuse has been lit and panic selling can force the share price much lower. Even if the shares rebound, the volatility will scare investors away over time, damaging share prices further. Distressingly, rules against naked short selling are still unenforced, while double- and triple-short ETFs remain a market mainstay with the potential to wreak havoc. Simply look at the unprecedented volatility in the last hour of daily trading to see how powerful these instruments can be.

Just who is trading in our capital markets remains murky. Sovereign wealth funds continue to grow in power and scope; dark pools and dark markets continue to spread. On May 6, 2011, the Dow lost nearly 1,000 points in about six minutes, erasing $900 billion from the market in the so-called "flash crash." Yet, despite multi-million-dollar investigations, we really don't know what or who caused the crash.[13] Most observers blame high-frequency, algorithm-based computerized trading. This indeed seems to be a growing problem. When the markets staged a mini-crash, losing $2.2 trillion in value in the first eight trading sessions of August 2011, high-frequency trading activity tripled. As of early August 2011, computer-driven trading had jumped from about a quarter of all trading in 2006 to around three-quarters.[14] The reality is that despite a great deal of talk, relatively little has been done to address the risk of algorithmic trading, let alone the possibility that the algorithms themselves could be manipulated or co-opted by terrorists. Quite simply, we can't verify who is trading or why.

The two firms identified in the "Red Flags" report as having been instrumental in the 2008 attack—Penson Financial Services and Wedbush Morgan Securities—are still finding new ways to dominate market action.

Both are extremely active in high-frequency trading and always seem near the top of trading data in one respect or another, especially when the markets are most volatile. Both are leaders in providing market bids and offers that rush the market and then are cancelled. Some argue that this adds liquidity, but regulators aren't sure. In fact, according to an August 2011 Bloomberg article, authorities are beginning to recognize the potential for manipulation: "U.S. prosecutors have joined a regulatory investigation into whether some high-speed traders are manipulating markets by posting and immediately canceling waves of rapid-fire orders, two officials said in April. Justice Department investigators are working with the SEC to review practices 'that are potentially manipulative,' according to Marc Berger, chief of the Securities and Commodities Task Force at the U.S. Attorney's Office for the Southern District of New York."[15]

Whether it's a result of manipulation or not, the markets are unquestionably volatile. Citing various academic studies, some argue that the benefits of liquidity outweigh the problems of hyper-trading. The problem with academic studies is that they hold a crucial assumption: "all other things being equal." The reality is that all other things are not equal—heightened volatility scares traditional investors out of the markets and that is detrimental overall.[16] The problem is that high volatility creates investor fatigue even if share prices bounce back after sharp declines. This is the emotional version of metal fatigue, a process in which a continual back-and-forth bending of a metal results in weakening and eventually failure.

THE REAL PROBLEM: PHASE THREE

Believe it or not, we have even bigger problems than those described above. The biggest problem is our mounting national debt and the monetary policy adopted to deal with it.

While Phases One and Two of the 2008 attack were deeply troubling, the U.S. economy eventually stabilized, at least in part, and the stock market has substantially recovered. But the response itself saddled the U.S. Treasury with massive new debts even as the Federal Reserve increased the money supply. In total, the U.S. government and monetary authorities put an estimated $12.8 trillion of economic stimulus into the pipeline by mid-2009, and more since then.

For context, $12.8 trillion is roughly in line with total U.S. GDP and is comparable to the value of all U.S. stocks in recent years. It is also about equivalent to the decline suffered by all American assets, peak to trough, as a result of the financial crisis. This effort will produce immense annual federal budget deficits over the next ten years that dwarf anything we've seen before. Meanwhile, the government's monetary response to the crisis risks stoking inflation; from the crisis of 2008 to April 2009, the annual percentage change in the monetary base was so high that at one point it even exceeded 100 percent.[17]

Economists continue to argue over the effects of the stimulus; one analysis showed it cost $500,000 per job created,[18] while other research purports to show that it prevented a second Great Depression. Either way, we have strong reason to believe that the cost of our recovery thus far has been far higher than normal recoveries because of financial terrorism. This is another major hit to United States finances, as it was when the government spent trillions of dollars on homeland security after a few box cutters and plane tickets took out the World Trade Center towers.

The Phase Three concern is that the response itself to the recent collapse has strained economic resources, creating large budget deficits and high inflation risks. And the situation will deteriorate dramatically in the event of another economic attack. In fact, we are watching this play out in Europe right now.

The European turmoil that began in Greece and spread across the continent undoubtedly stems partly from financial terrorism and economic warfare. As with our own collapse in 2008, Europe had serious economic vulnerabilities including structural weaknesses in its currency. Exploiting those problems, terrorists used credit default swaps and naked short selling as the same match to ignite the gasoline of economic chaos.

We know this for four reasons. First, in February 2010, a group of hedge funds—including Soros funds—met in New York to discuss how to exploit Greek vulnerability to press the euro. This was *before* Greek debt costs and CDSs rose to untenable levels.[19] Second, European spy agencies have acknowledged that European markets were attacked by financial terrorists.[20] Third, the German regulatory authorities recognized the problems and responded by banning naked credit default swaps and naked short selling.[21] Finally, the press reported that upon searching the bin Laden compound following his death, authorities discovered documents indicating he was planning an economic attack on Europe.[22] In short, the crisis across the Atlantic is Europe's 2008 with the twist that the attack is directed toward sovereign credit as well as the banking structure. In that respect, the attack on Europe is akin to a hybrid between our Phase Two and our coming Phase Three.

While it would be comforting to think the European crisis is self-contained, in fact it is already affecting our stock market and banking system. Morgan Stanley, one of the stronger survivors of 2008, has seen its CDS rates spike to levels untouched since the worst of the market collapse.[23] Much of this was attributed to rumors about the firm's European debt exposure that now appear false considering Morgan Stanley had a fully-hedged position.[24] This, of course, is reminiscent of the bear raids that brought down Lehman Brothers.

The one seemingly positive trend for us has been the relative strengthening of the U.S. dollar—as investors have dumped euros, they have turned to the greenback. The strong dollar, in turn, has benefited U.S. Treasury instruments, as the dollar is the world's primary reserve currency and the preferred way to hold dollars is in Treasury bonds. All this merely provides the illusion of security, however. Our research clearly indicates that the dollar and Treasury bonds will be nothing more than a temporary beneficiary. As the saying goes, "A one-eyed man is king in the land of the blind."

Make no mistake: the Phase Three attack will involve the dumping of U.S. Treasuries and the trashing of the dollar, ultimately removing it from reserve currency status. This is a foreseeable risk that is increasingly being discussed as an inevitable denouement. The S&P rating agency downgraded U.S. debt in early August 2011 based on its understanding of the U.S. fiscal situation. It understood that current rates of government spending and borrowing are unsustainable.[25] Announcement of the downgrade increased volatility on the stock markets, as if the downgrade was unexpected. Yet, our research provided to the Defense Department more than two years earlier had predicted the downgrade. We knew then that implementing the massive stimulus without equally impressive economic growth would ratchet up the deficit and the debt. You simply can't spend $1 million for every two jobs and make the economy healthy, especially when we allow financial terrorists to act without response. Ultimately, the combination of excessive domestic sovereign debt combined with the required monetary expansion seriously weakens the dollar and threatens the reserve currency status.

The implications are extremely serious. If the dollar lost its status as the reserve currency, foreign holders would dump their Treasuries en masse. This would hinder the government's ability to raise debt and drastically increase Treasury interest rates, further worsening the annual deficits due to sharply higher interest payments on expanding debts. Higher interest rates would further increase the deficit, and this in turn would force the government to raise taxes dramatically, further dampening growth—or alternatively, the Federal Reserve would be forced to monetize the debt, worsening inflation concerns. Pushed to the limit, our currency could experience the kind of hyperinflation that plagued Weimar Germany. These problems would surely infect Europe and elsewhere, which is why foreign leaders such as German Chancellor Angela Merkel have criticized U.S. monetary policies.[26]

Merkel isn't alone. Politicians around the globe are scared stiff by what the U.S. is doing with its currency. Others are positioning themselves to exploit the coming chaos. The answer in Europe, according to George Soros and others, is to create a Eurobond that would replace debt from individual currencies. That could give global investors a credible alternative to the U.S. bond market.

All these concerns will be sharply elevated if a concerted, planned attack is undertaken by holders of dollar-based instruments. As already explained, the largest holders of U.S. reserves, dollars, and Treasury debt include China, Russia, and the oil producing states. As financial threat expert James Rickards observes:

> The number one vulnerability is the dollar itself. We're printing them and shoving them out the door, and the Fed is basically out of bullets. So why hasn't the dollar collapsed? The short answer is, global investors don't have any other choice. That is, there simply aren't enough Euro- or Yen-backed securities for investors to shift their money out of dollars and into some other currency. But what if some kind of global coalition—say a trillion-dollar sovereign wealth fund allied with several countries around the world—banded together to create a gold-backed alternative to the dollar?

Rickards details the consequences: "That's the end of the dollar. You'd have high unemployment, deflation, and interest rates would go up. It would take what already looks like a strong recession and make it a Great Depression or worse."[27] He further explains, "The U.S. would reimport the hyperinflation which it has been happily exporting the past several years. U.S. interest rates would skyrocket to levels last seen in the Civil War, in order to preserve some value in new dollar investments."[28]

All the factors cited by Rickards are heightened today. Other analysts, such as Porter Stansberry, have called this scenario the "end of America."[29] As we have described, if allowed to happen, it will not be death by natural causes but rather murder by secret weapons.

THE CONTINUING ISLAMIC THREAT

A decade after the 9/11 attacks, America's leaders still refuse to acknowledge that our enemies would exploit all these loopholes and weaknesses throughout our economy—even though our enemies themselves are quite open about their efforts to do so.

In January 2011, *Inspire*, the English-language online magazine published by al Qaeda in the Arabian Peninsula, posted an article instructing jihadists to steal wealth from Western financial centers in general and from U.S. citizens in particular. The FBI quickly briefed Wall Street firms about the threat. FBI spokesman Jim Margolin declared, "In a post-9/11 world we routinely give security briefings to security personnel in various parts of the private sector. This was in the course of a periodic update in the evolving threat stream. I would stress that it's our belief that the information that was discussed was not imminent, not specific." CNBC Senior Editor John Carney commented, "What I think has probably caught the eyes of security officials are the articles advocating financing jihad with money stolen or embezzled from American banks, corporations, governments, and wealthy individuals."[30]

Carney further noted that the article's author, recently killed al Qaeda terrorist Anwar al-Awlaki, provided detailed guidelines for redistributing wealth stolen from the West: "Wealth taken from non-Muslims would have to be distributed according to how it was taken. When wealth is taken by force, it is divided up so that 4/5ths of it goes to the Muslim soldier who took it and 1/5 goes to either funding more jihad, spending for the poor or funding scholars and judges. Wealth that is [not taken] by force—basically, taxes imposed on non-Muslims—however, goes entirely to 'the Muslim treasury.' Money taken by theft or embezzlement is a special case.... There's no 4/5th rule—which means the thief gets to keep his wealth."[31]

As this book has detailed, Muslims wishing to follow al-Awlaki's instructions could use sharia-compliant finance to attack Western targets without breaking Islamic religious commandments. Instead of taking this threat seriously, however, the U.S. government appears to be *complicit* in it. When the government bailed out American Insurance Group (AIG), it also took over AIG's massive sharia-compliant insurance business. Andrew McCarthy of *National Review* explains, "Companies that practice SCF, including AIG, retain advisory boards of sharia experts. These boards, which often include Islamist ideologues, tell the companies which investments are permissible (*halal*) and which are not (*haram*). AIG's 'Shariah Supervisory Committee' includes a Pakistani named Imran Ashraf Usmani, who is the son and student of Taqi Usmani, a top cleric (a 'mufti') and a globally renowned sharia-finance authority. The mufti is author of a book that features a chapter urging Muslims to engage in jihad against the countries in which they live." For firms like AIG, this means that all the interest accrued through its SCF operations gets siphoned off to Islamic charities— many of which may be fronts for terrorism. In brief, says McCarthy, "An American company that practices SCF is, wittingly or not, advancing the jihadist agenda.... [With the takeover of AIG, you] get to fund the jihad, while the jihad gets to target you."[32]

AIG is not the only U.S. corporation involved in SCF. Citigroup, Dow Jones, HSBC, UBS, Visa, and Mastercard all have SCF branches. To ensure the probity of their SCF operations, the Accounting and Auditing Organization for Islamic Financial Institutions (AAOIFI) and the Islamic Finance Standards Board (IFSB) oversee branches of major Western institutions. Citibank's Islamic Investment Bank is a member of the AAOIFI, as is the law firm DLA Piper, Ernst & Young, HSBC, and PricewaterhouseCoopers. IFSB covers BNP Paribas, HSBC, and others.

This is problematic because the primary "scholars" who sit on these Islamic boards and guide companies' SCF activities have personal histories, relationships, and connections that some view as problematic.[33] For example, the AAOIFI board harbors Sheikh Yusuf al-Qaradawi, the charming fellow who celebrated Palestinian-style suicide bombing. Mufti Muhammad Taqi Usmani, chairman of AAOIFI and board member of HSBC, Dow Jones, Citigroup, and Guidance Financial, is another figure who raises concern. As Gadi Adelman and Joy Brighton report, Usmani told the *Times of London* that "aggressive military jihad should be waged by Muslims 'to establish the supremacy of Islam' worldwide." His son, Imran Ashraf Usmani, sits on the boards of AAOIFI, AIG, HSBC, Citigroup, Lloyds TSB Bank, and Credit Suisse. Sheikh Yusef Tala DeLorenzo, a board member of AAOIFI, IFSB, Barclays, Dow Jones, and Blackrock, was an advisor to the Pakistan government during the period the Taliban was established.[34] We can hope that these individuals would view SCF as merely a religious accommodation for Muslims to lawfully participate in the capital markets— and not as "jihad with money."

Far more attention needs to be paid to the activities of these "scholars," especially since the U.S. government now holds a stake in various firms involved in SCF. With $1 trillion in managed SCF assets, at least $10 billion or so is going to "charity" every year—and these charities have a strange tendency of acting as fronts for terrorism. In fact, Chubb, Ace, and Allstate have all sued various Islamic charities for their alleged complicity in funding the 9/11 attacks. Islamic banks comprise a big chunk of the suit.[35]

All this is not to say that everyone who follows SCF seeks to harm the West; but the system *was* created specifically for that purpose, and many of those who control it still subscribe to that mission. Out of political correctness, the U.S. government has been willfully blind to the dangers of SCF and has unwittingly propped up the entire system. For example, several years ago, the U.S. Federal Reserve provided seventy-three loans totaling more than $5 billion to the Libyan-owned Arab Banking Corporation. During that same time period, the Libya Investment Authority bought up banks like they were going out of style. Gary Johnson Jr. of Family Security Matters explained the implications: "The TARP bailouts and discount windows designed to buoy U.S. banking interests, then, were used by the Libya Investment Authority CEO Mohammad Hussain Layas to bail out failed European banks and to invest in First Energy Bank in Bahrain. The treasurer of ABC's New York branch, David Siegel, declined to comment because U.S. taxpayers footed the bill for a bailout of the Sharia Compliant Finance industry."[36]

Clearly, our enemies will exploit any vulnerabilities they can find—and they're adept at finding them. Walid Phares has reported that Ayman Zawahiri, the current leader of al Qaeda, recently

> called expressly and repetitively on the public to sell their US dollars and buy gold instead (Be'u al dullar washtaru al zahab). These were stunning statements ignored by most analysts at the time but that are making sense today. He predicted a collapse in the infidels' economy, starting from American markets. Was he a part of the lobbying effort in the OPEC game? Most likely not, but he seems to have been privy to the game, having insiders in the Wahhabi radical circles in the Peninsula: in the end there are too many political signs to dismiss and the analysis of price warfare is too evident to ignore.[37]

Apparently, Zawahiri's advice is being taken by the NASDAQ Dubai. In March 2009, that exchange created the first SCF tradable security "backed by gold to satisfy a growing demand for the precious metal as a safe haven in the global recession." Jeffrey Singer, chief executive of NASDAQ Dubai, proclaimed, "There is a huge demand for Sharia-compliant products in the region. You can use this product to diversify your portfolio. We are the gateway … and just made it very easy to buy gold." Marcus Grubb, managing director at the World Gold Council, noted—unsurprisingly—that "the product could also become interesting for the region's sovereign wealth funds."[38]

THE BRIC DANGER

The BRIC countries (Brazil, Russia, India, and China) are often at the forefront of international calls for a new reserve currency. These nations are all large holders of dollars and are looking to diversify in order to reduce their risk. Like the oil producers, the BRIC group has considerable clout due to its above-average long-term growth rates. Goldman Sachs chief economist Jim O'Neill finds that during the current economic downturn, the BRIC nations have grown even stronger vis-à-vis the West. Predicting that China and the other BRIC countries would overtake the world's developed economies in short order, O'Neill argues, "Their relative rise appears to be stronger despite the rather pitifully thought out views by some a few months ago that the BRIC 'dream' could be shattered by the crisis." O'Neill describes as "fascinating" a proposal by the governor of China's central bank that the International Monetary Fund create a new supranational currency that includes the Chinese yuan.[39]

Recently, the BRIC nations became the BRICS with the addition of South Africa. At an April 2011 summit, the quintet was not shy about announcing its goal of replacing the dollar as the world's reserve currency. The *Jakarta Globe* reported, "In a statement released at a summit on the southern island of Hainan, the leaders of Brazil, Russia, India, China and South Africa said the recent financial crisis had exposed the inadequacies and deficiencies of the current monetary order, which has the dollar as its linchpin. 'The era demands that the BRICS countries strengthen dialogue and cooperation,' Chinese President Hu Jintao said."[40]

Without perspective, this may all seem unremarkable. After all, the dollar is at risk and, in comparison with most of the BRICS, the debt-laden U.S. economy is moribund. Take a step back, however, and examine some key facts: the excessive U.S. government debt now totals about $15 trillion. Of that amount, however, about $5 trillion was accumulated *after* the financial collapse in 2008. Prior to that, the rate of debt growth was substantially lower. Contrary to the conventional wisdom, the dollar performed well during the crisis. In addition, the U.S. government and Federal Reserve made serious efforts to bail out many foreign banks, supporting the global economy at U.S. taxpayer expense. As we have demonstrated, much of the swing in commodity prices has been the result of foreign speculation. We have documented where sovereign wealth funds were active in the energy markets, and that oil speculation created much of the weakness leading up to the 2008 economic collapse. Much of the U.S. debt has gone directly to China, yet the Chinese have artificially pegged the yuan to the dollar, resulting in huge trade surpluses. What's important to recognize is that this BRICS summit is following precisely what we predicted in 2009 as a Phase Three attack on the U.S. dollar. The summit confirms our concerns.

The addition of South Africa to the group is a clear signal of intentions. South Africa is an unlikely BRIC member, with a long-term economic growth rate less than half that of the BRIC average. So why include it? Here's why: according to estimates from the U.S. Geological Survey, South Africa has around half the world's gold resources. If you were planning to replace the dollar, it couldn't hurt to have the world's top gold resource holder on your side.

According to popular belief, the BRIC concept arose spontaneously when certain people and groups began grouping the four nations together due to their high economic growth rates, and then the global investment community took notice with the aid of Goldman Sachs. The reality, however, is different. According to ISN Security Watch,

> A "strategic triangle" between Russia, India and China was first suggested by former Russian prime minister Yevgeny Primakov in 1998. Initially, the "strategic triangle" concept was dismissed by Beijing, while New Delhi's response was muted. Subsequently, the RIC foreign ministers have met five times in the past: twice on the sidelines of the UN General Assembly in 2002 and 2003; in Almaty in 2004; in Vladivostok in June 2006; and in Harbin in October 2007. However, repeated meetings of RIC top diplomats have brought very limited practical results. In the wake of the Yekaterinburg meeting, Russian officials reportedly argued that BRIC could have the potential to provide a new global leadership. Brazil's Amorim, likewise, reportedly said that the BRIC nations were "changing the world order."[41]

This implies BRIC was created for geopolitical reasons as much as economic ones. There are even hints that the Russians have adopted these alliances as well as their overall economic system in retribution for U.S. economic warfare initiatives undertaken during the Reagan years to bring down the Soviet Union.[42]

So, we have further evidence of planning for a three-phased attack as described in the 2009 Defense Department report. It appears that the elements are in place for this to begin in earnest following a resolution in Europe. If we are right, this will be one of the most dramatic attacks on our way of life in history. The worst part is that the global PR machine has been quite successful in convincing most of America that we have done this completely to ourselves. Unfortunately, these "checkmate" scenarios are entirely possible after nearly two decades as the world's sole superpower. It is clear that the American economy is under siege, endangering our military power and our very way of life.

A FAILURE OF IMAGINATION

If there is good news, it is that we are making progress in educating both the national security/intelligence community and also economists and market experts. That's a big change from just three years ago.

When we started this process, defense folks would tell me, "This isn't my area." They would then call a friend in the investment community who would refuse to even consider the feasibility of financial terrorism. The only way to overcome these objections was to go to back to the officials and educate them personally. The problem is that economists operate in the world of *ceteris paribus* (Latin, roughly translated as "all other things held constant"), while investors tend to believe in the efficient market hypothesis (holding that markets are rational and reflect all available information) and assume *Homo Economicus* (that people tend to act in an economically rational way). Underlying some prominent economic and investment theories, these assumptions work pretty well under certain circumstances.

If you hold to the assumptions, the market decline in 2008–2009 simply reflected the bad economy and poor future prospects for stocks and bonds. After all, the primary motive for each investor is to get the best possible return, right? But when you introduce the concept of non-economic motivations, the theories tend to break down, including the explanations of the 2008 crash.

Financial terrorism upsets established views on finance the same way suicide bombers once shook up our national security doctrine. Until 9/11, the prevailing view was that no hijacker would deliberately crash a plane because it would kill him. Thus, standard procedures focused on negotiations—but that changed with the suicide attacks of 2001. It goes to show that even well-worn doctrines need to be reconsidered in light of changing circumstances.

I have worked hard to educate national security officials about financial markets and the investment community about national security. The arduous task is made even more difficult by the planned secrecy of the financial attack and the purposed opacity of the financial markets. For years, free-market theorists at the SEC had allowed hedge funds and others to operate in the dark, assuming that as rational economic actors, the funds would be increasing market efficiency as long as they did not access inside information. So, to protect the market, officials focused on cracking down on insider trading. Unfortunately, financial terrorists who are motivated by malice, not by profit-seeking, fall well outside of these parameters.

Thus, to this day, measures are woefully inadequate for keeping financial terrorists from working through hedge funds. If you're wondering how opaque these funds really are, consider the disclosure statement from J. P. Morgan, which states, "Investing in hedge funds involves increased risk which include the following: leveraging, short-selling, lack of transparency and lack of regulation. Hedge funds are not subject to as much oversight from financial regulators as regulated funds, and therefore some may carry undisclosed structural risks."[43]

All this is to say that our inability to stop the 9/11 attacks stemmed from the same shortcoming as did our failure to stop the 2008 financial attack: a failure of imagination.

We learned our lesson quickly after 9/11; the same can't be said about the 2008 financial attack, which has not even been widely recognized as having occurred. After the market collapsed, pundits looked inward, assuming we brought this debacle upon ourselves through greed or bad government policy. Those explanations provided a convenient political narrative for Democrats and Republicans, respectively. Each side saw its view as a path to political victory. In that climate, the suggestion that it was financial terrorism disrupted each side's story and was rejected by all. That's how you get a failure of imagination.

THE STRUGGLE

When I first sent my report on the 2008 financial attack to the group at Irregular Warfare/SOLIC (Special Operations, Low-Intensity Conflict) in the Department of Defense, the initial positive response was short-lived. For one thing, the project was conceived in the waning days of the Bush presidency, meaning there may have been some knee-jerk opposition to it once Obama's team took charge. There was also the typical institutional reluctance to think outside the box and challenge long-held beliefs. Never mind that the financial terror hypothesis matched precisely with credible warnings starting as early as 2004 from sources in the Middle East and North Africa of planned economic attacks—I was simply told that my report had "too many assumptions." So I went page by page, listed each assumption, and provided supporting documentation, to the point that the objections required far more assumptions than the report did.

I had demonstrated motive, means, and opportunity, but in the end I could not overcome the failure of imagination. One would think national security officials would be obligated to consider all plausible theories in line with the 1 percent doctrine toward terrorism articulated by former Vice President Dick Cheney: "Even if there's just a 1 percent chance of the unimaginable coming due, act as if it is a certainty."[44] But even my simple requests for further study were too much for the establishment to handle.

Some officials, in fact, seemed anxious to suppress my work, including a threat to classify it. I tried to explain that my work was completely "open source"—presumably anyone could find the same information from publicly available sources. I was told that while the source data was public, my analysis was not. If classified, I could be put in jail for even discussing it, I was told.

So, if my analysis was so full of assumptions, why would it need to be classified? Wouldn't it simply be laughed off by the more enlightened? Or, perhaps the powers that be feared that my work would start a market panic? Only later did one official tell me the truth: no one wanted the report to surface because it "did not fit the narrative."

I called Patrick Maloy, who had been an indispensable guide to the Pentagon. He was a former executive for Morgan Stanley, interacting with great economists like Art Laffer. As a former Marine officer stationed in Iraq and throughout the Middle East, he also deeply understood the Islamic terrorist mindset. Maloy was indignant at the attempts to suppress my report. I discovered later he immediately gave my report to Jim Woolsey, CIA Director under Clinton, for safekeeping. In turn, Woolsey sent copies to three prominent senators. Maloy then told the officials who threatened to classify my report that if they did so, it might be read publicly from the Senate floor. At that point the group backed down. One of them even told Maloy they were only considering classifying my report for my own protection—from whom, they didn't say.

Unexpectedly, at this point the Pentagon seemed to warm up to my research. I was told the higher-ups were impressed and that they were considering commissioning a second study, this time in cooperation with one of the architects of Reagan's economic warfare strategy. But then I encountered a months-long series of delays, receiving around a dozen explanations ranging from personnel changes to funding problems. With each excuse, I was told not to undertake any major commitments because the follow-up study would be exhaustive. Eventually, a SOLIC official admitted I was being strung along, and that there was no intention to conduct another study. Worse, the purpose of keeping me "on the hook" was to prevent me from moving forward on my own or pursuing other funding.

By that point we had formed a solid team intent on getting this information disseminated. Between my contacts and Maloy's, we had a "who's who" list of national security officials interested in our project. Jim Woolsey, who became a key supporter of our efforts, set up a meeting with the legendary Robert Morganthau, long-serving District Attorney of New York. Maloy and I went to New York to meet Morgenthau, who was fresh from his big bust of major banks that had been money-laundering for the Iranian government. (As a side note, Morganthau's father had been FDR's Treasury Secretary and even assisted in planning U.S. economic warfare activities during World War II.) Morgenthau seemed convinced by our work; having experience both with terrorists and with Wall Street, he understood that financial terrorism was not only possible but inevitable. Unfortunately, as he noted, we'd need a forensic study to definitively prove criminality, and he was set to retire. "If I were ten years younger," he sighed.

Morgenthau did share some valuable advice; this was a national security matter, he noted, and thus best handled by the defense/intelligence community. Criminal justice is slow and the requirements of evidence complicated. The only problem, we all agreed, was that the relevant agencies and congressional committees were now controlled by the Obama administration and its supporters, who seemingly had zero interest in addressing the situation.

Over the next two years, our team held dozens of briefings with senators, congressmen, national security officials, and many others across the country, all at our own expense. The plan was to establish a base of understanding so that when a favorable political change occurred, we'd be ready to act against the threat. We just hoped it wouldn't be too late.

David Hemenway and his wife Ducky were instrumental in opening doors for us in Washington, as were Rachel Ehrenfeld, Frank Gaffney, E. J. Kimball, Marilyn Britten, Larry Arnn, Michael Del Rosso, and many others. David has been an ongoing part of the team, chauffeuring me around D.C. and attending many of the critical meetings. Eventually, we met with two former Attorneys General, Ed Meese and Michael Mukasey, who separately confirmed that this was a matter of national security meriting further study at a minimum. They both warned, however, that the issue could only be addressed by executive authority, meaning it would need White House support.

We met with at least a half dozen current and former generals. Half of them had three stars, including former head of the Defense Intelligence Agency Harry (Ed) Soyster and former Deputy Undersecretary of Defense for Intelligence William (Jerry) Boykin. Maloy also got us briefly in front of former Secretary of Defense Rumsfeld. Overall, the group has been very supportive, especially Lieutenant General Boykin, Brigadier General David Reist (USMC), and former CIA Director James Woolsey, though they all warned us that we could encounter a lot of resistance due to the political sensitivity of our findings.

We met with dozens of members and staff from the House and Senate. We met with the permanent staff from the key committees, including Armed Services and Intelligence. On Capitol Hill, as we had been warned, we often ran into political resistance. Republicans wanted to blame the 2008 crash on the Community Reinvestment Act, Democrat-backed subprime loans, and on Democrats who sold out to Fannie Mae and Freddie Mac lobbyists. In turn, Democrats pointed the finger at Republican-backed tax cuts for the rich, Wall Street greed, and George W. Bush. Undoubtedly, we did get through to many responsible people genuinely interested in protecting our country. But too often we met with the arrogant claim, "If this were a problem, we would already know about it."

Maloy continued to add to the team with great contacts like Steve Zidek, a cyber-intelligence expert who was a former Deputy National Intelligence Officer with extensive experience at State and at the DoD. Steve also led the team charged with following Saddam's money that uncovered the Iraqi Oil for Food Scandal. Zidek remains a Lieutenant Colonel in the Marine Reserves and is well connected in the intelligence community. He has accompanied me on a variety of briefings as has his former colleague from the State Department, Paul Janiczek.

Special Agent Nancy Duncan arranged briefings for the FBI. We also presented our research to representatives of the DIA, DEA, FDIC, SEC, and CIA. We met with heads of policy groups and think-tanks, among whom Frank Gaffney at the Center for Security Policy became a particularly energetic supporter of our work. Similarly, Dr. John Lenczowski of the Institute for World Politics, Clifford May of the Foundation for Defense of Democracy, and Rachel Ehrenfeld of the Economic Warfare Institute have been supportive. Dr. Larry Arnn, President of Hillsdale College, has been a friend for many years and was an early supporter.

But inside government, we constantly heard that our theory "doesn't fit in our lane." Our response consisted of two prongs. First, we sent a copy of the report to the Financial Crisis Inquiry Commission (FCIC), which was established to investigate the causes of the financial collapse. If there ever were a "lane" for our research, this was it. Ann Canfield, whose firm publishes the GSE Report and has a "who's who" list of contacts in the financial markets and government, first recommended and then facilitated getting a copy to the FCIC. Ultimately, the commission seemed to appreciate getting the report but required an "official" copy straight from the Pentagon with a fully-pedigreed chain of custody. We directed them to formally request a copy from SOLIC, via the Office of the Secretary of Defense, which they did.

The Defense Department, however, dragged its feet in providing an official copy to the commission. DoD said they needed a "copyright free" version from me—an odd request, since they had contractual permission to use it for any government purpose, and the FCIC clearly qualified. I turned it around immediately but by the time it was finally delivered to the FCIC, about two months after the request, the commission had collapsed into partisan bickering, splitting along the dividing line of the political narrative.[45] As Commissioners Peter Wallison and Arthur Burns sum up the problem in their dissenting statement, "Accordingly, the Commission majority's report ignores hypotheses about the causes of the financial crisis that any objective investigation would have considered, while focusing solely on theories that have political currency but far less plausibility."[46]

Recall that the 9/11 Commission had seriously investigated the possibility that Osama bin Laden had been short-selling stocks ahead of the 9/11 attacks.[47] Yet inexplicably, when the locus of devastation was the financial markets themselves, the Financial Crisis Inquiry Commission, charged with investigating the causes of the economic collapse, did not even consider the possibility of financial terrorism. Don't forget that the 9/11 Commission ultimately ruled out al Qaeda trading due to market transparency—and there was a lot less transparency in 2008 and even less today.

Our other strategy was to force a federal agency to address the issue of financial terrorism via congressional mandate in the Dodd-Frank bill. On that track, a senator added language requiring that the Treasury Department be made responsible for issues of financial terrorism. Unsurprisingly, the White House struck the language. We were told that the task didn't belong at DoD, That Treasury didn't want it, and that the FCIC and SEC seemed unable to address the problem. Week after week the team continued to visit Washington for briefings, hoping to draw some attention somewhere, somehow.

THE BREAKTHROUGH

We knew we had to broadcast our message to a wider audience. We received some international publicity when Alexandra Frean covered our report for the *Times of London*, but the U.S. media mostly ignored the story.[48] Then, we had a breakthrough when some people we'd briefed passed our report to Bill Gertz of the *Washington Times*. Gertz is perhaps America's premier defense/intelligence reporter, with innumerable contacts in the DoD, CIA, and across Washington. Finding our report credible, Gertz wrote a front-page story about it in which he asked key questions that remain unanswered: If there is even a small possibility that my report is right, why hasn't there at least been a second study? The answer he received was that the Deputy Assistant Secretary over SOLIC wanted to spike the report. That official has since been promoted to the Undersecretary of Defense for Intelligence.[49] Amazingly, his wife was on the FCIC Commission staff, suggesting a reason why it took so long for the DoD to get the report to them.[50]

Gertz's article sparked extensive news coverage, including a front and center link on the Drudge Report. Drudge draws extraordinary attention, so any mention there makes an issue nuclear. Soon, reporters from CNBC, Fox News, and MSNBC were calling me to ask if the Pentagon had really commissioned a study of financial terrorism and what were the risks of a future attack. I spoke on the air with Megyn Kelly from Fox News and Maria Bartiromo from CNBC's *The Closing Bell*, and had the satisfaction of watching Glenn Beck read parts of my report on the air.

My research garnered a lot of attention on the blogosphere, with some praising my work and others denouncing me as everything from an Obama shill to a Wall Street stooge to a Muslim-hater. Someone uploaded the report on the Internet and overnight more than 30,000 copies were downloaded.

Shortly thereafter, bloggers began noting how the 2008 financial attacks coincided with the U.S. presidential race, and how the downfall of Lehman Brothers had erased John McCain's lead in the polls, paving the way for Obama's election. Noting al Qaeda's successful attempt to change the Spanish government by bombing the Madrid train system just before Spain's 2004 elections, bloggers asked whether al Qaeda may have reprised the tactic in Washington using a financial attack instead of a bombing.

I was on national radio with Ron Insana, Steve Malzberg, Doug Urbanski, and Ray Dunaway, among others. Hundreds of blog postings and articles kept the discussion going. As a result, I received tips about financial terrorist activities from around the world. Tellingly, several representatives from foreign governments contacted me because they wanted to hold discussions with their U.S. counterparts but could not identify who in our bureaucracy was responsible for monitoring financial terrorism.

Eventually some FBI agents began showing an interest. One is now heading a project for the Director of National Intelligence that is seeking innovative firms to devise a program that would monitor potentially malicious trading activity. Another has moved from a traditional counter-terrorist role to studying global financial markets—that agent told me he used to fear suicide bombers coming to America, but now stays up at night worrying that our financial markets could be attacked again. A third is a forensic accountant with the Bureau, drilling down on the data. My friend Nancy was promoted to D.C. and now works in policy on the Director's floor.

We've made progress in the research community as well. I sat in on a development stage "war game" built around economic threats. In fact, financial terrorism has become something of a trendy topic of study, propelled by rising interest among Europe's intelligence community. We've also received support from people we term "fallen angels"—CEOs or former CEOs whose companies were victims of bear raids. Dr. Kevin Hassett, who heads the economics study at the American Enterprise Institute, graciously took several hours to dig into the research. He also brought me before top economists from the Fed, Wall Street, academia, and even FCIC commissioners. In the end, the consensus was that this risk was much higher than the 1 percent threshold and at a minimum worthy of further study.

One of the biggest breakthroughs came through our efforts in Congress. Congressman Mac Thornberry had language added to the defense bill requiring that the Pentagon's think-tank review my research and report back to the House Armed Services Committee. Congressman Thornberry even went on CNBC to explain the importance of the effort. Congressman Posey has introduced similar language for the House Financial Services Committee. We are also developing a multi-jurisdictional task force to study and respond to the economic warfare threat.

Overall, despite the challenges, our team has made measurable progress—and none too soon. Phase Three has already begun, and our enemies are playing to win.

CHAPTER NINE

THE NEXT ATTACK

Almost half the planet's wealth was destroyed in the 2008 financial crisis, according to the Blackstone Group. "This is absolutely unprecedented in our lifetime," explained Blackstone CEO Stephen Schwarzman.[1] As Elizabeth Wurtzel, author of *Prozac Nation*, observed in early 2009, "The market has lost a dozen years worth of wealth in a matter of months.... The whole system is warped."[2]

The Asian Development Bank reports that the value of stocks, bonds, and currencies dropped over $50 trillion during 2008, equivalent to losing everything produced on the planet for a full year. "The loss of financial wealth is enormous, and the consequences for the economies of the world will unfortunately [be] commensurate," lamented Claudio Loser, former IMF director. "There are serious economic and political stumbling blocks that may well cause the recovery to be costly and slow to consolidate.... Poor macroeconomic and regulatory policies allowed the global economy to exceed its capacity to grow and contributed to a buildup in imbalances across asset and commodity markets. The previous sense of strength and invulnerability is now gone." Former IMF Managing Director Michel Camdessus agreed. "This crisis is the first truly universal one in the history of humanity," he stated. "No country escapes from it. It has not yet bottomed out."[3]

It isn't even close, actually. Worse, our continuing vulnerabilities invite further financial attacks. As early as February 2009, the Associated Press reported that the recession, bailout, and stimulus "pose U.S. security risks" and "may have weakened some U.S. security interests abroad and hampered the nation's ability to respond financially to an attack at home."[4]

Potential attackers across the globe are already conducting dry runs, especially in Europe. In February 2010, the Spanish newspaper *El Pais* reported that Spain's intelligence services were investigating foreign speculation they believed was intended to bring down the Spanish economy.[5] Likewise, Greece's intelligence service has investigated U.S. and London-based firms for allegedly launching financial attacks on their money markets.[6] This is all just the tip of the iceberg. And, as we have demonstrated, it can be nearly impossible to trace the true origins of financial attacks.

In the United States, China is now the chief cause of concern over economic warfare and financial terrorism. In February 2009, the office of the Director of National Intelligence warned the Chinese government that if it sold off mass quantities of U.S. bonds, the United States would consider it "financial warfare."[7]

The concern is well-founded, of course. Over the last decade, China has stacked foreign trade in its own favor. By depressing the value of the yuan, China has essentially used the exchange rate to subsidize its exports and put tariffs on imports. This makes American goods expensive for Chinese consumers and Chinese goods cheap in America. The net effect is that our goods can't compete, we build up an enormous trade deficit, and the Chinese end up with huge amounts of dollars. Our manufacturing base is hollowed out and China's booms. Normally, this process is self-adjusting; China's acquisition of so many dollars should weaken the dollar against the

Chinese yuan, boosting the competitiveness of U.S. exports to China. But the Chinese peg their currency to the dollar and keep it artificially low. This effectively exports jobs to China. To keep this system functioning over time, China returns the dollars by buying our Treasury debt. In other words, we get their goods, they get our jobs, and we end up owing them bundles of money.

Some of our politicians berate China for its currency manipulation, but the Chinese have us over a barrel since they already hold trillions of dollars of government debt. In addition, the Chinese effectively lobby both Democrats and Republicans in Washington, so that any meaningful suggestions to address the problem are met with dire warnings about sparking a "trade war."

Now, this system also makes China dependent on the value of American currency; if the dollar collapsed, or if the United States could no longer pay off its debts, then China would lose money. This creates confidence that the Chinese would never attack the dollar. That is why the Chinese have been buying U.S. bonds at record rates—they want to allow the United States to spend its way out of depression so that we can keep buying Chinese products.

Or do they?

Contrary to popular belief, there is a perfectly rational reason why China may be willing to tank the dollar: they might do it if they can substitute the yuan as the world's reserve currency. That would create a mass market for the yuan and dramatically strengthen it. If this happened, China would be able to have centralized U.S. dollars in order to shore up its economy, sell them off to destroy the dollar, and then allow other countries to invest heavily in China as they move toward the yuan.

Consider how a company becomes a monopoly: it gains a strong position in the market, then lowers its prices so much that it drives all competitors out of business. Then, it can raise prices as much as it wants.

The Chinese could be behaving in a similar way. They have depressed their currency in order to achieve and maintain a dominant position in the world economy. American politicians are now pushing to have the yuan appreciate against the dollar to correct the existing imbalances. But what if the pendulum swings back too far? Is it possible that the Chinese could manipulate their currency in *that* direction? Of course it is. In fact, as recently as 1983 the Chinese pegged their currency at the rate of 2.8 yuan to the dollar, a massive overvaluation. That was a time when the Chinese leadership wanted cheap imports and infrastructure development.[8] Americans would initially cheer the yuan's appreciation, but it could portend something disastrous: the end of the reign of the dollar, and with it, the end of America's global dominance.

The downfall of the U.S. dollar is discussed increasingly openly throughout the world. For example, Nobel Prize-winning economist Joseph Stiglitz in April 2011 advocated a new global currency.[9] Beijing clearly agrees with him. In August 2011, Reuters reported, "China's yuan could overtake the U.S. dollar as the world's principal reserve currency as soon as the next decade.... Beijing has been promoting the use of the yuan beyond its borders since 2009 to settle trade transactions. The resulting build-up of deposits in Hong Kong has spawned a thriving yuan bond market. Internationalizing the yuan, also known as the renminbi, brings with it a host of financial and political benefits. Notably, it allows China to build up claims on the rest of the world in yuan rather than increasing exposure to foreign currencies, especially a dollar that it distrusts."[10]

Indeed, China views the dollar's demise as a vital part of its efforts to eclipse the United States on the world stage. Said Arvind Subramanian, senior fellow at the Peterson Institute for International Economics, "Chinese economic dominance is more imminent and more broad-based—encompassing output, trade, and currency—than is currently recognized." In fact, Subramanian commented, "By 2030, [China's] dominance could resemble that of the United States in the 1970s and the United Kingdom around 1870. And this economic dominance will in turn elevate the renminbi to premier reserve currency status much sooner than currently expected."[11]

WOULD CHINA DO IT?

Right now, China is supposedly prevented from attacking the dollar because doing so would raise the value of the yuan and slow its economy. That's the opinion of Fareed Zakaria, a liberal thinker who writes for CNN.com. According to him,

> Here in the U.S. you hear many people worry that the Chinese government might stop buying American T-Bills. I think these fears are vastly overblown. The economic situation between China and the U.S. is the financial version of mutually assured destruction—that cold war doctrine of nuclear deterrence. If you destroy me, I will destroy you.... [Destroying the dollar] would in turn hurt the U.S. economy, which is China's number one export market (not a good idea if you are the Beijing government trying to keep workers occupied in factories across China). China is addicted to a strategy of export-led growth, which requires that it keep its goods cheap. This means keeping its currency undervalued. That's why it buys dollars.[12]

But China is a communist country, after all. Any government that can force a "one child policy" can control domestic production and consumption. At some point, Beijing will be forced to stop subsidizing exports. The regime understands there are benefits to a rising yuan; and it will explain how its citizens will benefit as consumers. If China can tolerate such a deflation, and if it can transition effectively, it will be sitting in the shade. There's a reason top economists believe 40 percent of trade between China and Africa will be conducted in yuan by the year 2015—and that would kick off the reserve currency substitution war.[13]

That's precisely what China is looking to do. "We now conceive of China challenging the US for number one slot by 2027," said Goldman Chief Economist Jim O'Neill. "They are dominating the world growth picture even more than when the world was booming.... China has had a good crisis. In terms of China's role in the world the crisis has arguably been very helpful because it has forced China to realize that the next stage of their development cannot be led by export growth."[14] Under purchasing power parity, the Chinese economy will expand to $19 trillion by 2016; the U.S. economy will be just $18.8 trillion at that point. A survey in June 2011 by UBS of major central bank reserve managers found that more than half thought the United States would lose its reserve status over the next twenty-five years. "Right now there is great concern out there around the financial trajectory that the US is on," fretted Larry Hatheway, UBS chief economist. Robert Zoellick of the World Bank has already proposed a new monetary system that would be a basket of currencies, including the yen, pound, and renminbi. Most of the managers said that gold would be the prudent investment in years to come.[15]

Arguments against Chinese economic warfare incorrectly presuppose a monolithic China. In January 2011, for example, Secretary of Defense Robert Gates visited China and was shocked to learn that President Hu was unaware of the test flight of the new Chinese stealth fighter. It was a clear attempt by the People's Liberation Army to show military independence from civilian authority. This was the same PLA that once proposed that Beijing consider entering into a nuclear exchange with the United States if China could secure a tactical advantage. This army is obviously not afraid to suffer short-term casualties in the pursuit of long-term objectives.

Some Chinese are willing to do anything to boost the country's economic power against the United States. According to one estimate, as much as 30 percent of China's economic growth over the past decade was the direct result of intellectual property theft—and that figure was probably an *underestimate*. Unfortunately, U.S. companies face a troubling dilemma: China is where the growth is, and American executives feel driven to do business there. Yet, all should know that China's ascendancy compromises our nation's future. Frighteningly, China's corporate espionage and currency manipulation are peanuts compared to the PLA's economic warfare plans. The Chinese are seeking to achieve both economic and military superiority over the United States within a decade, and they recognize the value of economic weapons, including collapsing the dollar, if needed to achieve their goals. For example, in August 2011, the Chinese Communist Party's official *People's Daily* newspaper suggested that China "punish" America for our arms sales to Taiwan: "Now is the time for China to use its 'financial weapon' to teach the United States a lesson if it moves forward with a plan to sale arms to Taiwan. In fact, China has never wanted to use its holdings of U.S. debt as a weapon. It is the United States that is forcing it to do so."[16]

According to Jim Rickards, "The struggle between China and the United States, between the yuan and the dollar, is the centerpiece of global finance today and the main front in Currency War III."[17] Rickards further explains, "The value of a nation's currency is its Achilles' heel. If the currency collapses, everything else goes with it."[18]

Another official publication of the Communist Party, *Qiushi Journal,* acknowledged the coming currency war. In a lengthy essay, *Qiushi* made the case that China must show the United States that it isn't afraid of war—and that China should use its key weapons:

> What is the most powerful weapon China has today? It is our economic power; especially our foreign exchange reserves ($2.8 trillion). The key is to use it well. If we use it well, it is a weapon; otherwise it may become a burden.... Of course, the most important condition is still that China must have enough courage to challenge the US currency. China can act in one of two ways. One is to sell US dollar reserves, and the second is not to buy US dollars for a certain period of time. The first option may cause the U.S. dollar to devalue, so China must consider whether it can take a loss resulting from the depreciation of the

U.S. dollar. However, the U.S's over-printing currency will also cause the dollar to depreciate and will cause the foreign exchange reserve to shrink even more in value. Thus, in comparison, we will probably end up losing less.

For the second option, if we do not buy the U.S. debt, what should we buy instead to increase our foreign exchange reserves? Options are the Euro, the British sterling, Japanese yen, Indian rupee, Russian ruble, and Brazilian currency. At the same time, buying the debt of these countries will help promote good relations and economic and trade cooperation between China and these countries. It will enhance China's economic influence in these countries. Therefore, this is a highly cost-effective tactic, and, more importantly, China is the biggest buyer of U.S. debt. China's actions will have a demonstrable effect on the market. If China stops buying, other countries will pay close attention and are very likely to follow. Once the printed excess dollars cannot be sold, the depreciation of the dollar will accelerate and the impact on Americans [sic] wealth will be enormous.... The key to success is that China needs to have enough courage and determination to take the U.S. pressure. This is exactly what we need. It just shows how much the U.S. needs China. The more pressure we can take, the more successful this strategy. It will indicate that this "weapon" is highly effective and the U.S. will start to fear us.[19]

Beyond simply letting the dollar collapse by restricting purchases of Treasury debt, the *Qiushi* essay outlines plans for financial war as a major Chinese strategy designed to directly attack the dollar:

Financial War: The fact that the U.S. dollar is the world's reserve currency makes the U.S. a financial superpower. Currently, China's increased share in the International Monetary Fund and its increased voting rights are a very big step forward. The problem is not that the value of this share is expressed in U.S. dollars, but that it would be best if the share could be expressed in RMB. Therefore, for China to challenge the position of the U.S. dollar, it needs to take a path of internationalization and directly confront the U.S. dollar. [20]

The article goes on to explain that these moves, though clearly intended as acts of warfare and even labeled as such, would be hidden as "market driven" policies so that China could escape blame. Essentially, they view the approach as a "sneak attack" that would go unrecognized until it was too late to respond. Jim Rickards explains the process in his book *Currency Wars*: "The Chinese could shift the mix of their Treasury holdings from longer to shorter maturities without selling a single bond and without reducing their total holdings.... The shift would make the Chinese portfolio more liquid, vastly facilitating a full Chinese exit from Treasury securities. The Chinese would not have to dump anything but merely wait the six months or so it takes the new notes to mature. The effect is like shortening the time on a detonator."[21]

No wonder columnist Gideon Rachman of the *Financial Times* wrote in early October, "The dark interpretation of China's actions is that nationalist forces and the country's military are becoming more influential in Beijing. A younger generation is coming to power, schooled to believe that China has been victimized by the outside world because it has been weak. The current contrast in the economic fortunes of China and America has also increased China's confidence and assertiveness."[22]

THE DRY RUN

The PLA has already engaged in economic warfare against the United States via cyberwarfare. That's straight from the *Unrestricted Warfare* playbook, which states, "The goal should be to use all means whatsoever—to force the enemy to serve one's own interests.... Financial warfare has become a 'hyperstrategic' weapon that is attracting the attention of the world. This is because financial war is easily manipulated and allows for concealed actions, and is also highly destructive.... The most unsettling aspect of financial terrorism is 'hot money' which is able to launch destructive attacks upon a nation's economy within several days, and the target varies from national central banks to poor people."[23] Cyberattacks are a big part of this strategy.

There are many indications that the Chinese have an extensive program for conducting cyberattacks. In November 2010, 15 percent of the world's internet traffic was suddenly routed through Chinese servers by hackers. The redirection, according to a congressional commission, could have allowed "surveillance of specific users or sites [and]...could even allow a diversion of data to somewhere that the user did not intend.... Perhaps most disconcertingly, control over diverted data could possibly allow a telecommunications firm to compromise the integrity of supposedly secure encrypted sessions."[24]

In another incident, in February 2011, Chinese-based hackers infiltrated computer networks of five international oil companies that contained confidential information including bids. McAfee Security chief technical officer George Kurtz announced the hack, stating, "Starting in November 2009, covert cyber attacks were launched against several global oil, energy, and petrochemical companies. The attackers targeted proprietary operations and project-financing information on oil and gas field bids and operations." How bad was the hack? According to Kurtz, the information "is highly sensitive and can make or break multibillion dollar deals in this extremely competitive industry."[25]

The hacks were highly sophisticated, indicating the culprits were full-time professionals. The Chinese government brushed off the report, remarking, "As for these types of reports, we see them quite often."[26] Yet a 10-second clip on the Chinese military affairs television station showed Colonel Du Wenlong explaining cybersecurity issues—and the video then showed a screen demonstrating a PLA-driven "distributed denial-of-service attack." "However modest, ambiguous—and, from China's perspective, defensive—this is possibly the first direct piece of visual evidence from an official Chinese government source to undermine Beijing's official claims never to engage in overseas hacking of any kind for government purposes," said Andrew Erickson and Gabe Collins of the China SignPost analytical service.[27]

It turns out the attack was even more extensive than first believed. McAfee revealed in August 2011 that the cyber-espionage had hit seventy-two governments. Victims included the UN, Taiwan, the United States, the International Olympic Committee, Vietnam, and Canada. Six U.S. government agencies and thirteen defense contractors were hacked. In 2010, China also hacked Google.

Firmly implanting its head in the sand, the White House refused to say anything of substance. "Cyberthreats to information and communications infrastructure pose an economic and national security challenge for the United States and our partners, which is why the president has made cyber-security one of his top priorities," said White House Press Secretary Jay Carney, in typical bureaucratic doublespeak.[28]

In February 2011, the NASDAQ announced it had found suspicious files on its computer servers. The National Security Agency was called to investigate. "By bringing in the NSA, that means they think they're either dealing with a state-sponsored attack or it's an extraordinarily capable criminal organization," said Joel Brenner, former head of U.S. counterintelligence in the Bush and Obama administrations.[29] An FBI investigation into a simultaneous attack on the computer networks of the International Monetary Fund found that China was likely behind it.[30]

Congressman Mike Rogers, chairman of the House Intelligence Committee, took the opportunity to lambaste the Chinese government. "Beijing is waging a massive trade war on us all, and we should band together to pressure them to stop," he declared. "Combined, the United States and our allies in Europe and Asia have significant diplomatic and economic leverage over China, and we should use this to our advantage to put an end to this scourge." Michael Hayden, former director of the CIA and NSA, said at the hearing, "I say that as a professional intelligence officer, I step back in awe at the breadth, depth, sophistication and persistence of the Chinese espionage effort against the United States of America."[31]

As we've explained, America's high volume trading system is a systemic vulnerability that could have catastrophic consequences. In April 2010, the European Union attempted to crack down on high frequency trading, believing it could be used to manipulate prices.[32] They weren't fast enough. Remember that in the flash crash of May 6, 2010, a trillion dollars in equity was lost in six minutes, triggered by algorithm activity. Who's to say the codes weren't stolen, hacked, or altered? MIT researchers have also pointed out that even without algorithms or trading codes, markets could still be manipulated based on high-frequency trading.[33]

Beyond algorithms and trading codes, the SEC investigated whether so-called "quote stuffing" occurred during the flash crash—situations in which high frequency traders manipulate stock prices and attack other investors by making enormous numbers of trades and then quickly cancelling them. These situations, in fact, comprise the bulk of the market. On February 18, 2010, the NASDAQ traded 1.247 billion shares—but traders submitted offers to buy or sell stock for almost 90 billion shares.[34]

Could the flash crash have been economic terrorism? As Leon Cooperman, chairman of Omega Advisors, said, "There is no economic reason for markets to go up 5% a day and down 5% a day. There are definitely things going on." Are we vulnerable to another flash crash? You bet we are. "We will have another flash crash, yes without question," warned James Angel, associate professor of finance at Georgetown University. "The combination of human nature, markets and technology means that at some point, something will misfire."[35] Former SEC Chairman Harvey Pitt told Newsmax that the chances of another flash crash are "still high.... What troubles me is that if you read the May 6 Flash Crash report that the SEC and CFTC did, it doesn't instill one with a great deal of confidence. What is absolutely critical is to have a trail of accountability or an audit trail.... What we want are markets that operate fairly and that aren't subject to the kinds of wild gyrations that go unexplained for as long a period of time that happened after May 6."[36] Added Senator Ted Kaufman, "Why would [people] not be concerned? We are playing with dynamite here."[37]

This wasn't the only flash crash. August 2011 saw a flash crash in slower motion when the stock market erased $2.2 trillion in value from August 1 to August 10. The volume of trading spiked sharply, again largely due to high frequency trading and leveraged ETF activity. "We're seeing a tremendous amount of high-frequency trading," explained Gary Wedbush, head of capital markets at Wedbush Securities, the largest broker supplying bids and offers on the NASDAQ and one of the two trading firms singled out in the "Red Flags" report. "Their business is a trading business, and volatility creates far more opportunities. Some of their algorithms and automated systems are trading two, three or five times as many shares as they would have in a more normalized volatility environment."[38]

And *Barron's* reported the possibility of an even more dangerous crash occurring—a "splash crash" in which "a dislocation by high-speed trading computers…could simultaneously splash across many more asset classes and markets."[39] Essentially, everything melts down all at once. While *Barron's* dismissed the notion that foreigners caused the flash crash, it did report that "witnesses before an informal convocation of the House Committee on Homeland Security on July 20 [2010] were united in their conviction that the nation's 10 or so stock exchanges and 50-plus related trading venues are absolutely vulnerable to attacks from traders overseas."[40] In September 2011, CNBC commentator Jon Najarian reported that another flash crash was underway, with high-frequency trading driving market volatility through the roof.

None of this should come as a surprise. The Chinese laid out this methodology years ago in *Unrestricted Warfare*: "The Americans have not been able to get their act together in this area. This is because proposing a new concept of weapons does not rely on the springboard of new (military) technology, it just demands lucid and decisive thinking. However, this is not a strong point of the Americans who are slaves to technology in their thinking.... As we see it, a single man-made stock market crash, a single computer virus invasion, or a single rumor or scandal that results in a fluctuation in the enemy country's exchange rates...can all be included in the ranks of new-concept weapons."[41]

THE BEGINNING

If the Chinese were to undercut the dollar, they'd begin by encouraging investment in gold—and that's precisely what they're doing. In the first quarter of 2011, China became the world's largest buyer of gold bars and coins. Between January and March, Chinese investors bought 93.5 tons of gold, a 55 percent jump from 2010. China now accounts for one quarter of all gold investment demand; India comes in second with 23 percent. Chinese citizens are running to gold to avoid domestic inflation, of course, but their government would not allow this unless it suited their purposes—in this case, by artificially inflating the price of gold against the dollar.[42] "In March 2010, we predicted that gold demand in China would double by 2020; however, we believe that this doubling may in fact be achieved sooner," the World Gold Council's Managing Director for the Far East, Albert Cheng, stated.[43]

During just the first two months of 2011, China imported 200 metric tons of gold. China trails far behind the United States in gold holdings—which were once used to bolster the dollar's status as reserve currency—but if China keeps picking up gold at anywhere near that pace, within just four years it would overtake America's holdings. Gold is the easiest currency in which to trade, since none of the other currencies are yet stable enough to become a reserve currency.[44] Nonetheless, China, Russia, Brazil, India, and the Mid-East oil powers have been moving into the euro, despite its structural weakness, rather than the dollar. China's foreign exchange reserves grew by $200 billion from January to April of 2011, and most of that was invested in currencies other than the dollar. "It certainly appears that

China's finally following through on its policy to diversify its foreign reserve holdings away from the U.S. dollar," said Stephen Green of the Standard Chartered Bank. It's difficult to tell just how much China is doing that, since they disguise their trading via London and Hong Kong.[45]

Secret Chinese gold buying has also been hidden behind sovereign wealth fund buying from 2004 to 2009 in a "clandestine operation," according to Jim Rickards. He continues, "What other financial operations are being pursued in secret today? While the Chinese proceed on numerous fronts, the United States continues to take its dollar hegemony for granted. China's posture toward the U.S. dollar is likely to become more aggressive as its reserve diversification becomes more advanced. China's hard asset endgame is one more ticking time bomb for the dollar."[46]

By May 2011, Reuters was reporting that "Americans worried about a weaker dollar may want to get used to it.... If the yuan appreciates between an annual 5-7 percent against the dollar over the next five years, as some analysts and traders expect, then the dollar is likely to slide anywhere between 20 to 30 percent on trade weighted and other indexes based on baskets of currencies." Investors were already predicting that a rise in the value of the yuan against the dollar would mean less lending to the United States by China, undercutting the spending ability of the country. If the value of the yuan jumped, so would the value of Latin American, Australian, Canadian, and New Zealand currencies.[47]

That wasn't idle speculation. In April 2011, the Treasury Department reported that China was dramatically reducing its holdings of U.S. debt. China's ownership of U.S. treasuries hit its apex in October 2010 and then declined each month thereafter, from $1.1753 trillion in October to $1.1541 trillion by the end of February 2011. Just how vulnerable is the United States to such sell-offs? As of February 2011, the total U.S. debt amounted to $14.195 trillion; $9.566 of that was public treasuries. And 47 percent of that total was owned by foreign entities. Overall, China owned 12 percent of all publicly held U.S. debt.[48] By September, China was signaling it wanted to invest its foreign reserve holdings in companies and physical assets rather than treasuries. "Once the US Treasury market stabilizes we can liquidate more of our holdings of Treasuries," said Li Daokui, a key rate-setter for China's central bank.[49]

In July, the Bank of China worried that the U.S. sovereign debt problem was far worse than the European debt crisis. It further indicated its belief that the risk would continue to rise—a great excuse for unloading it. The *China Daily* adhered to the same rationale: "The debt crisis in Europe and uncertainty in Japan could mean that there will be no strong alternatives to dollar assets, so it has a great chance that the US might walk away from its debts and, at the same time, borrow more money from other countries."[50]

Sadly, China isn't wrong. As of July 2011, while Greece's debt-to-GDP ratio was 143 percent, America's was already 97 percent—and that doesn't count the $5 trillion for which American taxpayers are obligated to Fannie and Freddie, or the $62 trillion in total liabilities and unfunded obligations for Social Security and Medicare, or the bailouts. "By some measures," wrote Addison Wiggin of *Forbes* magazine, "the United States is even more deeply in hock than Greece."[51] Foreign countries continue to invest in gold at record rates. "It is very scary: the flight to gold is accelerating at a faster and faster speed," lamented Peter Hambro, chairman of Britain's biggest pure gold lister. "One of the big US banks texted me today to say that if [the next round of inflation] actually happens, we could see gold at $5,000 and silver at $1,000. I feel terribly sorry for anybody on fixed incomes tied to a fiat currency because they are not going to be able to buy things with that paper money."[52]

The timing here is fortuitous for a Chinese move. In a little-noticed development, Reuters reported in March 2011 that the Chinese national bank announced that due to overseas demand that the yuan be used as a reserve currency, it would pursue a policy of forcing all its exporters and importers to pay for cross-border trades in Chinese currency.[53] Meanwhile, as China was divesting itself of U.S. debt and buying up massive amounts of gold, it was discussing the possibility of a multicurrency reserve and trading system with the other BRICS nations. In April 2011, those countries held a conference in Southern China.[54] The BRICS announced they wanted to see a "broad-based international reserve currency system providing stability and certainty." China's President Hu Jintao led the way, proclaiming, "The world economy is undergoing profound and complex changes. The era demands that the BRICS countries strengthen dialogue and coopera- tion." The BRICS also agreed to establish enormous credit lines in their local currencies for one another, rather than via the dollar.[55]

China's allies like Venezuela are more than eager to help sink the U.S. currency by investing elsewhere and using other forms of currency. As of August 2011, Venezuela announced its intention to transfer $6.3 billion in cash reserves to banks in BRIC members Russia, China, and Brazil, and in the process undercut the dollar. Venezuelan strongman Hugo Chavez will also shift 211 tons of physical gold back into Venezuela. Venezuelan Foreign Minister Nicolas Maduro announced the goal: the dollar, he said, "had entered into a crisis of uncertainty and we are planning to construct a new international monetary system, and especially in South America, protect ourselves from this situation."[56]

While baffled economists claimed the move doesn't make any financial sense, it makes perfect sense from a geopolitical anti-American perspective, which is Chavez's driving motivation. It is no coincidence that China gave Venezuela a $20 billion credit line in 2010 (Venezuela has also received additional credit lines of $4 billion each from China, Russia, and Brazil), or that Russia has supplied incredible amounts of arms to Chavez.[57] Speak- ing of Russia, Vladimir Putin agrees with the Venezuelan geopolitical outlook: "They [Americans] are living like parasites off the global economy and their monopoly of the dollar. Countries like Russia and China hold a significant part of their reserves in American securities.... There should be other reserve currencies."[58] He says that U.S. monetary policy is "hooli- ganism.... Look at their trade balance, their debt, and budget. They turn on the printing press and flood the entire dollar zone—in other words, the whole world—with government bonds. There is no way we will act this way anytime soon."[59] Both the UN and the IMF have also endorsed a non-dollar reserve currency.

The U.S. has been caught totally unprepared for the mini-run on the dollar currently underway. In April 2011, Treasury Secretary Tim Geithner told the press there was "no risk" the United States would lose its AAA credit rating. "Washington is a hard place to read. And it's hard for people to look past the political rhetoric and try to understand whether the leadership of Washington is going to take the tough steps necessary to get ahead of this problem," Geithner said. "I think the prospects for a bipartisan agreement are better than they've been in a long period of time. Of course, we have to turn that into action."[60]

Naturally, that didn't happen—the Obama administration has shown no intention of shoring up the dollar by cutting spending and curbing inflation. In June 2011, a Chinese ratings house announced the U.S. was already in default.[61] By August 2011, China's rating agency, Dagong Global, cut the credit rating on U.S. debt to A from A+, putting us in the same boat as Russia. Dagong maintained that the U.S. needed to cut its deficit by $4 trillion within five years to maintain its debt load. China also hinted that the Treasury market was not going to be a steady ride.[62] China's official Xinhua news outlet warned that there should be "international supervision over the issue of U.S. dollars" and—surprise, surprise!—the creation of "a new, stable and secured global reserve currency."[63] The newspaper proclaimed, "China, the largest creditor of the world's sole superpower, has every right now to demand the United States to address its structural debt problems and ensure the safety of China's dollar assets.... [The United States] should also stop its old practice of letting its domestic electoral politics take the global economy hostage and rely on the deep pockets of major surplus countries to make up for its perennial deficits."[64]

Meanwhile, the committee of bond dealers and investors that advises the U.S. Treasury warned that the dollar could lose its world reserve status. "The idea of a reserve is that it is built on strength, not typically that it is 'best among poor choices," the committee reported. "The fact that there are not currently viable alternatives to the U.S. dollar is a hollow victory and perhaps portends a deteriorating fate."[65]

And we cannot forget the piggybacking short sellers—at the end of July, somebody made a $1 billion trade betting that the U.S. government would lose its AAA status. As Jack Barnes of *Money Morning* wrote, "You only do this if you see an edge. This means someone is confident that the United States is either going to default or is going to lose its AAA rating. That someone is willing to bet the proverbial farm that U.S. interest rates will be going up."[66] Sure enough, at the beginning of August, right around the time that China was cutting the U.S.'s credit rating, Standard & Poor's downgraded the U.S. government's credit rating from AAA to AA+.[67] Some believe that the bettor was none other than George Soros.[68]

Beijing isn't prepared for the big showdown just yet—it still fears what would happen if its currency appreciated too quickly. But make no mistake about it—China is testing the waters.

THE EUROPEAN DOMINO THEORY

The weakness of the dollar, and not coincidentally, of the euro, means that we're seeing renewed interest in credit default swaps. With people worried about the risk of default, they're buying insurance against it. "The U.S. CDS market is much less liquid than other sovereign markets as up until recently no one thought the chance of a U.S. credit event was very high," explained Ira Jersey of Credit Suisse. "The market is getting nervous over the risk of a default."[69] And just as before, heavy investment in CDSs precipitates bear raids.

In February 2010, several major hedge funds made enormous bets against the euro, shorting it in incredible amounts. The *Wall Street Journal* said that CDSs were pushing down the market.[70] Said George Soros, "This crisis is still the continuation of the same crisis. In 2008, the financial system collapsed and it had to be put on artificial life support. The authorities managed to save the system. But the imbalances that caused the crisis have not been removed.... Of course, speculation will always make a crisis worse. If there is a weak point, it will expose it. And you are right, the CDS market is a very dangerous instrument and I think it should not be allowed. I am one of the very few people who argue that the CDS is a dangerous instrument because it is so lop-sided in favor of a negative outcome."

That didn't stop Soros from using it, though—in fact, it was Soros who sparked the February 2010 short selling spree targeting Greece.[71] So we should respond with skepticism when Soros proclaims, "There is only one choice.... You have got to allow the members of the euro zone to be able to refinance the bulk of their debt on reasonable terms. So you need this dirty word: 'euro bonds.'"[72] No wonder John Taylor, chairman and CEO of hedge fund FX Concepts, which specializes in currency speculation, says that Soros is plotting against the euro. Soros himself stated, "Financial markets have a very safe way of predicting the future. They cause it."[73]

In early August 2011, the Dow underwent a mini-crash of more than 500 points precipitated by direct assaults on the Italian, Spanish, French, and Belgian economies by market participants. Weaker players were targeted in much the same way Lehman Brothers was in 2008. Wall Street hedge funds took the blame, but as in 2008, we believe that whoever is moving the markets may have more than profits in mind. Without transparency, there is the overwhelming risk of financial terrorism or economic warfare with the intention of destroying the euro and even the European Union. The collapse of a major European economy will set us up as a future target. Dominoes can and do fall. Once the United States' reserve currency status is destroyed, our dollar will be just as vulnerable as these other assets—perhaps far more so.

Meanwhile, the nature of Europe will change. The *New York Times* reported in September 2011 that European leaders are now discussing the rise of "something resembling a United States of Europe." The head of the IMF's European unit recently stated, "If today's policy makers want to successfully stay the course, they will have to press ahead with structural changes and deeper economic integration. To put the crisis behind us, we need more Europe, not less. And we need it now."[74]

How does all of this help China? Chinese premiere Wen Jiabao said that China would help Europe—but only if Europe recognized China as a "full market economy." That, he said, was "a way a friend recognizes a friend."[75] That would only help China's mission of divesting itself of so much foreign currency. Beijing is already looking toward full convertibility. Senior advisor to the People's Bank of China Li Daokui said, "With a fully convertible currency there will be both inflows and outflows of currency. So currently there is a great, great potential for our households and enterprises to get our foreign currency reserves and go out and invest abroad."[76]

Despite China's phenomenal economic growth of recent decades, some analysts believe its economy is heading for disaster. Although this is a minority view, there is some evidence supporting it; Beijing artificially inflated its real estate market domestically in much the same way that the United States did over the last decade—it funneled enormous resources into building new infrastructure and new housing, only to see demand level off, a trend that can cause severe economic dislocations. These observers will often dismiss our warnings about Beijing's economic warfare capabilities, arguing that China is essentially doomed.

The problem is, economic catastrophe could make Beijing just as aggressive as economic strength does. In 2005, Defense Minister Chi Haotian said that he feared that if the Chinese economy began to sink, the Communist Party would collapse. The government would not allow that to happen. "If we do not have good ideas," he said, "China will inevitably change...and we will all become criminals in history. After some deep pondering, we finally came to this conclusion: only by turning our developed national strength into the force of a fist striking outward—only by leading the people to go out—can we win forever the Chinese people's support and love for the Communist Party."

Overall, according to columnist J. R. Nyquist, "The rationale behind Chinese capitalism is not to eliminate Communism. The rationale is to fight fire with fire—to defeat capitalism by capitalist means."[77] When that fails, war becomes inevitable. The Chinese have even suggested biological warfare. "It is indeed brutal to kill one or two hundred million Americans," General Chi said in 2005. "But that is the only path that will secure a Chinese century." Chi even took a poll to determine whether the "people [of China] would rise up against us if one day we secretly adopted resolute means to 'clean up' America." Eighty percent of those polled approved the secret methods.[78] Why then would they shy away from economic warfare?

In addition to China and other foreign threats, the United States faces a significant challenge from U.S.-based anti-capitalist leftists. We've already discussed the plan of the SEIU's Stephen Lerner to crash the stock market by destabilizing the banks.[79] There are many similar actors in America with similar goals. One of them is the computer hacking group known as "Anonymous," which is backing the Occupy Wall Street protesters and is threatening to "erase the New York Stock Exchange from the Internet."[80]

None of this is coincidence. It even appears loosely coordinated. According to the *Huffington Post*, "Lerner currently directs SEIU's banking and finance campaign, mobilizing SEIU members and other community groups across the country into action to break the decades-long stranglehold Wall Street and big banks have had on our economy and democracy. Through this campaign SEIU is also partnering with unions and groups in Europe, South America, and elsewhere to build a campaign to hold financial institutions accountable in a global economy."[81] Some have questioned if George Soros was funding the protests.[82]

The other financial terror suspects also have connections to the Occupy Wall Street protests and their spinoffs around the country, including radical Islamic elements.[83] Arab newspapers report almost gleefully that these protests are the American version of the Arab Spring.[84] Connections have also been cited between the SEIU and Hamas.[85] This is in line with Osama bin Laden's long-term plans to join Marxism and Islam in bringing down America.[86] If the goal is to crash the stock market as the Lerner tape indicates, and the players clearly include radical Islamic elements working with the domestic hard Left, there should be no doubt that this is financial terrorism. Add to this efforts in the Middle East to displace the dollar, and the risks increase exponentially.[87] In combination with the Phase Three plans of the Chinese, the outcome will be devastating.

★ ★ ★

Rather than directly confronting our military might, some of America's enemies have chosen to use secret weapons to attack us. They have done it before, and they will do it again. Yet our government is unwilling to imagine the possibility of a catastrophic economic attack. When Phase Three fully arrives, it will make Phase Two look like a picnic.

So what can you do to protect yourself? Keep reading.

CONCLUSION

Despite compelling evidence that points to financial terrorists as the culprits of the 2008 financial meltdown, there will always be skeptics who blame our own leaders and especially our own corporations for the crash. This narrative is being used for political ends, including by the "Occupy Wall Street" crowd. Some are even co-opting the terms "financial terrorism" and "economic warfare" to fit the narrative, applying them to the Federal Reserve or to major banks that were themselves targets of financial terrorists.

None of this will negate the essential point that our financial system remains vulnerable to enemies with motive, means, and opportunity to do us harm. The government's response to the current threat—a Phase Three attack—has been muted at best, willfully negligent at worst. That means we citizens must protect ourselves even as a few educated patriots are beginning to address the problem.

Since the 2008 crash, our 401(k)s have become 201(k)s. With the next attack, they could easily become 101(k)s, or even zeroes across the board. With that in mind, here's how you can protect yourself from the next attack.

It seems we've now got the worst of both worlds economically—rising prices for what we consume (especially food and energy) and decreasing value of our investments (such as stocks and real estate). There are sophisticated players—some might say market manipulators—like George Soros who have thrived in recent years, but most regular folks who invested hoping to help pay for their retirement or their kids' college tuition have not done well. The best thing you can do is stay flexible and not become wedded to a single strategy. The dynamics of the next financial attack will be swift and multi-dimensional, meaning the best defense is to diversify. Now, this is no magic elixir—during a panic, contagion spreads and nearly everything may go down at once. Over time, however, the benefits of diversification re-emerge. The key is not to panic. If this requires that you keep some money under your mattress, do so. Just make sure you have more than one currency!

Don't listen to salesmen advising you to put all your money into bars of gold and bury them in the back yard. Gold prices could easily plunge if the largest holders of gold—global central banks—begin dumping their supplies. This happens periodically anyway and may become a common response as currencies come under fire. By the same token, gold will be a terrific investment if they don't. And even in the event of a selloff by central banks, gold prices will rebound as uncertainty grows. So gold prices will probably prove highly volatile in the near future but ultimately move higher. This means gold could be a meaningful part of your investment mix, though not the whole mix. When you buy gold, diversify within the asset class—buy gold in various forms, from physical gold (coins and bullion) to exchange traded funds and gold-mining shares. You can also buy poor man's gold—silver—which is even more volatile but has industrial uses as well as monetary ones.

Agriculture can be another good investment, since it's always needed and will inflate in price as the currency declines. The United States retains a competitive edge in many crops, and the growing worldwide demand for quality food will make our production attractive. Once again, diversify within the sector—you can buy farmland, farm equipment, seeds, fertilizer, and the commodities themselves. You can also buy futures or the shares of producer companies. The global demand for food will increase dramatically over time, and the value of it will increase even faster in tough times.

That isn't to say all investments are created equal. Based on your needs, stocks may be better than bonds in this environment, and quality corporate bonds may be better than government debt. Government bonds rely on the government to pay them back and are subject to manipulation by outside forces with political motivations.

For many, treasury bonds may well be, by far, the single worst investment at present, subject as they are to Chinese manipulation, not to mention massive overspending by our government. And 10-year Treasuries were paying around 2 percent in the fall of 2011 after Standard & Poor's downgraded their credit rating. This means the U.S. federal government—the largest debtor in world history with expectations of running trillion-dollar deficits over the next decade—is offering a 2 percent annual return to investors who loan them money.

Let's put this in context. Imagine a family that earns $250,000 annually, spends $400,000 per year, and owes $1.5 million—and has no plan to alter that course. Would you loan them money at 2 percent for a decade, especially when that return is being outpaced by inflation? Surely not, yet that is roughly the situation our federal government is in, if you multiply the figures by ten million. If the government were a family, its shaky finances would mean it would have to pay exorbitant interest rates to borrow money. But the government has been paying around 2 percent for a 10-year loan. Over time, that rate will have to rise, and when it does, bond prices will fall.

By contrast, dividends from common stocks can provide an excellent source of income, especially from a diversified portfolio comprising shares of quality companies with strong balance sheets, low price-to-earnings ratios, and good growth (that can result in higher future payouts). Companies with strong overseas earnings are a good bet, since they will benefit from a weaker dollar. This reminds me of the story Sir John Templeton once shared with me about his experience investing in Latin America: even during periods of hyperinflation and government default, his patient investments in well-selected common stocks with good fundamentals paid off beautifully.

At present, dividend-paying stocks have substantially greater potential and provide higher income than the so-called "safe" government bonds. We've seen the risk of sovereign defaults in Europe and, as we have explained, there are good reasons to believe those risks will soon spread to America.

These concerns are unlikely to sway one group of pessimists that love Treasury bonds: the deflation crowd. This group believes that international debt problems will cause such a severe economic collapse that cash—especially U.S. dollars—will provide the only safe haven. Their theory, however, ignores the risks of financial terrorism and economic warfare, and discounts the Federal Reserve's likely reaction if their doomsday scenario comes true, which would be a massive expansion of the money supply that would devalue the dollar.

Another group of pessimists foresee a currency collapse but recommend simply buying gold regardless of price. This solution is also deficient—who can know that, say, $2,000 per ounce is the proper price for gold? Or is it $20,000 per ounce, or perhaps just $200? Gold can't be eaten, produces nothing, and has expenses associated with storing and insuring it. All the gold ever mined would fit inside three Olympic swimming pools with room to spare. As indicated above, gold could be part of your investment mix, but not an overwhelming part. In Warren Buffett's words, "Gold gets dug out of the ground in Africa, or someplace. Then we melt it down, dig another hole, bury it again and pay people to stand around guarding it. It has no utility. Anyone watching from Mars would be scratching their head."[1] Of course, Earthlings understand that people have used gold for money for thousands of years. In that sense, it has utility—but so do food and many other consumer goods.

Gold enthusiasts insist that the price of gold will never fall to zero. That is true—there will always be demand for the shiny metal. It is also true, however, that the price of a properly diversified portfolio of quality stocks won't go to zero either. Yet both investments can suffer serious declines. We last saw gold drop in price by more than 50 percent following the panic peak of the late 1970s. Gold topped $800 per ounce in 1979 and traded under $300 per ounce more than twenty years later. Since then, gold has risen for more than a decade without pause. The last time an asset class appreciated like that was the technology stocks of the 1990s—which, of course, crashed around 2000 and are still down 50 percent from their peak.

That's why we preach diversification. In the short term, it's possible for all assets to decline simultaneously as investors panic. Over years, however, some will rebound as others may continue to fall. So, diversification is really a long-term strategy, one that should incorporate myriad inflation or crisis hedges. In addition to the investments mentioned above, these could include (depending on your circumstances):

- Productive assets that have pricing power even in the event of serious inflation (including technology shares and other businesses that can prosper during inflation)
- Foreign currencies and assets priced in other currencies such as shares in emerging markets including the BRIC nations
- Various types of energy (oil, coal, nuclear, natural gas, and solar) in various forms (commodities, shares of producers, equipment makers, etc.)
- Agricultural commodities such as livestock, grains, soft commodities (cotton, cocoa, coffee, sugar, and lumber, fruits), and fertilizers
- Precious metals aside from gold (silver, platinum, and palladium)
- Other commodities including copper, zinc, and lumber, as well as shares of materials producers and equipment makers

It's important to understand that any of these investments could rapidly rise or fall in bursts of greed or fear. Diversification helps to smooth these swings over the long term, although it may seem less helpful during bursts of contagion. Of course, every investor must do his or her own homework and evaluate options carefully. Timing is important and so is valuation.

Amidst the global uncertainty, your best bet may be to put your money in the hands of a professional. Professional management, for all the stigmas attached to it, still can offer huge benefits—but your money manager must understand the nature of the global economic threat, which affects everything from oil to stocks to bonds. Sadly, such understanding is rare even among the best of professionals as evidenced by the cover quote from the July/August issue of the CFA Institute magazine: "The investment industry is not equipped to understand the impact of political instability."[2] That's an understatement. Most professional investors remain oblivious to geopolitics, but we are gradually training them in the art. Some investors—even small investors—are not only weathering the current storm but are actually making money. They follow the market closely and recognize the impact of geopolitical change. And they are always ready to adapt at a moment's notice. If you are caught during a bear raid, you will lose money. If you want to be in the markets in the near future, be ready to move and move quickly, or put your money in the hands of somebody who is.

★ ★ ★

In terms of policy solutions, we have made a number of recommendations, some of which are being taken seriously. First, a task force should be formed that cross-pollinates understanding among the national security community, those with economic expertise, and those with real-world experience on the financial markets. This group should focus on the next phase of study, left fallow by the Department of Defense, as well as real-time monitoring of global financial activity through all available means.

Our second recommendation is a practical approach to reducing the risks of terrorism. We must develop and implement a comprehensive national energy policy that favors domestic production. According to the Truman National Security Project, "The one billion dollars a day that Americans send overseas on oil floods a global oil market that enriches hostile governments, funds terrorist organizations, and props up repressive regimes. Former CIA Director Jim Woolsey explains it this way: 'Except for our own Civil War, [the war on terror] is the only war that we have fought where we are paying for both sides.'"[3]

An energy solution would go a long way toward protecting our nation from economic warfare. This should include a "drill, drill, drill" strategy as Larry Kudlow advocates, focused on the development of our own domestic energy production from traditional sources.[4] It can also include market-led alternative energies whenever such opportunities can be made truly cost effective. One proposal that should draw serious consideration is that of T. Boone Pickens' plan for across-the-board energy production, including the development of domestic natural gas as a transitional transportation fuel and the cultivation of wind energy for electricity.[5]

Regardless of the specifics, defunding hostile nations is essential for our economic security. Developing a good domestic energy plan would greatly reduce the risks of both a Phase One and Phase Two terror attack and would strengthen our economy in the process. The risk is that we do nothing, resulting in a projected direct cost of $10 trillion to our economy over the next ten years and "putting our security in the hands of potentially unfriendly and unstable foreign nations."[6] With an additional $10 trillion working against us, we'll lose the economic war.

Regarding a Phase Three financial attack, a relatively simple solution has to do with how we treat foreign earnings from U.S. companies. The present structure encourages corporations to keep their foreign income offshore, meaning that more than $1 trillion is currently unavailable to our domestic economy.[7] That represents lost tax revenues that could otherwise help reduce our budget deficit, boost our domestic economy, and support the dollar. As one example, Cisco has more than $30 billion outside the United States, about 90 percent of the firm's cash holdings.[8] Brought home, this cash could provide domestic tax revenues, employ workers, and reward investors. This is like creating new money and strengthening the dollar in the process.

Finally, we must undertake sensible regulatory reform to address the numerous structural vulnerabilities identified throughout this book. These steps must include limiting credit default swaps and enforcing bans on naked short selling. Additionally, since manipulation can often be stopped simply by exposing it, we need meaningful reforms to increase market transparency. Well-informed markets will self-correct many problems, but that healthy mechanism breaks down when trading is hidden in dark pools and the like.

This is a national security issue, not a partisan one—and we have our work cut out for us. As a nation, we must acknowledge the risks of economic warfare and financial terrorism and seriously address them. The future of our currency, our economy, and our way of life may depend on it.

ACKNOWLEDGMENTS

The process of writing a book is interesting and challenging in and of itself, requiring a great deal of help from many people. The whole story behind *Secret Weapon* made it even more interesting and challenging, as it was like living out a spy novel in the real world and then writing about it. When investment banker turned novelist H. T. Narea was set to roll out his latest work, *The Fund*, he learned about my research. He immediately contacted me so I would know that he hadn't borrowed the story, even though his novel was eerily similar to our work. Sometimes life does imitate fiction.

One result of experiencing and writing a real-life spy novel is that there are many people to thank. First and above all, I must express thanks to God for His mercy and Grace. Without His Holy Spirit, none of this would be possible. Next, I owe so much to my wife and children. They have been wonderfully supportive despite the overabundance of travel and innumerable late nights dedicated to the research and book based on a zealous passion to keep our nation safe. I must also thank the team of people who worked with me directly or indirectly to complete the research and get the word out. Of course, I must also thank my extended family, friends, clients, and our Church. Thank you for always being there. I've been blessed with a rather large group of people praying or otherwise supporting me, the team, and our mission. I am also thankful for a curious media that found the concept intriguing as well as a great group of professionals who helped turn the research into the book you are now holding. Finally, I am grateful for the large and growing number of dedicated men and women in the fields of politics, national security, law enforcement, academics, research, economics, and financial markets who were willing to listen to our findings. Some of them are currently helping to address the problem.

Because the number of people to thank is extensive, I am just listing names without title or personal comment. I have grouped them into categories. Some fit into more than one group so names may be repeated. They are mostly listed alphabetically by first name.

THE TEAM, VOLUNTEERS, AND OTHERS WHO PLAYED A PART

Even though I was the primary author of both the report to the Department of Defense and the book you are now reading, there was a significant team and numerous volunteers who made these projects possible. Thank you to Ann Canfield, Caren Wheaton, Carol Taber, David Hemenway, Ducky Hemenway, EJ Kimball, Frank Gaffney, John Actis, John Guandolo, Jonathan Low, Marilyn Britton, Michael Del Rosso, Mitchell Morgan, Pat Calhoun, Patrick Maloy, Paul Janiczek, Rachel Ehrenfeld, Roger Robinson, Stephen Coughlin, Steve Zidek, Steven Tipton, and many others, some of whom must remain unnamed.

THOSE WHO PROVIDED SUPPORT, ENCOURAGEMENT, OR PRAYER

There is an even broader group who supported me in a variety of ways including prayer. At the top of this list are my wife and our children, family, and extended family (including Miss Joy). My heartfelt thanks go to Aaron Wronko, Adam and Tara Ross, Al Proo, Al and Tracie Denson, Alan and Michelle Schnacke, Allen and Dolores Wood, Allen and Leslee Unruh, Ambree Stone, Amy Duncan, Amy Dunn, Andy and Jenny Hickl, Andy and Jennifer Strachan, Angie and John Anderson, Ann and Bill Quest, Ann and Cliff Bruder, Annette McPhetridge, Arch Bonnema, Barry Armstrong, Ben and Melanie Lasoi, Bernie and Lee Reese, Beth Palmer, Bill Garaway, Bill Mauerman, Bill and Anne Ashton, Bill and Carolyn Doughty, Bill and Patty Stoner, Blake and Margaret Keating, Bill and Caren Wheaton, Bill and Jane Mason, Billy Joe and Sharon Daughtery, Bob Reccord, Bob and Char Reehm, Bob and Rita Fisher, Brad and Patty Harber, Brad and Tammy Worley, Brannon and Noelle Preston, Brent and Carrie Blake, Bridget and Rick Losa, Bruce Hallett, Bruce and Laura Bellamy, Buddy and Hazel Atkinson, Byron and Sally Todd, Carl and Sue Richards, Carlos and Marilyn Morales, Carolyn Hunt, Casey and Amy Cook, Casey and Angela Jones, Charles and Jana Fay Bacarisse, Chris and Amy Davis, Chris and Kathy Howard, Chris McKinzie, Chuck and Elaine Hewitt, Cindi Sherrod, Clynt Taylor, Dale Gibson, Dan Sullivan, Dana Pollard, Dane and Twyla Bartel, Darin and Christy Sloan, Dave and Michael Cook, David and Cheryl Barton, David and Rochelle Bader, David and Shelli Manuel, David Keyston, Dean Forman, Dean and Kim Gillitzer, Dean and Michelle DeCavitte, Deb Gatzke, Denise Gerrich, Dennis and Beth Dribin, Don and Tiffany Willet, Don and Vivian Blakeman, Doug and Cynthia Nurss, Doug and Suzanne Wright, Doug and Sylvia Carter, Drew and Linda Springer, Ed Belan, Ed Smith, Elizabeth Tolhurst, Ellen Grigsby, Evan Loomis, Erik and Lori Davidson, Foster and Lynn Friess, Fran Sherwood,

Frank Bragg, Gabe and Karen Joseph, Gail Gause, Gateway Church Pastoral Staff, Gene and Barbara Graves, George Mauerman, Gordon and Nita Chen, Hiram Sasser, Jack and Rose Fredricks, James and Lynda Dickey, Jamie Waller, Jason and Abi Landry, Janet Sullivan, Jason Noble, Jay and Shonda Wagner, Jensine Bard, Jerry and Martina Ledzinski, Jeff and Carolyn Wakefield, Jeff and Kim Hassell, Jeff and Melanie Burns, Jen and Zach Neese, Jessica Juarez, Jessica Spawn, Jim Czirr , Jim and 'Gene Edwards, Jim and Jeanne White, Jim and Laurie Bolton, Jim and Tisha Ghormley, Jim and Patti Jo Peevy, Jim Griffith, Joe Musser, Joe and Peggy Smith, John Anderson, John and CJ Early, John and Kelley Kasperbauer, John and Lynn Pohanka, John Hemenway, John Spurling, John Templeton Jr., Johnson and Feyi Obamahinti, Jonathan and Jennifer Weiss, Jonathan Low, Jonathan Rotenberg, Jonathan Saenz, Joshua and Casey Tolhurst, Julie and Jeff Luke, KT Freeman, Kay and Paco Jordan, Ken Davidson, Kent and Christie Glesener, Keet Lewis, Kellie Black, Kelly and Scott Luttenberg, Kelly and Karen Shackelford, Ken and Joanna Wiesinger, Ken and Sandy Campbell, Kerrie and Phillip Oles, Kerry and Donna Freeman, Kevin and Liz Horn, Kevin Blacquiere, Kirk and Nancy Freeman, Kris Humber, Kristi Davis, Kyden and Melanie Reeh, Larry and Joan Ezell, Larry and Staci Wallace, Lawrence and Joanne Kersten, Les Pierce, Liberty Institute Prayer Team, MM Freeman, Madge and Forest Williams, Marc and Libba Hanna, Marla and Chad Swandt, Mark and Rebecca Ritchie, Mark and Robyn Tolhurst, Mark Swafford, Mark Yearout, Mary K. Boston, Matthew Taylor, Michael Farris, Michael and Peggy Lee, Michael Del Rosso, Michelle Smith, Mike and Julie Katzorke, Mike and Jayne Carter, Mike and Lisa Moore, Mike McGuire, Mike Studer, Miriam (Joy) Mager, Mitchell and Deana Morgan, Nathan and DeeDee Ng, Nic and Janine Stevens, Ollie and Marlaina Wick, Pat and Deborah Calhoun, Patrick and Amy Maloy, Patricia Lee, Paul and Grace Hallen, Paul and Nancy Pressler, Paul and Paula Martin, Peggy Dau, Phil Wiltfong, Phillip Jauregui, Prasad and Beulah Rao, Randall Swanson, Randy and Becky Isbell, Ray and

Sharon Loveless, Rebecca Hagelin, Rex and Janie Lake, Richard and Jac-
quie Patterson, Richard Bott, Richard Headrick, Rob Smith, Rod and
Sherri Martin, Roger and Moe Westfall, Rolla and Lisa Goodyear, Ron and
Christy Brooks, Roy Stuart, Russ and Laura Finlay, Russell and Karen Lake,
Salina Duffy, Sarah and David Area, Scott and Gaylynn McBrayer, Scott
and Megan Richards, Shay Beard, Shawn and Anita Maloney, Simon Bull,
Stephen Luttenberg, Steve and Wendy Riach, Steve Dulin, Steve Gritton,
Steve Monson, Steve Weinberg, Steve and Tracy Gallemore, Steven and
Emily Dilla, Steven and Kim Tipton, Sue Freeman, Sue and Lanny Peden,
Sue Richardson, Tarek Saab, Ted Baehr, Tim and Tuyet Cahill, Tim and
Virginia Shepherd, Tim and Amy LeFever, Tod and Tammy Williams,
Todd and Maria Horchner, Todd and Salina Lorch, Tommy Jarrell, Trayce
and Scott Bradford, Travis and Vanessa Howard, Troy and Erica Andrews,
Tricia Erickson, Vicki and Dan Nohrden, Wade Parkhill, Wanda and Bev
Brown, Will and Kelly Angus, Will King, and all others who have prayed
and helped so much.

MEDIA WILLING TO REPORT

While financial terrorism, economic warfare, and secret weapons are
intriguing concepts, it took a courageous media to look beyond the popular narrative for the truth. I appreciate all who have studied and/or reported
on the story, including Alex Frean, Anthony Martin, Ben Shapiro, Bill
Gertz, Bill Lunden, Brad Watson, Bryan Biggs, Chris Graham, Craig John-
son, Dan Cofall, David Arnett, David Hahn, David Morris, Doug Urban-
ski, Frank Beckman, Gayle Ruzicka, Glenn Beck, Hugh Vail, Joseph and
Elizabeth Farah, JR Nyquist, Jeff Stoffer, Jerry Corsi, Joey Bourgoin, Ken
Chandler, Maria Bartiromo, Mark Mitchell, Matt Drudge, Megyn Kelly,
Michael Reagan, Mike Porenta, Paul Sperry, Ray Dunaway, Rich Bott,
Richard Miniter, Robert England, Ron Insana, Steve Malzberg, and Stuart
Epperson.

THOSE WHO HELPED ME WITH THE BOOK

The professionals at Regnery have been terrific, as have other success-ful authors who have provided wise insights. I especially want to thank Ben Shapiro and Jack Langer for sharing their experienced wisdom in crafting this book. Others who have helped make this book a reality include Gene Brissie, HT Narea, Harry Crocker, Marji Ross, Mary Beth Baker, Maria Ruhl, Lisa Pulaski, Laura Bentz, Jeff Carneal, Joe Musser, and Randy Tunnell.

SOME OF THOSE WHO
WERE WILLING TO LISTEN

I went through my travel schedule and emails over the past three years to get an idea of how many briefings I had given all across the country. There were hundreds of people involved, some of whom I briefed as many as six times each. I can't list all the names, as some must be withheld for security reasons. Thank you to all who took serious time to listen, includ-ing Adam Kaufman, Adam Miller, Al Micallef, Al Santoli, Alan Jackson, Alec Bierbauer, Alida Jacob, Andrew Davenport, Andy Wehrle, Andy Polk, Ann Canfield, Anthony Arend, Avi Lipkin, Bill Federer, Bill Floyd, Bill Pascoe, Bill Posey, Bill Tucker, Bill Walton, Bob Reccord, Bob McEwen, Boone and Madeleine Pickens, Brady Cassis, Brett Heimov, Brian Kennedy, Brian Halstead, Carol Taber, Chris Barkley, Charles Worrell, Christian Beckner, Clarine Nardi-Riddle, Cliff May, Connie Hair, Craig Shirley, Dan Brandt, Dana Crane, Dane Bartel, David Bobb, David Britz, David Hamon, David Jackson, David Kotz, David Lane, David Patch, David Reist, David Yerushalmi, Diana Banister, Ed Koch, Ed McCallum, Ed Royce, Ed Soyster, Edwin Meese, EJ Kimball, Eric Bleiken, Everett Piper, Erik Davidson, Fos-ter Friess, Frank Bragg, Frank Gaffney, Frank Wolf, Fred Grandy, Gary Fletcher, George Cecala, George Strake, Harold Lanier, Herman Cain, Howard Kaloogian, HT Narea, James Hoge, James McGarrah, Jason Lee, Jay Rosser, Jeff Staubach, Jeff Taylor, Jeffrey Roach, Jerry Boykin, Jerry

Jones, Jim Woolsey, John Craig, John Guandolo, John Lenczowski, John Mauldin, John Miri, John Russo, John Ryan, John Sandoz, John Shadegg, John Sloan, Johnny A. Moncayo, Jon Kyl, Kara Schoeffling, Keith Poole, Kelly Shackelford, Ken Jensen, Kevin Gates, Kevin Gentry, Kevin Hassett, Larry Arnn, Lisa Pollard, Luke Miller, Mac Thornberry, Marc Colby, Marcus Brubaker, Mark Hafner, Matthew Elias, Michael Del Rosso, Michael Hoehn, Michael Leary, Michael Mukasey, Michele Bachmann, Mike Moen, Mike Moore, Mike Moncrief, Mike Pillsbury, Mike Rogers, Nancy Duncan, Neal Freeman, Newt Gingrich, Patrick Byrne, Patrick Maloy, Paul Blocher, Paul McRory, Paulette Standefer, Peter King, Peter Wallison, Rachel Ehrenfeld, Rich Higgins, Richard Stoyeck, Richard Viguerie, Rick Bremseth, Rinelda Bliss, Rob Schwazwalder, Robert Boland, Robert Maguire, Robert Morgenthau, Roger Robinson, Roger Staubach, Ron Burgess, Roscoe Bartlett, Russ Ramsland, Ryan Morfin, Serge Kabud, Sharron Angle, Shaun Brady, Stephen Coughlin, Steve Feiss, Steve Stockman, Steve Weinberg, Stuart Burns, Stuart Epperson, Ted Cruz, Thomas Connolly, Thomas Culligan, Tim Cahill, Tim Morrison, Tim Slemp, Todd Wagnor, Tom O'Connell, Tom Pauken, Tony Perkins, Van Taylor, Walid Phares, and William Wright.

My final acknowledgement recognizes the reality that our American way of life has clearly been under attack. We must understand, however, that our vulnerabilities are the natural result of spiritual and moral failure. There has been too much greed on Wall Street, cutting corners through efforts of financial alchemy—hoping to earn profits without real productivity. Likewise, there has been too much corruption in the government and bureaucracy—using the strong arm of the law and regulation to advance partisan political agendas rather than supply liberty which creates opportunity. On Main Street, we have too often forgotten compassion and have placed too much faith in government to solve our problems. These are not the principles from our nation's founding. From my heart, I know that the best means of achieving a moral and spiritual renewal is to return to God in repentance and restore the greatness of our land. In the words of Ronald Reagan:

I believe with all my heart that standing up for America means standing up for the God who has so blessed our land. We need God's help to guide our nation through stormy seas. But we can't expect Him to protect America in a crisis if we just leave Him over on the shelf in our day-to-day living.

May we return our hearts to Him, and may God bless the United States of America.

NOTES

INTRODUCTION

1. Phillip J. Cooper and Claudia Maria Vargas, *Sustainable Development in Crisis Conditions* (United States of America: Rowman & Littlefield Publishers, Inc., 2008), p. 65.

CHAPTER ONE

1. "Study: Economic Impact of 9/11 Was 'Short-Lived,'" NBCLosAngeles.com, January 7, 2010, http://www.nbclosangeles.com/news/business/Study-bin-Ladens-Strategy-Was-Short-Lived.html (accessed September 2011).
2. Stephen E. Atkins, ed., *The 9/11 Encyclopedia* (ABC-CLIO, LLC, 2011), 151–52.
3. Merrill Goozner, "9/11 and the $5 Trillion Aftermath," *Fiscal Times*, September 6, 2011, http://www.thefiscaltimes.com/Articles/2011/09/06/911-and-the-War-on-Terror-A-5-Trillion-Choice.aspx–page1 (accessed September 2011).
4. "How the terrorists extract huge indirect economic costs," *New York Times*, September 11, 2011, available at http://articles.economictimes.indiatimes.com/2011-09-11/news/30139612_1_terrorist-attack-terrorist-profile-families (accessed September 2011).

5.   BBC, 17 September 2001.

6.   Henry Weinstein, "European Stock Trading Scrutinized," *Los Angeles Times*, September 18, 2001, http://articles.latimes.com/2001/sep/18/news/mn-46931 (accessed October 2011).

7.   William Bergman, "A Money Aggregate That Matters," Sandersresearch.com, September 16, 2005, quoted in www.historycommons.org/timeline. jsp?timeline=complete_911_timeline&before_9/11=insidertrading (accessed October 2011).

8.   "Fed offers explanation for $5 billion surge," Mucker Report, May 29, 2007, http://www.apfn.net/messageboard/05-30-07/discussion.cgi.23.html (accessed November 2011).

9.   National Commission on Terrorist Attacks on the United States, Staff Report to the Commission, Appendix A: The Financing of the 9/11 Plot, p. 150, http://www.9-11commission.gov/staff_statements/911_TerrFin_Monograph.pdf (accessed September 2011).

10.   For the University of Illinois study: Allen M. Poteshman, "Unusual Option Market Activity and the Terrorist Attacks of September 11, 2001," *The Journal of Business*, 2006, vol. 79, no. 4, http://www.journals.uchicago.edu/doi/ abs/10.1086/503645 (accessed November 2011); for the University of Zurich study (also Swiss Finance Institute): Marc Chesney, et al, "Detecting Informed Trading Activities in the Options Markets," Social Sciences Research Network, January 13, 2010, http://papers.ssrn.com/sol3/papers.cfm?abstract_id=1522157, accessed November 2011; for the Hong Kong Baptist University, University of Wisconsin, and National University of Singapore studies: Wing-Keung Wong, et al, "Was There Abnormal Trading in the S&P 500 Index Options Prior to the September 11 Attacks?" Social Sciences Research Network, April 2010, http://papers.ssrn.com/sol3/papers.cfm?abstract_id=1588523 (accessed November 2011); for the Charles Sturt University study: Bruce Andrews, "9/11 terrorists made millions on the stock market: CSU academic," CSU News, September 10, 2011, http://news.csu.edu.au/director/features.cfm?itemID=4C5F5C13C6A53 8CCE83C67E0784596AA (accessed November 2011).

11.   Board of Governors of the Federal Reserve System, "SUBJECT: Suspicious Activity Report Database," FederalReserve.gov, August 2, 2001.

12.   "More unusual market activity reported before attacks," Reuters, September 20, 2001, http://www.rediff.com/money/2001/sep/20usmkt.htm (accessed September 2011).

13.   Ibid.

14.   Ibid.

15.   Allen M. Poteshman. "Unusual Option Market Activity and the Terrorist Attacks of September 11, 2001," op. cit.

16.   Ibid.

17.   "Stock-trading probe expands to Canada," SFGate.com, October 3, 2001, http://www.sfgate.com/cgi-bin/article.cgi?file=/chronicle/archive/2001/10/03/BU187948.DTL (accessed September 2011).

18.   Bruce Andrews, "9/11 terrorists made millions on the stock market: CSU academic," Alumni.csu.edu.au, September 10, 2011, http://alumni.csu.edu.au/news/202-911-terrorists-made-millions-on-the-stock-market-csu-academic (accessed September 2011).

19.   Ibid.

20.   *The City Uncovered with Evan Davis*, BBC 2, video available at http://www.youtube.com/watch?v=ZjN-RN27uSk (accessed September 2011).

21.   Adam Sage, "SocGen rogue trader Jerome Kerviel 'hit the jackpot' on 7/7," *The Times* (UK), January 23, 2009, article available to subscribers at http://business.timesonline.co.uk/tol/business/industry_sectors/banking_and_finance/article5568518.ece (accessed September 2011).

22.   Phillip J. Cooper and Claudia Maria Vargas, *Sustainable Development in Crisis Conditions* (Rowman & Littlefield Publishers, Inc., 2008), p. 65.

23.   Lawrence Wright, *The Looming Tower: Al-Qaeda and the Road to 9/11* (Vintage Books, 2007), p. 361.

24.   Donald Rumsfled, "Rumsfeld's war-on-terror memo," USAToday.com, May 20, 2004, http://www.usatoday.com/news/washington/executive/rumsfeld-memo.htm (accessed September 2011).

25.   "Bin Laden: Goal is to bankrupt U.S.," CNN.com, November 1, 2004, http://articles.cnn.com/2004-11-01/world/binladen.tape_1_al-jazeera-qaeda-bin?_s=PM:WORLD (accessed September 2011).

26. Dan Eggen and John Lancaster, "Al Qaeda Showing New Life," *Washington Post*, August 14, 2004, http://www.washingtonpost.com/ac2/wp-dyn/A63897-2004Aug13?language=printer (accessed September 2011).

27. "Bin Laden deplores climate change," AlJazeera.net, January 29, 2010, http://english.aljazeera.net/news/middleeast/2010/01/20101277383676587.html (accessed September 2011).

28. "Osama bin Laden aide who was set to 'attack Europe's economy' is arrested," Metro.co.uk, September 6, 2011, http://www.metro.co.uk/news/874586-osama-bin-laden-aide-who-was-set-to-attack-europes-economy-is-arrested (accessed September 2011).

29. Beth Rowen, "The Biggest One-Day Declines in the Dow Jones Industrial Average," Infoplease.com, http://www.infoplease.com/business/economy/declines-dow-jones-industrial-average.html (accessed November 2011).

CHAPTER TWO

1. Tor Egil Førland, "The History of Economic Warfare: International Law, Effectiveness, Strategies," *Journal of Peace Research*, Vol. 30, No. 2 (May 1993), pp. 151–62, http://jpr.sagepub.com/content/30/2/151.abstract (accessed September 2011).

2. Ibid.

3. Ibid.

4. *History of World War II: Origins and Outbreak* (Marshall Cavendish Corporation, 2005), p. 580.

5. Ibid., pp. 302–4.

6. Winston S. Churchill, *The Second World War: The Grand Alliance* (Houghton Mifflin Company, 1951), pp. 426–27.

7. Ibid., p. 586.

8. Ibid., p. 599.

9. *History of World War II: Origins and Outbreak*, pp. 302–4.

10. Dean Acheson, *Present at the Creation: My Years in the State Department* (Doubleday and Company, 1969), pp. 48–50.

11. Ibid., pp. 48–50, 52–53

12.   Andreas Schroeder, *Scams! Ten Stories That Explore Some of the Most Outrageous Swindlers and Tricksters of All Time* (Annick Press Ltd., 2004), pp. 72–87, and Larry Allen, *The Encyclopedia of Money* (Greenwood Publishing Group, 2009), p. 306.

13.   David Rose, "North Korea's Dollar Store," *Vanity Fair*, August 5, 2009, http://www.vanityfair.com/politics/features/2009/09/office-39-200909 (accessed September 2011).

14.   Ibid.

15.   "Embargoes and Sanctions – Cold War sanctions," Encyclopedia of the New American Nation, http://www.americanforeignrelations.com/E-N/Embargoes-and-Sanctions-Cold-war-sanctions.html (accessed September 2011).

16.   Matthew French, "Tech sabotage during the Cold War," *Federal Computer Week*, April 26, 2004, http://fcw.com/articles/2004/04/26/tech-sabotage-during-the-cold-war.aspx (accessed September 2011).

17.   Peter Schweizer, *Victory: The Reagan Administration's Secret Strategy That Hastened the Collapse of the Soviet Union* (Atlantic Monthly Press, 1996), p. xviii.

18.   Matthew French, "Tech sabotage during the Cold War," op. cit.

19.   Ibid.

20.   James P. Hubbard, *The United States and the End of British Colonial Rule in Africa, 1941-1968* (McFarland & Company, Inc., 2010), pp. 153–54.

21.   Catherine R. Schenk, *The Decline of Currency: Managing the Retreat of an International Currency* (Cambridge University Press, 2010), p. 112–13, and Jerald A. Combs, *The History of American Foreign Policy: From 1895* (M.E. Sharpe, Inc.), p. 163.

22.   *History of Britain and Ireland* (DK Publishing, 2011), p. 367.

23.   Daniel Yergin, *The Prize* (Simon & Schuster, 1991), p. 591.

24.   Ibid., p. 593.

25.   Ibid., p. 598.

26.   Ibid., p. 604.

27.   Ibid., pp. 609–11.

28.   Dan Briody, *Inside the Secret World of the Carlyle Group* (John Wiley & Sons, Inc., 2003).

29.   Ibid.

30. Michael T. Kaufman, *The Life and Times of a Messianic Billionaire* (Random House, Inc., 2002).

31. Col. Qiao Liang and Col. Wang Xiangsui, *Unrestricted Warfare* (Pan American Publishing Company, 2002), p. 36.

32. Ibid.

CHAPTER THREE

1. Erick Stakelbeck, *The Terrorist Next Door* (Regnery, 2011), pp. 57–58.

2. Matt Apuzzo and Eileen Sullivan, "Recession, Bailout, Stimulus: US Security Threats?" Associated Press, February 26, 2009, http://www.memphisdailynews. com/editorial/ArticleEmail.aspx?id=41112 (accessed October 2011).

3. Zachary A. Goldfarb, "SEC Faults Its Handling Of Tips on Short Sales," *Washington Post*, March 19, 2009, http://www.washingtonpost.com/wp-dyn/content/ article/2009/03/18/AR2009031803459.html (accessed October 2011).

4. George Soros, "One Way to Stop Bear Raids," *Wall Street Journal*, March 23, 2009, http://online.wsj.com/article/SB123785310594719693.html (accessed October 2011).

CHAPTER FOUR

1. Sean Hannity, *Deliver Us From Evil* (Regan Books, 2004), p. 185.

2. Matt Pyeatt, "Clinton Paid 'Lip Service' to Terror Attacks, Expert Charges," CNSNews.com, December 6, 2001, http://archive.newsmax.com/archives/ articles/2001/12/5/142108.shtml (accessed August 22, 2011).

3. President Clinton's Address to the Nation, August 20, 1998.

4. Daryl Lindsey, "One cowardly attack," Salon.com, October 14, 2000, http://www. salon.com/news/feature/2000/10/14/bombing (accessed August 2011).

5. "6 Dead, Dozens Hurt in Attack on Navy Ship," ABC News, October 12, 2000, http://abcnews.go.com/International/story?id=80798&page=1 (accessed November 2011).

6. Charles Duelfer and James Rickards, "Financial Time Bombs," *New York Times* Op-Ed, December 21, 2008, www.nytimes.com/2008/12/21/opinion/21duelfer. html (accessed May 2009).

7.   Shawn O'Connell, "Economic Terrorism: The Radical Muslim War Against the Western Tax Base," *Small Wars Journal*, July 2005.

8.   Hamza Idris and Yahaya Ibrahim, "Nigeria: Boko Haram – Why We Are Attacking Banks – Sets Terms For Ceasefire," AllAfrica.com, July 14, 2011, http://allafrica.com/stories/201107140416.html (accessed August 2011).

9.   Baron Bodissey, Centurean2's Weblog, "A Shariah-Compliant Future," June 18, 2009, article available at Centurean2's Weblog, http://centurean2.wordpress.com/2009/06/18/a-sharia-compliant-future/ (accessed October 2011).

10.   Muhammad Ashraf, "Shariah-compliant Financial Products," *Accountancy*, March 15, 2007, http://www.accountancy.com.pk/articles.asp?id=174 (accessed October 2011).

11.   Ibid.

12.   Rachel Ehrenfeld and Alyssa A. Lappen, "The Fifth Generation Warfare (5GW) Shari`ah Financing and the Coming Ummah," published in *Armed Groups: Studies in National Security, Counterterrorism, and Counterinsurgency*, chapter 28, US Naval War College, June 2008, http://www.acpr.org.il/nativ/0811-6-rehrenfeldE1.pdf (accessed June 2009).

13.   Magdi Abdelhadi, "Controversial preacher with 'star status,'" BBC News, July 7, 2004, http://news.bbc.co.uk/2/hi/uk_news/3874893.stm (accessed August 22, 2011).

14.   Oren Kessler, "Analysis: Yusuf al-Qaradawi – a 'man for all seasons,'" JPost.com, February 20, 2011, http://www.jpost.com/MiddleEast/Article.aspx?ID=208978&R=R (accessed August 22, 2011).

15.   Dr. Rachel Ehrenfeld, "The 'Union of Good' and the Lost Peace," FrontPageMagazine.com, March 7, 2005, http://archive.frontpagemag.com/readArticle.aspx?ARTID=9368 (accessed August 22, 2011).

16.   "Panorama: Faith, Hate and Charity," BBC, July 30, 2006, http://www.bbc.co.uk/pressoffice/pressreleases/stories/2006/07_july/30/panorama.shtml (accessed August 22, 2011).

17.   Lt. Col. Jonathan D. Halevi, "What Drives Saudi Arabia to Persist in Terrorist Financing? Al-Jihad bi-al-Mal–Financial Jihad Against the Infidels," *Jerusalem Viewpoints*, no. 531, June 1, 2005, www.jcpa.org/jl/vp531.htm (accessed June 2009).

18.   "Full text: bin Laden's 'letter to America,'" *Guardian* (UK), November 24, 2002, http://www.guardian.co.uk/world/2002/nov/24/theobserver (accessed August 22, 2011).

19.   Osama Bin Laden, FBIS translated text of message carried on Al-Jazirah's satellite channel television, December 27, 2001, http://groups.yahoo.com/group/MewNews/message/4339 (accessed March 2009).

20.   Senate Committee on Governmental Affairs, *Terrorism Financing: Origination, Organization, and Prevention*, 108th Congress, 1st sess, July 31, 2003. Washington, DC: U.S. Government Printing Office, 2004, p. 194.

21.   Matthew Levitt, "TERRORISM SALON: Matthew Levitt on Al Qaeda's Economic Warfare," TheWashingtonNote.com, July 30, 2008, http://www.thewashington note.com/archives/2008/07/terrorism_salon_29/ (accessed September 2011).

22.   Andrew C. McCarthy, *The Grand Jihad: How Islam and the Left Sabotage America* (Encounter Books, 2010), 181–85.

23.   Robert Siegel, "Sayyid Qutb's America," NPR *All Things Considered*, May 6, 2003, http://www.npr.org/templates/story/story.php?storyId=1253796 (accessed September 2011).

24.   Andrew C. McCarthy, *The Grand Jihad: How Islam and the Left Sabotage America*, 181–85.

25.   Lahem Al Nasser, "Islamic Banking and the Collapse of Capitalism," Asharq Al-Awsat, December 15, 2008, http://www.asharq-e.com/news.asp?section=6&id=15051 (accessed October 2011).

26.   Rachel Ehrenfeld and Alyssa A. Lappen, "The Fifth Generation Warfare (5GW) Shari`ah Financing and the Coming Ummah," op cit.

27.   Patrick Sookhdeo, *Understanding Shari'a Finance: The Muslim Challenge to Western Economics* (Isaac Publishing, 2008), p. 49 (book information available: http://www.amazon.com/Understanding-Sharia-Finance-Challenge-Economics/dp/0978714172/ref=sr_1_1?ie=UTF8&s=books&qid=1246048343&sr=8-1, accessed June 2009).

28.   Frank Gaffney, Jr., "Treasury submits to Shariah," *Washington Times*, November 4, 2008, http://www.washingtontimes.com/news/2008/nov/04/treasury-submits-to-shariah/ (accessed June 2009).

29.   Gamal Essam El-Din, "A financial jihad," *Al-Ahram Weekly*, November 21–27, 2002 (Issue No. 613), http://weekly.ahram.org.eg/2002/613/ec2.htm (accessed June 2009).

30.   Michael T. Kaufman, *The Life and Times of a Messianic Billionaire* (Random House, Inc., 2002).

31.   Commanding Heights interview with Dr. Mahathir bin Mohamad, conducted July 2, 2001 for PBS, http://www.pbs.org/wgbh/commandingheights/shared/ minitext/int_mahathirbinmohamad.html (accessed September 2011).

32.   "Malaysian ex-premier Mahathir and billionaire Soros end feud," ABC (Australian Broadcasting Corporation) News, December 15, 2006, http://www.abc.net. au/news/2006-12-15/malaysian-ex-premier-mahathir-and-billionaire/2154878 (accessed September 2011).

33.   Gadi Adelman and Joy Brighton, "Exclusive: Are We Financing Our Own Demise?" FamilySecurityMatters.org, March 2, 2010, http://www.familysecuri tymatters.org/publications/id.5632/pub_detail.asp (accessed August 22, 2011).

34.   "Ahmadinejad calls for economic jihad," PressTV.IR, April 3, 2011, http://www. presstv.ir/detail/172938.html (accessed August 22, 2011).

35.   "Iran Ends Oil Transactions In U.S. Dollars," CBS News, February 11, 2009, http://www.cbsnews.com/stories/2008/04/30/business/main4057490.shtml (accessed September 2011)

36.   Dan Murphy, "Egypt revolution unfinished, Qaradawi tells Tahrir masses," *Christian Science Monitor*, February 18, 2011, http://www.csmonitor.com/World/ Middle-East/2011/0218/Egypt-revolution-unfinished-Qaradawi-tells-Tahrir-masses (accessed August 22, 2011).

37.   Ibid.

38.   Gary H. Johnson, Jr., "Sharia Compliant Finance Slips Past Libya Sanctions," FamilySecurityMatters.org, April 2, 2011, http://www.familysecuritymatters.org/ publications/id.9137/pub_detail.asp (accessed August 22, 2011).

39.   "Shariah, Law and 'Financial Jihad': How Should America Respond?" McCormick Foundation, 2008, pp.55–57, http://www.scribd.com/doc/15955083/ Shariah-Law-and-Financial-Jihad-How-Should-America-Respond (accessed June 2009).

40.   "Expert: China Sees U.S. as Top Enemy," Newsmax.com, September 9, 2005, http://archive.newsmax.com/archives/articles/2005/9/8/161513.shtml (accessed August 22, 2011).

41.   "Chinese army develop first-person shooter game…with U.S. troops as the enemy," *Daily Mail*, May 20, 2011, http://www.dailymail.co.uk/news/arti

cle-1388867/Chinese-army-PLA-develop-military-game-Glorious-Revolution-shoot-U-S-troops.html (accessed August 22, 2011).

42.   Robert Kagan, "China's No. 1 Enemy," *New York Times*, May 11, 1999.

43.   "Kuhner: Obama's betrayal to China," *Washington Times*, November 11, 2011, http://www.washingtontimes.com/news/2011/nov/11/book-review-obamas-betrayal-to-china/.

44.   Jack H. Barnes, "China devalues US buying power by 30%, Protects US Treasury Holdings," BusinessInsider.com, January 19, 2011, http://www.businessinsider.com/china-devalues-us-buying-power-by-30-protects-us-treasury-holdings-2011-1 (accessed August 22, 2011).

45.   Col. Qiao Liang and Col. Wang Xiangsui, *Unrestricted Warfare* (Pan American Publishing Company, 2002), p. 5.

46.   Brett M. Decker and William C. Triplett II, *Bowing to Beijing* (Regnery, 2011), 111–28.

47.   Bill Gertz, "N. Korea general tied to forged $100 bills," *Washington Times*, June 2, 2009, http://www.washingtontimes.com/news/2009/jun/02/n-korea-general-tied-to-forged-100-bills/ (accessed June 2009).

48.   "Russia: Iran nuclear plant to start up this year," Haaretz.com, January 21, 2010, http://www.haaretz.com/news/russia-iran-nuclear-plant-to-start-up-this-year-1.261846 (accessed August 22, 2011).

49.   Hao Li, "China-Russia currency agreement further threatens U.S. dollar," IBTimes.com, November 24, 2010, http://www.ibtimes.com/articles/85424/20101124/china-russia-drop-dollar.htm (accessed August 22, 2011).

50.   Anne Applebaum, "The Russia Reset Button Doesn't Work," *Washington Post*, March 24, 2009, http://www.washingtonpost.com/wp-dyn/content/article/2009/03/23/AR2009032302138.html (accessed August 22, 2011).

51.   Micah Morrison, "Iran Threat 'Deadly Serious' to U.S.," Fox News, 6 March 2009, http://www.foxnews.com/politics/2009/05/06/morgenthau-iran-threat-world/ (accessed June 2009).

52.   "Chavez's colourful quotations," BBC News, November 12, 2007, http://news.bbc.co.uk/2/hi/7090600.stm (accessed August 22, 2011).

53.   Nasser Karimi, "Hugo Chavez Receives Iran's Highest Honor," Associated Press, July 30, 2006, http://www.breitbart.com/article.php?id=D8J6NURG0&show_article=1 (accessed October 2011).

54.   Tom Ramstack, "Hezbollah's Latin American influence worries Congress," *Homeland Security News*, SSI, 6 July 2011, http://www.homelandsecurityssi. com/ssi/content/view/599/296/ (accessed August 22, 2011).

55.   Johan Freitas and Luis Garcia, "9/11: Chavez financed Al Qaeda, details of $1M donation emerge," *Militares Democraticos*, December 31, 2002, article available at Free Republic, http://www.freerepublic.com/focus/news/814934/posts (accessed June 2009).

56.   "Venezuela's Chavez: 'Capitalism Needs to Go Down,'" Associated Press, April 3, 2009, http://www.foxnews.com/story/0,2933,512395,00.html (accessed May 2009).

57.   Matthew Clark, "Arabs' new favorite leader: Hugo Chávez!?!" *Christian Science Monitor*, May 20, 2009 http://features.csmonitor.com/globalnews/2009/05/20/ arabs-new-favorite-leader-hugo-chavez/ (accessed June 2009).

58.   YVKE Mundial, "Chávez and Ahmadinejad Call for Breaking Free from Free Trade," MRZINE, http://mrzine.monthlyreview.org/2009/veniran020409p.html (accessed October 2009).

59.   Hilary Keenan, "Hugo Chávez: the most popular leader in the Middle East," 21st Century Socialism, May 25, 2009, http://21stcenturysocialism.com/article/ hugo_chvez_the_most_popular_leader_in_the_middle_east_01857.html (accessed June 2009).

60.   George Soros, World Economic Forum 2009, interview, Davos, Switzerland, video available at http://www.infowars.com/soros-admits-lindsey-williams-assertion-oil-is-a-weapon/ (accessed October 2011).

61.   "Two Japanese citizens arrested for carrying $134 billion of bonds," IBTimes, June 16, 2009, http://uk.ibtimes.com/articles/20090612/japanese-citizens-bonds-arrests_all.htm (accessed October 2011), and FT Reporters, "Mafia blamed for $134 bn fake Treasury bills," *Financial Times*, June 18, 2009, http://www.ft.com/ intl/cms/s/0/82091ec2-5c2f-11de-aea3-00144feabdc0.html#axzz1XCuXQyAh (accessed September 2011) (subscription required).

62.   Kyle Alspach, "Markopolos on Madoff: 'It took me about five minutes to figure out he was a fraud,'" *Patriot Ledger*, February 5, 2009, http://www.patriotledger. com/archive/x1717608693/Harry-Markopolos-Madoff-tipster-from-Whitman-assails-SEC (accessed June 2009).

63. Frankie Saggio and Fred Rosen, *Born to the Mob: The True-Life Story of the Only Man to Work for All Five of New York's Mafia Families* (Thunder's Mouth Press, 2004), p. 139.

64. "Stephen Lerner," *Huffington Post*, http://www.huffingtonpost.com/stephen-lerner (accessed September 2011).

65. Henry Blodget, "CAUGHT ON TAPE: Former SEIU Official Reveals Secret Plan To Destroy JP Morgan, Crash The Stock Market, And Redistribute Wealth In America," BusinessInsider.com, March 22, 2011, http://www.businessinsider.com/seiu-union-plan-to-destroy-jpmorgan (accessed September 2011).

66. George Soros, "One Way to Stop Bear Raids," *Wall Street Journal*, March 24, 2009, http://online.wsj.com/article/SB123785310594719693.html (accessed September 2011).

67. Mark Milner, "Soros in £1.4m fine for insider trading," *Guardian*, December 21, 2002, http://www.guardian.co.uk/world/2002/dec/21/france.markmilner (accessed September 2011).

68. Matthew Vadum, "Communism-Loving George Soros Wants To Kill Capitalism," NewsRealBlog.com, March 28, 2011, http://www.newsrealblog.com/2011/03/28/communism-loving-george-soros-wants-to-kill-capitalism/ (accessed September 2011).

69. "The Economy Fell Off The Cliff," *Der Spiegel*, November 24, 2008, http://www.spiegel.de/international/business/0,1518,592268,00.html (accessed September 2011).

70. George Soros, "No alternative to a new world architecture," *Japan Times* online, November 8, 2009, http://search.japantimes.co.jp/cgi-bin/eo20091108a1.html (accessed September 2011).

71. For a list of Soros-funded radical groups, see http://www.discoverthenetworks.org/individualProfile.asp?indid=977.

CHAPTER FIVE

1. Col. Qiao Liang and Col. Wang Xiangsui, *Unrestricted Warfare*, p. 167.

2. Ibid.

3. Ibid., p. 191.

4.   Richard S. Eckaus, "The Oil Price Really Is a Speculative Bubble," Center for Energy and Environmental Policy Research, June 13, 2008, p. 1, http://web.mit.edu/ceepr/www/publications/workingpapers/2008-007.pdf (accessed June 2009).

5.   "Did Speculation Fuel Oil Price Swings?" CBSNews *60 Minutes*, April 14, 2009, http://www.cbsnews.com/stories/2009/01/08/60minutes/main4707770.shtml (accessed September 2011).

6.   Ibid.

7.   Testimony of Blythe Masters, Managing Director, Head of Global Commodities, JPMorgan Chase & Co. and Chairman, Securities Industry and Financial Markets Association Before the Subcommittee of Energy of the Senate Committee on Energy and Natural Resources, September 16, 2008, http://energy.senate.gov/public/_files/BlytheMastersEaglestestimony091608.doc, accessed November 2011.

8.   "Did Speculation Fuel Oil Price Swings?" *60 Minutes*, CBSNews April 14, 2009, http://www.cbsnews.com/stories/2009/01/08/60minutes/main4707770.shtml, accessed September 2011.

9.   Diana B. Henriques, "JPMorgan Questioned on Oil Bets," The *New York Times*, September 17, 2008, http://www.nytimes.com/2008/09/18/business/18speculate.html, accessed November 2011.

10.   David Teather, "The woman who built financial 'weapon of mass destruction,'" The *Guardian*, September 19, 2008, http://www.guardian.co.uk/business/2008/sep/20/wallstreet.banking, accessed November 2011.

11.   Robert Lenzner, "ExxonMobil CEO Says Oil Price Should Be $60 To $70 A Barrel," *Forbes*, 14 May 2011, http://www.forbes.com/sites/robertlenzner/2011/05/14/exxon-mobil-ceo-says-oil-price-should-be-60-70-a-barrel/, accessed September 2011.

12.   Catherine Boyle, "Oil Price Fall Driven by 'Speculation': OPEC," CNBC.com, September 20, 2011, http://www.cnbc.com/id/44590407/Oil_Price_Fall_Driven_by_Speculation_OPEC, accessed September 2011.

13.   "Did Speculation Fuel Oil Price Swings?" op cit.

14.   James D. Hamilton, "Historical Oil Shocks," University of California, San Diego, February 1, 2011, http://dss.ucsd.edu/~jhamilto/oil_history.pdf (accessed September 2011).

15.   "OPEC Oil Embargo, 1973-1974," U.S. Department of State *Milestones*, http://history.state.gov/milestones/1969-1976/OPEC (accessed October 2011).

16.   Walid Phares, "OPEC War against America's Economic Independence?" CounterTerrorism Blog, October 10, 2008, http://counterterrorismblog.org/2008/10/opec_war_against_americas_econ.php (accessed June 2009).

17.   Krishna Guha, "Paulson claims Russia tried to foment Fannie-Freddie crisis," *Financial Times*, January 29, 2010, http://www.ft.com/intl/cms/s/0/ffd950c4-0d0a-11df-a2dc-00144feabdc0.html#axzz1XCuXQyAh (accessed September 2011) (subscription needed).

18.   Michael McKee and Alex Nicholson, "Paulson Says Russia Urged China to Dump Fannie, Freddie Bonds," Bloomberg News, January 29, 2010, http://www.bloomberg.com/apps/news?pid=newsarchive&sid=afbSjYv3v814 (accessed September 2011).

19.   "Chinese Economist Warns Of Risks In Freddie Mac, Fannie Mae Bonds," Dow Jones Newswires, February 10, 2011, previously available at http://www.foxbusiness.com/markets/2011/02/10/chinese-economist-warns-risks-freddie-mac-fannie-mae-bonds/#ixzz1ZwZqz0d2 (accessed September 2011).

20.   Xu Yunhong, "How China Deals with the U.S. Strategy to Contain China," *Quiushi*, December 10, 2010.

21.   James Rickards, *Currency Wars, The Making of the Next Global Crisis* (Portfolio/Penguin, 2011), pp.165–67; "Iran president calls U.S. dollar 'worthless,'" Associated Press, November 18, 2007, http://www.msnbc.msn.com/id/21870271/ns/business-world_business/t/iran-president-calls-us-dollar-worthless/ (accessed November 2011); and "BRICS push for end of dollar dominance," Reuters, April 15, 2011, article available at, http://www.khaleejtimes.ae/biz/inside.asp?xfile=/data/business/2011/April/business_April256.xml&section=business (accessed November 2011).

22.   "'Bear Raid' Stock Manipulation: How and When It Works, and Who Benefits," Knowledge@Wharton, April 16, 2008, http://knowledge.wharton.upenn.edu/article.cfm?articleid=1939 (accessed May 2009).

23.   Sebastian Mallaby, "'Go for the Jugular,'" *The Atlantic*, June 4, 2010, http://www.theatlantic.com/business/archive/2010/06/go-for-the-jugular/57696/2/?single_page=true (accessed September 2011).

24. George Soros, "One Way to Stop Bear Raids," *Wall Street Journal*, March 23, 2009, http://online.wsj.com/article/SB123785310594719693.html (accessed June 2009).

25. Warren Buffett, Berkshire Hathaway 2002 Letter to Shareholders, February 21, 2003, p.14, http://www.berkshirehathaway.com/letters/2002pdf.pdf (accessed May 2009).

26. Matthew Philips, "The Monster That Ate Wall Street," *Newsweek*, September 27, 2008 (from the magazine issue dated October 6, 2008), http://www.newsweek.com/id/161199 (accessed June 2009).

27. "The Bet That Blew Up Wall Street," CBS News, January 11, 2010 (from a news report October 2008), http://www.cbsnews.com/stories/2008/10/26/60minutes/main4546199.shtml (accessed November 2011).

28. Dan Weil, "Soros Urges Strict Regulation of Derivatives," MoneyNews.com, Friday, June 19, 2009, http://www.moneynews.com/FinanceNews/soros-derivatives/2009/06/19/id/331030 (accessed June 2009).

29. Floyd Norris, "Get Shorty," *New York Times*, September 17, 2008, http://norris.blogs.nytimes.com/2008/09/17/get-shorty (accessed June 2009).

30. George Soros, "One Way to Stop Bear Raids," op cit.

31. Andy Kessler, "Have We Seen the Last of the Bear Raids?" *Wall Street Journal*, March 26, 2009, http://online.wsj.com/article/SB123802165000541773.html (accessed June 2009).

32. John Finnerty, "Short Selling, Death Spiral Convertibles, and the Profitability of Stock Manipulation," March 2005, p. 8, http://papers.ssrn.com/sol3/papers.cfm?abstract_id=687282 (accessed May 2009).

33. John Keefe, "The Big Picture, Strange end-of-day phenomenon sets pundits thinking," *Financial Times*, May 10, 2009, http://www.ft.com/cms/s/0/f65adb32-3cc0-11de-8b71-00144feabdc0.html (accessed May 2009) (subscription needed).

34. Tom Lauricella, Susan Pulliam, and Diya Gullapalli, "Are ETFs Driving Late-Day Turns?" *Wall Street Journal*, December 15, 2008, http://online.wsj.com/article/SB122929670229805137.html (accessed June 2009).

35. Jason Zweig, "Will Leveraged ETFs Put Cracks in Market Close?" *Wall Street Journal*, April 18, 2009, http://online.wsj.com/article/SB124000593149930309.html (accessed September 2011).

36. "What is a SWF?" About Sovereign Wealth Funds, Sovereign Wealth Fund Institute, www.swfinstitute.org/funds.php (accessed June 2009).

37. Testimony by Dr. Gal Luft, executive director, Institute for the Analysis of Global Security (IAGS) presented before House Committee on Foreign Affairs, "Sovereign Wealth Funds, Oil, and the New World Economic Order," May 21, 2008, p. 2, http://www.iags.org/Luft_HFRC_SWF_052108.pdf (accessed June 2009).

38. Robert Kimmitt, "Public Footprints in Private Markets," *Foreign Affairs*, January/February 2008, http://www.foreignaffairs.com/articles/63053/robert-m-kimmitt/public-footprints-in-private-markets (accessed September 2011).

39. Lawrence Summers, "Funds that shake capitalist logic," *Financial Times*, July 29, 2007, http://www.ft.com/intl/cms/s/2/bb8f50b8-3dcc-11dc-8f6a-0000779fd2ac.html#axzz1ZsTzct8x (accessed September 2011).

40. "Shariah, Law and Financial Jihad: How Should America Respond?" McCormick Foundation, 2008, p.55-57, http://www.scribd.com/doc/15955083/Shariah-Law-and-Financial-Jihad-How-Should-America-Respond, accessed June 2009.

41. Ibid.

42. James Rickards, *Currency Wars: The Making of the Next Global Crisis*, p. 8.

43. Donna Block and Bill McConnell, "Oil on Ice," *The Deal* magazine, July 3, 2008, http://www.thedeal.com/magazine/ID/017540/featuresold/oil-on-ice.php (accessed June 2009).

44. Press Release of Senator Cantwell, "Senators Cantwell and Snowe Push for More Oversight in Energy Markets," Cantwell.Senate.gov, May 22, 2008, http://cantwell.senate.gov/news/record.cfm?id=298325 (accessed September 2011).

45. Ibid.

46. Ibid.

47. Donna Block and Bill McConnell, "Oil on Ice," op cit.

48. Ellen Hodgson Brown, *Web of Debt* (Third Millennium Press, 2007), p.194, http://www.amazon.com/Web-Debt-Shocking-Sleight-Trapped/dp/0979560802 (accessed June 2009).

49. "Where's the Heat on Hedge Funds?" *Business Week*, June 19, 2006, www.businessweek.com/magazine/content/06_25/b3989062.htm (accessed June 2009).

50. "Statement of Senator Carl Levin on Treasury Withdrawal of Proposed Rule to Require Anti-Money Laundering Controls at Hedge Funds," press release dated November 3, 2008, http://levin.senate.gov/newsroom/release.cfm?id=304790 (accessed June 2009).

51. Anuj Gangahar, "It is time to shine some light into these dark pools," *Financial Times*, July 5, 2008, www.ft.com/cms/s/0/ 9eea52be-4a2d-11dd-891a-000077b07658.html (accessed June 2009) (subscription needed).

52. Darren Boey, "Dark Pools Pose Risk to Markets, Hong Kong's Arculli Says," Bloomberg, December 9, 2009, http://www.bloomberg.com/apps/news?pid=n ewsarchive&sid=aBFcQ8EMJV.4 (accessed October 2011).

53. Reinhardt Krause, "Dark Pools Let Big Institutions Trade Quietly," *Investors Business Daily*, November 26, 2008 www.conatum.com/presscites/Quietly.pdf (accessed June 2009).

54. "Shining a light on dark pools," *The Economist*, August 18, 2011, http://www. economist.com/blogs/schumpeter/2011/08/exchange-share-trading (accessed September 2011).

55. Nina Mehta, "Top SEC Trading Chief Takes Aim at Dark Pools," TradersMaga zine.com, May 20, 2009, http://www.tradersmagazine.com/news/sec-dark-pools-james-brigagliano-103787-1.html (accessed June 2009).

56. Ibid.

57. "Shining a light on dark pools," op cit.

58. Nina Mehta, "Gloves Off," TradersMagazine.com, April 2009, http://www.trad ersmagazine.com/issues/20_293/-103612-1.html (accessed June 2009).

59. Ibid.

60. Ibid.

61. "Shining a light on dark pools," op cit.

62. "The Impact of High-frequency Trading: Manipulation, Distortion or a Better-functioning Market?" Knowledge@Wharton, September 30, 2009, http://knowl edge.wharton.upenn.edu/article.cfm?articleid=2345 (accessed September 2011).

63. Robert Iati, "The Real Story of Trading Software Espionage," The Tabb Group Perspective, July 10, 2009.

64. Bob Sullivan, "Agency warns banks of al-Qaida risk," MSNBC, July 24, 2003, http://www.msnbc.msn.com/id/3072757/ns/business-world_business/t/agency-warns-banks-al-qaida-risk/ (accessed September 2011).

65. Ibid.

66. Shanthi Bharatwaj, "UBS Execs Booted for Rogue Trader Blowup," *The Street*, October 5, 2011, http://www.thestreet.com/story/11269155/1/ubs-execs-booted-for-rogue-trader-blowup.html?cm_ven=GOOGLEN (accessed October 2011).

67. Nicola Clark, "Rogue Trader at Société Générale Gets 3 Years," *New York Times*, October 5, 2010, http://www.nytimes.com/2010/10/06/business/global/06bank. html?pagewanted=all (accessed September 2011).

68. Joanna Slater, "When Hedge Funds Meet Islamic Finance," *Wall Street Journal*, August 9, 2007, http://online.wsj.com/article/SB118661926443492441.html (accessed June 2009).

69. Ian King and Patrick Hosking, "Government prevented from taking Barclays stake by deal with Abu Dhabi," *The Times*, January 22, 2009, http://business. timesonline.co.uk/tol/business/industry_sectors/banking_and_finance/arti cle5563223.ece (accessed October 2011) (subscription needed).

70. Landon Thomas Jr. and Eric Dash, "Saudi Prince Is Humbled by Citigroup," *New York Times*, February 27, 2009, http://www.nytimes.com/2009/02/28/business/ worldbusiness/28prince.html (accessed June 2009).

71. Will McSheehy and Bradley Keoun, "Citigroup to Raise $7.5 Billion from Abu Dhabi State," Bloomberg News, November 27, 2007, http://www.bloomberg. com/apps/news?pid=20601087&sid=a0X4zgNm8Ibs (accessed June 2009).

72. Ian King and Patrick Hosking, "Government prevented from taking Barclays stake by deal with Abu Dhabi," op cit.

73. Kirk Shinkle "Saudi Prince Burned By Citigroup," *US News & World Report* The Ticker, January 21, 2009, http://www.usnews.com/blogs/the-ticker/2009/01/21/ saudi-prince-burned-by-citigroup.html.

74. Souhail Karam, "Saudi Kingdom Hldg says posts Q4 profit after review," Reuters, January 24, 2009, http://www.reuters.com/article/businessNews/idUSTRE50N 1GW20090124?feedType=RSS&feedName=businessNews (accessed June 2009).

75. James Pethokoukis, "Should Dubai Buy Part of the Nasdaq?" *US News & World Report*, September 21, 2007, http://money.usnews.com/money/blogs/capital-commerce/2007/09/21/should-dubai-buy-part-of-the-nasdaq (accessed September 2011).

CHAPTER SIX

1. Securities and Exchange Commission, "SEC Concept Release: Short Sales," SEC. gov, October 20, 1999, http://www.sec.gov/rules/concept/34-42037. htm#P56_11734 (accessed September 2011).

2. Robert Sloan, *Don't Blame the Shorts: Why Short Sellers Are Always Blamed for Market Crashes and How History is Repeating Itself* (The McGraw-Hill Companies, 2010), p. 107.

3. Securities and Exchange Commission, "Amendments to Regulation SHO and Rule 10a-1," February 12, 2007, p. 6.

4. Robert Sloan, *Don't Blame the Shorts*, p. 107.

5. Gretchen Morgenson, "Why the Roller Coaster Seems Wilder," *New York Times*, August 26, 2007, http://select.nytimes.com/2007/08/26/business/yourmoney/26gret.html?_r=1 (accessed September 2011).

6. "To require the Securities and Exchange Commission to reinstate the uptick rule on short sales of securities," HR 6517, 110th Cong., http://thomas.loc.gov/cgi-bin/bdquery/z?d110:HR06517:@@@P (accessed September 2011).

7. Robert Holmes, "Uptick Rule: Meaningful or Meaningless," TheStreet.com, February 26, 2009, www.thestreet.com/story/10466532/uptick-rule-meanigful-or-meaningless.html (accessed June 2009).

8. "SEC Seeks Comments on Short Sale Price Test and Circuit Breaker Restrictions," SEC.gov, April 8, 2009, http://www.sec.gov/news/press/2009/2009-76.htm (accessed September 2011).

9. Nina Mehta, "SEC May Reinstate Uptick Rule," *Traders* magazine, October 7, 2008, http://www.tradersmagazine.com/news/102225-1.html (accessed September 2011).

10. James Armstrong, "Short Sale Rule Catching Long List of Stocks," *Traders* magazine May 9, 2011, http://www.tradersmagazine.com/news/short_sale_rule-107506-1.html (accessed October 2011).

11. International Monetary Fund, "Global economy on track for continued strong growth, says IMF," *IMF Survey* Vol. 36, No. 6, April 11, 2007, http://www.imf.org/external/pubs/ft/survey/2007/041107.pdf, p. 84 (accessed May 2009).

12. The Futurist, "Economic Growth is Exponential and Accelerating, v2.0," July 12, 2007, http://www.singularity2050.com/2007/07/economic-growth.html (accessed May 2009).

13. Paul Krugman, "How Did Economists Get It So Wrong?" *New York Times Magazine*, September 6, 2009, http://www.nytimes.com/2009/09/06/magazine/06Economic-t.html?_r=1&pagewanted=all (accessed October 2011).

14. "In come the waves," *The Economist*, June 16, 2005, http://www.economist.com/node/4079027?story_id=4079027 (accessed September 2011).

15. David R. Henderson and Jeffrey Rogers Hummel, "Greenspan's Monetary Policy in Retrospect: Discretion or Rules?" CATO Institute Briefing Papers, November 3, 2008, http://www.cato.org/pubs/bp/bp109.pdf (accessed September 2011).

16. Peter J. Wallison and Edward J. Pinto, "A Government-Mandated Housing Bubble," *Forbes*, February 16, 2009, http://www.forbes.com/2009/02/13/housing-bubble-subprime-opinions-contributors_0216_peter_wallison_edward_pinto.html (accessed September 2011).

17. Herman M. Schwartz, *Subprime Nation: American Power, Global Capital, and the Housing Bubble* (Cornell University Press, 2009), p. 180.

18. Peter Wallison, "Fannie, Freddie and Other Villains," *BARRON'S Book Review*, July 2, 2011, http://online.barrons.com/article/SB50001424053111903617204576411781103509242.html#articleTabs_panel_article%3D1 (accessed November 2011).

19. Peter Wallison and Edward J. Pinto, "A Government-Mandated Housing Bubble," op cit.

20. Ibid.

21. Ibid.

22. Andrew Redleaf and Richard Vigilante, *Panic: The Betrayal of Capitalism By Wall Street and Washington* (Richard Vigilante Books, 2010), pp. 132–39.

23. Floyd Norris, "Financial alchemy couldn't turn these loans into gold," *New York Times*, June 29, 2007, http://www.nytimes.com/2007/06/29/business/worldbusiness/29iht-wbmarket30.1.6406777.html (accessed November 2011).

24. Lawrence Carrel, "Managers: Subprime Blame Lies With Rating Agencies," TheStreet.com, July 2, 2007, http://www.thestreet.com/story/10365816/2/managers-subprime-blame-lies-with-rating-agencies.html (accessed November 2011).

25. "The Financial Crisis Inquiry Report," GPOAccess.gov, January 2011, http://www.gpoaccess.gov/fcic/fcic.pdf (accessed September 2011).

26. Kathleen M. Howley, "US Mortgages Enter Foreclosure at Record Pace," Bloomberg.com, June 14, 2007, http://www.bloomberg.com/apps/news?pid=newsarchive&sid=aLwz4ThaWzAg&refer=home (accessed September 2011).

27. Tim Devaney, "Probe faults many for financial collapse," *Washington Times*, April 13, 2011, http://www.washingtontimes.com/news/2011/apr/13/probe-faults-many-financial-collapse/?page=all (accessed October 2011).

28.   Ibid.

29.   Joseph G. Carson, Alliance Bernstein Global Economic Research, "Will the US Debt Burden Undermine the Economy's Long-Term Growth?" *US Weekly Economic Update*, June 5, 2009, p. 2, https://www.bernstein.com/CmsObjectPC/pdfs/EconomicUpdates/B62685_EconomicUpdate_JC_090605.pdf (accessed June 2009).

30.   Ibid., p. 3.

31.   "The Long Demise of Glass-Steagall," PBS/KERA Frontline, May 8, 2003, http://www.pbs.org/wgbh/pages/frontline/shows/wallstreet/weill/demise.html (accessed November 2011).

32.   Consumer Education Foundation, "Sold Out: How Wall Street and Washington Betrayed America," WallStreetWatch.org, March 2009, p. 24, http://www.wallstreetwatch.org/reports/sold_out.pdf (accessed October 2011).

33.   Cyrus Sanati, "10 Years Later, Looking at Repeal of Glass-Steagall," NYTimes.com, November 12, 2009, http://dealbook.nytimes.com/2009/11/12/10-years-later-looking-at-repeal-of-glass-steagall/ (accessed September 2011).

34.   Consumer Education Foundation, "Sold Out: How Wall Street and Washington Betrayed America," op cit.

35.   Cyrus Sanati, "10 Years Later, Looking at Repeal of Glass-Steagall," op cit.

36.   Consumer Education Foundation, "Sold Out: How Wall Street and Washington Betrayed America," op cit.

37.   Ibid.

38.   Christopher Cox, SEC Chairman, "Testimony Concerning Turmoil in U.S. Credit Markets: Recent Actions Regarding Government Sponsored Entities, Investment Banks and Other Financial Institutions," before the Committee on Banking, Housing, and Urban Affairs, United States Senate, September 3, 2008, http://www.sec.gov/news/testimony/2008/ts092308cc.htm (accessed June 2009).

39.   Consumer Education Foundation, "Sold Out: How Wall Street and Washington Betrayed America," op cit.

40.   Ibid.

41.   Ibid.

42.   Hernando De Soto, "Toxic Assets Were Hidden Assets," *Wall Street Journal*, March 25, 2009, http://online.wsj.com/article/SB123793811398132049-email.html (accessed October 2011).

43.   Gary Matsumoto, "Naked Short Sales Hint Fraud in Bringing down Lehman," Bloomberg, March 19, 2009, www.bloomberg.com/apps/news?pid=20601109& sid=aB1jlqmFOTCA&refer=home (accessed June 2009).

44.   David Kotz, "Practices Related to Naked Short Selling Complaints and Referrals," US Securities and Exchange Commission Office of Inspector General Office of Audits, March 18, 2009, http://www.sec-oig.gov/Reports/AuditsInspections/ 2009/450.pdf (accessed September 2011).

45.   Ibid.

46.   Gary Matsumoto, "Naked Short Sales Hint Fraud in Bringing down Lehman," op cit.

47.   Leslie Boni, Ph.D., "Strategic Delivery Failures in U.S. Equity Markets," September 24, 2005, p. 1, http://www.investigatethesec.com/drupal-5.5/files/Leslie Boni. pdf (accessed June 2009).

48.   Susanne Trimbath, Ph.D., "Naked shorting's crux: BD failure to deliver," *Investment News*, Letter to Editor, June 25, 2007, www.investmentnews.com/apps/ pbcs.dll/article?AID=/20070625/FREE/70621011/1006/TOC&template= printart (accessed September 2011).

49.   Ibid.

50.   Richard Evans, Christopher Geezy, David Musto, and Adam Reed, "Failure *is* an Option: Impediments to Short Selling and Options Pricing," revised version, December 7, 2005, pp. 1, 18, http://finance.wharton.upenn.edu/~musto/papers/ egmr.pdf (accessed June 2009).

51.   Gary Matsumoto, "Naked Short Sales Hint Fraud in Bringing down Lehman," op cit.

52.   Susanne Trimbath, Ph.D., "Naked shorting's crux: BD failure to deliver," op cit.

53.   Liz Moyer, "Naked Horror," *Forbes*, August 25, 2006, www.forbes. com/2006/08/25/naked-shorts-global-links-cx_lm_0825naked.html (accessed June 2009).

54.   Ibid.

55.   Greg Land, "Short-Selling Sparks RICO Suit Against Financial Giants," Law.com, May 15, 2009, www.law.com/jsp/article.jsp?id=1202430726911 (accessed June 2009).

56.   Bob Drummond, "Double Voting in Proxy Contests Threatens Shareholder Democracy," Bloomberg, February 27, 2006, http://www.bloomberg.com/apps/ news?pid=newsarchive&sid=a4OuCsU8r2Yg (accessed June 2009).

57. Karey Wutkowsi, "SEC staff saw Madoff as a voice of authority," Reuters, December 17, 2008, http://www.reuters.com/article/2008/12/17/us-madoff-sec-remarks-idUSTRE4BG6US20081217 (accessed September 2011).

58. Kyle Alspach, "Markopolos on Madoff: 'It took me about five minutes to figure out he was a fraud,'" *Patriot Ledger*, February 5, 2009, http://www.patriotledger.com/archive/x1717608693/Harry-Markopolos-Madoff-tipster-from-Whitman-assails-SEC (accessed June 2009).

59. "SEC staff saw Madoff as a voice of authority," Reuters, December 17, 2008, http://www.reuters.com/article/2008/12/17/us-madoff-sec-remarks-idUSTRE4BG6US20081217.

60. Consumer Education Foundation, "Sold Out: How Wall Street and Washington Betrayed America," op cit.

61. Brian S. Wesbury, "Why Mark-To-Market Accounting Rules Must Die," *Forbes*, February 24, 2009, http://www.forbes.com/2009/02/23/mark-to-market-opinions-columnists_recovery_stimulus.html (accessed October 2011).

62. Ibid.

63. "Barclays buys core Lehman assets," BBC News, September 17, 2008, http://news.bbc.co.uk/2/hi/business/7620306.stm (accessed October 2011), and Michael J. de la Merced, "Barclays Seeks Dismissal of Lehman Estate Suit," *New York Times*, January 29, 2010, http://www.nytimes.com/2010/01/30/business/global/30barclays.html (accessed October 2011).

64. Steve Wunsch, "From Bankers to Speculators," *Barrons*, October 9, 2010, http://online.barrons.com/article/SB50001424052970204044404575479704056364196.html?mod=djembwr_h (accessed October 2011).

65. Sean Hendelman and Brandon Rowley, "SEC Should Rethink Reg NMS To Fix HFT Liquidity Problem," September 30, 2010, http://www.istockanalyst.com/article/viewarticlepaged/articleid/4546293/pageid/1 (accessed November 2011).

66. National Commission on Terrorist Attacks, *The 9/11 Commission Report* (W.W. Norton & Company, Inc., 2004), p. 169.

67. Ibid.

68. Dan Eggen, "U.S. Is Given Failing Grades By 9/11 Panel," *Washington Post*, December 6, 2005, http://www.washingtonpost.com/wp-dyn/content/article/2005/12/05/AR2005120500097.html (accessed September 2011).

69.   David Yerushalmi, "The Threat of Shariah-Compliant Finance," *National Review*, December 2, 2009, http://www.nationalreview.com/corner/191091/threat-shariah-compliant-finance/david-yerushalmi (accessed September 2011).

70.   Paul Richter, "Gaddafi salted away about $200 billion," *Sydney Morning Herald*, October 22, 2011, http://news.smh.com.au/breaking-news-world/gaddafi-salted-away-about-200-billion-20111022-1md9z.html (accessed November 2011).

71.   Scott Cohn, "Court Filing: Libyans Knew Stanford Was Running Scam When They Withdrew Millions," CNBC.com, June 23, 2011, http://www.cnbc.com/id/43518221 (accessed September 2011).

72.   Frank Jack Daniel and Brian Ellsworth, "Well-off Venezuelans say Chavez led them to Stanford," Reuters, February 20, 2009, http://uk.reuters.com/article/2009/02/20/stanford-venezuela-chavez-idUKN1930711820090220 (accessed October 2011).

73.   Bob Sullivan, "Agency warns banks of al-Qaida risk," MSNBC.com, July 24, 2003, http://www.msnbc.msn.com/id/3072757/ns/business-world_business/ (accessed September 2011).

74.   Senator Jon Kyl and Senator Dianne Feinstein, *Three Years After September 11: Keeping America Safe*, United States Senate Committee on the Judiciary, Subcommittee on Terrorism, Technology, and Homeland Security, March 2005, p. 79.

75.   Dr. Rachel Ehrenfeld and Alyssa A. Lappen, "Financial Jihad," *Human Events*, September 22, 2005, http://www.humanevents.com/article.php?id=9235 (accessed October 2011).

CHAPTER SEVEN

1.   Paul Krugman, "How Did Economists Get It So Wrong?" *New York Times Magazine*, September 6, 2009, http://www.nytimes.com/2009/09/06/magazine/06Economic-t.html?_r=1&pagewanted=all (accessed October 2011).

2.   Gene Koprowski, "Samuelson: Economists Missed the Financial Crisis," MoneyNews.com, July 10, 2009, http://www.moneynews.com/StreetTalk/financial-crisis/2009/07/10/id/331462 (accessed October 2011)

3.   Erik Holm, "Buffett Buys Goldman Stake in 'Economic Pearl Harbor,'" September 24, 2008, http://www.bloomberg.com/apps/news?pid=20601087&sid=aRef_DUx6AcU&refer=worldwide (accessed June 2009).

4. (Name of Author Withheld), "Red Flags of Market Manipulation Causing a Collapse of the U.S. Economy," March 2, 2009, p.1.

5. Col. Qiao Liang and Col. Wang Xiangsui, *Unrestricted Warfare*, p. 114.

6. Richard S. Eckaus, "The Oil Price Really is a Speculative Bubble," June 13, 2008, p. 8. http://web.mit.edu/ceepr/www/publications/workingpapers/2008-007.pdf (accessed June 2009).

7. Walid Phares, "OPEC War against America's Economic Independence?" CounterTerrorism Blog, October 10, 2008, http://counterterrorismblog.org/2008/10/opec_war_against_americas_econ.php (accessed June 2009).

8. "Did Speculation Fuel Oil Price Swings?" CBSNews *60 Minutes*, April 14, 2009, http://www.cbsnews.com/stories/2009/01/08/60minutes/main4707770.shtml (accessed September 2011).

9. "Commodity Futures Market Reform," Petroleum Marketers Association of America, May 2010, http://www.pmaa.org/userfiles/file/Legislative/2010/COMMODITY%20FUTURES%20MARKET%20REFORM(2).pdf (accessed October 2011).

10. Walid Phares, "OPEC War against America's Economic Independence?" op cit.

11. Testimony by Dr. Gal Luft, executive director, Institute for the Analysis of Global Security (IAGS) presented before House Committee on Foreign Affairs, "Sovereign Wealth Funds, Oil, and the New World Economic Order," May 21, 2008, p. 1, http://www.iags.org/Luft_HFRC_SWF_052108.pdf (accessed June 2009).

12. Kenneth B. Medlock, III, "Who Is In the Oil Futures Market and How Has It Changed?" James A. Baker III Institute for Public Policy, August 26, 2009, http://bakerinstitute.org/publications/EF-pub-MedlockJaffeOilFuturesMarket-082609.pdf (accessed October 2011).

13. Matt Taibbi, "Wall Street's Naked Swindle," *Rolling Stone*, April 5, 2010, http://www.rollingstone.com/politics/news/wall-streets-naked-swindle-20100405 (accessed October 2011).

14. Gary Matsumoto, "Bringing Down Bear Began as $1.7 Million of Options," Bloomberg, August 11, 2008, http://www.bloomberg.com/apps/news?pid=newsarchive&sid=aGmG_eOp5TjE (accessed October 2011).

15. Matt Taibbi, "Wall Street's Naked Swindle," op cit.

16. Ibid.

17. Ibid.

18. George Soros, "One Way to Stop Bear Raids," *Wall Street Journal*, March 23, 2009, http://online.wsj.com/article/SB123785310594719693.html (accessed June 2009).

19. "EMERGENCY ORDER PURSUANT TO SECTION 12(k)(2) OF THE SECURITIES EXCHANGE ACT OF 1934 TAKING TEMPORARY ACTION TO RESPOND TO MARKET DEVELOPMENTS," Release No. 58166, July 15, 2008, http://www.sec.gov/rules/other/2008/34-58166.pdf (accessed October 2011).

20. Adam Davidson, "Global Nightmare: If Fannie And Freddie Had Failed," NPR, September 9, 2008, http://www.npr.org/templates/story/story.php?storyId=94424809.

21. Michael McKee and Alex Nicholson, "Paulson Says Russia Urged China to Dump Fannie, Freddie Bonds," Bloomberg News, January 29, 2010, http://www.bloomberg.com/apps/news?pid=newsarchive&sid=afbSjYv3v814 (accessed October 2011).

22. Gary Matsumoto, "Naked Short Sales Hint Fraud in Bringing down Lehman," Bloomberg, March 19, 2009, www.bloomberg.com/apps/news?pid=20601109&sid=aB1jlqmFOTCA&refer=home (accessed June 2009).

23. Ibid.

24. Representative Kanjorski, "$550 Billion Disappeared in 'Electronic Run On the Banks,'" *Live Leak*, February 7, 2011, http://www.liveleak.com/view?i=ca2_1234032281 (accessed November 2011).

25. Statement of Richard S. Fuld, Jr. before the United States House of Representatives Committee on Oversight and Government Reform, October 6, 2008, http://online.wsj.com/public/resources/documents/fuldtestimony20081006.pdf (accessed October 2011).

26. Andy Kessler, "Have We Seen the Last of the Bear Raids?" *Wall Street Journal*, March 26, 2009, http://online.wsj.com/article/SB123802165000541773.html (accessed October 2011).

27. Ibid.

28. Ibid.

29. Ibid.

30. EMERGENCY ORDER PURSUANT TO SECTION 12(k)(2) OF THE SECURITIES EXCHANGE ACT OF 1934 TAKING TEMPORARY ACTION TO RESPOND TO MARKET DEVELOPMENTS, SECURITIES EXCHANGE ACT

OF 1934 RELEASE NO. 34-58592 / September 18, 2008, http://www.sec.gov/
rules/other/2008/34-58592.pdf (accessed October 2011).

31. Ibid.

32. (Name of Author Withheld), "Red Flags of Market Manipulation Causing a
Collapse of the U.S. Economy," March 2, 2009, pp. 1–65.

33. Ibid.

34. Michael McKee and Vivien Lou Chen, Bloomberg, "Yellen Signals Letting
Lehman Collapse Was a Mistake," Bloomberg, April 17, 2009, www.bloomberg.
com/apps/news?pid=20601087&sid=aycrixRelVc0# (accessed June 2009).

35. Reuters, "The Lehman Failure Seen as Straw that Broke the Credit Market,"
Insurance Journal, October 13, 2008, www.insurancejournal.com/news/
national/2008/10/13/94566.htm (accessed June 2009).

36. George Soros, Bill Bradley, Niall Ferguson, Paul Krugman, Nouriel Roubini,
Robin Wells, et al., "The Crisis and How to Deal with It," *New York Review of
Books*, Volume 56, Number 10, June 11, 2009, www.nybooks.com/articles/22756
(accessed June 2009).

37. George Soros, "One Way to Stop Bear Raids," op cit.

38. Stephen Taub, "Brother, Can You Spare a Billion?" *Institutional Investor*, March
23, 2009, http://www.institutionalinvestor.com/Article/2165684/Brother-Can-
You-Spare-a-Billion.html (accessed June 2009).

39. Floyd Brown and Lee Troxler, *Obama Unmasked* (Merril Press, 2008), p. 98; and
Susan Page, "Poll: Convention lifts McCain over Obama," *USA Today*, September
8, 2008, http://www.usatoday.com/news/politics/election2008/2008-09-07-
poll_N.htm (accessed October 2011).

40. "Red Flags of Market Manipulation Causing a Collapse of the U.S. Economy," op
cit., pp. 1–65.

41. Ibid.

42. Ibid.

43. Jason Zweig, "Will Leveraged ETFs Put Cracks in Market Close?" *Wall Street
Journal*, April 18, 2009, http://online.wsj.com/article/SB124000593149930309.
html (accessed September 2011).

44. "Texas billionaire Stanford arrested in U.S.," CNN, June 18, 2009, http://articles.
cnn.com/2009-06-18/justice/stanford.fraud.charge_1_stanford-international-
bank-allen-stanford-ponzi-scheme?_s=PM:CRIME (accessed November 2011).

45. Ana Isabel Martinez, "Venezuela seizes Stanford bank after online run," Reuters, February 19, 2009, http://uk.reuters.com/article/2009/02/19/uk-stanford-vene zuela-bank-sb-idUKTRE51I54I20090219 (accessed November 2011).

46. "Cricket mogul Stanford unfit for trial: judge," ABC News, January 27, 2011, http://www.abc.net.au/news/2011-01-27/cricket-mogul-stanford-unfit-for-trial-judge/1919622 (accessed November 2011).

47. "SEC Proposes New Rule to Effectively Prohibit Unfiltered Access and Maintain Market Access Controls," SEC Press Release, January 13, 2010, http://www.sec.gov/news/press/2010/2010-7.htm (accessed October 2011).

48. Jonathan Spicer, "'Naked access' now 38 pct of U.S. trading – report," Reuters, December 14, 2009, http://uk.reuters.com/article/2009/12/14/uk-trading-nake daccess-idUKTRE5BD0FQ20091214 (accessed October 2011).

49. "Red Flags of Market Manipulation Causing a Collapse of the U.S. Economy," op cit., p.1.

50. James Ramage, "Firms Sound Off on SEC's Sponsored Access Proposal," *Traders* magazine, Online News, April 14, 2010, http://www.tradersmagazine.com/news/sponsored-access-naked-clearing-high-frequency-trading-105494-1.html (accessed November 2011).

51. James Rickards, *Currency Wars: The Making of the Next Global Crisis* (New York, Portfolio/Penguin, 2011), p. 8.

52. Mike Caswell, "Multivision's Nazerali wins order against U.S. site," StockWatch, October 21, 2011, http://www.stockwatch.com/News/Item.aspx?bid=Z-C:MTV-1891609&symbol=MTV&news_region=C (accessed November 2011).

53. William K. Wolfrum, "Overstock.com CEO Patrick Byrne's attacks on financial journalists are false," March 11, 2009, http://www.williamkwolfrum.com/2009/03/11/overstockcom-ceo-patrick-byrnes-attacks-on-financial-jour nalists-are-false/ (accessed November 2011).

54. "America's dodgy financial plumbing: Too big a fail count," *The Economist*, June 2, 2011, http://www.economist.com/node/18774844 (accessed November 2011); and Cade Metz, "Patrick Byrne: 'See, I told you America's economy was busted,'" *The Register*, June 14, 2011, http://www.theregister.co.uk/2011/06/14/patrick_byrne_on_dodgy_american_financial_plumbing/ (accessed November 2011).

55. The Friedman Foundation for Educational Choice, Dr. Patrick Byrne (Chairman), http://www.edchoice.org/About-Us/Board-of-Directors/Dr--Patrick-

Byrne-(Chairman).aspx (accessed November 2011); and "New Chairman Named For Friedman Foundation," InsideINdianaBusiness.com, July 21, 2008, http://www.insideindianabusiness.com/newsitem.asp?ID=30535 (accessed November 2011).

56. Mark Mitchell, "The Miscreants' Global Bustout," Chapters 1–20, www.deep capture.com, accessed October 2011. [Note: This website was shut down by court order on October 19, 2011 through at least December 2, 2011.]

57. Barry Ritholz, "Terror Attack on US Financials? Details of SEC Short Ban," *The Big Picture*, September 19, 2008, http://www.ritholtz.com/blog/2008/09/terror-attack-on-us-financials-details-of-sec-short-ban/ (accessed November 2011).

58. "Economic Terrorism – Is The Stock Market Being Manipulated?" NationalTerrorAlert.com, October 16, 2008, http://www.nationalterroralert.com/2008/10/16/economic-terrorism-is-the-stock-market-being-manipulated/.

59. Gene Koprowski, "Paulson: British Screwed U.S. on Lehman Bailout," MoneyNews.com, February 5, 2010, http://www.moneynews.com/StreetTalk/Paulson-British-Screwed-US/2010/02/05/id/349081 (accessed October 2011).

60. Louise Armitstead and Philip Aldrick, "Barclays may lose control to Gulf investors," *The Telegraph*, January 21, 2009, http://www.telegraph.co.uk/finance/newsbysector/banksandfinance/4309296/Barclays-may-lose-control-to-Gulf-investors.html (accessed October 2011).

61. "SWFs involved in Barclays £4.5 billion share off," CentralBanking.org, http://www.centralbanking.com/central-banking/news/1431097/swfs-involved-bar clays-gbp4-billion-share (accessed October 2011) (subscription required).

62. "70% of Hedge Funds Lost Money in 2008; Average Fund Plunges 21.44% in 12 Months," BarclayHedge Blog, January 22, 2009, http://barclayhedge.blogspot.com/2009/01/70-of-hedge-funds-lost-money-in-2008.html (accessed October 2011).

63. "Larger/Younger Hedge Funds Reported Better Returns for 2008: Study," Team Hedge Fund, May 31, 2009, http://www.teamhedgefund.com/largeryounger-hedge-funds-reported-better-returns-for-2008-study/ (accessed October 2011).

64. James Rickards, "Recession, bailout and stimulus: Are they US security threats?" Associated Press, February 26, 2009, available at the *Jerusalem Post*, http://www.jpost.com/Business/BusinessFeatures/Article.aspx?id=135938 (accessed October 2011).

65.   Matt Taibbi, "Wall Street's Naked Swindle," *Rolling Stone*, April 5, 2010, http://www.rollingstone.com/politics/news/wall-streets-naked-swindle-20100405 (accessed October 2011).

CHAPTER EIGHT

1.   Joshua Schneyer and Timothy Gardner, "US sues big oil traders for 2008 manipulation," Reuters, May 25, 2011, http://www.msnbc.msn.com/id/43165610/ns/business-oil_and_energy/t/us-sues-big-oil-traders-manipulation/ (accessed October 2011).

2.   Gretchen Morgenson, "Speculators Get a Break in New Rule," *New York Times*, September 24, 2011, http://www.nytimes.com/2011/09/25/business/economy/new-rule-gives-commodities-speculators-a-break.html (accessed October 2011).

3.   Agustino Fontevecchia, "Dodd-Frank Failing On Volcker Rule, Derivatives, Credit Rating Agencies," *Forbes*, June 6, 2011, http://www.forbes.com/sites/afontevecchia/2011/06/06/dodd-frank-failing-on-volcker-rule-derivatives-credit-rating-agencies/ (accessed October 2011).

4.   Luke Mullins, "The Obama Housing Fix: 5 Things to Know," *US News & World Report*, February 18, 2009, http://money.usnews.com/money/personal-finance/real-estate/articles/2009/02/18/the-obama-housing-fix-5-things-to-know (accessed October 2011).

5.   Ibid.

6.   Gretchen Morgenson, "Mortgage Giants Leave Legal Bills to the Taxpayers," *New York Times*, January 24, 2011, http://www.nytimes.com/2011/01/24/business/24fees.html?pagewanted=all (accessed October 2011).

7.   Gretchen Morgenson, "Strong Enough for Tough Stains?" *New York Times*, June 26, 2010, http://www.nytimes.com/2010/06/27/business/27gret.html (accessed October 2011).

8.   Scott Patterson and Victoria McGrane, "Volcker Rule May Lose Its Bite," *Wall Street Journal*, September 22, 2011, http://online.wsj.com/article/SB10001424053111904563904576585181202426862.html (accessed October 2011).

9.   Zach Carter and Nouriel Roubini, "Nouriel Roubini: How to Break Up the Banks, Stop Massive Bonuses, and Rein in Wall Street Greed," Alternet.org, May 18, 2010, http://www.alternet.org/news/146900/nouriel_roubini%3A_how_to_

break_up_the_banks,_stop_massive_bonuses,_and_rein_in_wall_street_
greed?page=entire (accessed October 2011).

10. Chris V. Nicholson, "The Dodd-Frank Bill Up Close," *New York Times*, June 28, 2010, http://dealbook.nytimes.com/2010/06/28/the-dodd-frank-bill-up-close/ (accessed October 2011).

11. "Congressionally-Mandated Study Says Improve, Do Not Suspend, Fair Value Accounting Standards," SEC.gov, December 30, 2008, http://sec.gov/news/press/2008/2008-307.htm (accessed October 2011).

12. Craig Torres and Scott Lanman, "Bernanke Urges Rules Overhaul to Stem Risk Build-Ups," Bloomberg, March 10, 2009, http://www.bloomberg.com/apps/news?pid=newsarchive&sid=agtjbFBcR1Gw&refer=home (accessed October 2011).

13. Ronald D. Orol, "SEC still lacks tools to prevent 'flash crashes,'" *MarketWatch*, May 6, 2011, http://www.marketwatch.com/story/sec-still-lacks-tools-to-prevent-flash-crashes-2011-05-06 (accessed October 2011).

14. Nina Mehta, "High-Frequency Firms Tripled Trades Amid Rout, Wedbush Says," Bloomberg, August 12, 2011, http://www.bloomberg.com/news/2011-08-11/high-frequency-firms-tripled-trading-as-s-p-500-plunged-13-wedbush-says.html (accessed September 2011).

15. Ibid.

16. Whitney Kisling, "Fund Withdrawals Top Lehman as $75 Billion Taken From Stocks," Bloomberg, September 19, 2011, http://www.businessweek.com/news/2011-09-19/fund-withdrawals-top-lehman-as-75-billion-taken-from-stocks.html (accessed October 2011).

17. Arthur B. Laffer, "Get Ready for Inflation and Higher Interest Rates," *Wall Street Journal*, June 11, 2009, http://online.wsj.com/article/SB124458888993599879.html (accessed June 2009).

18. Matt Kelley, "Tracking the stimulus: Some jobs cost more to create," *USA Today*, March 22, 2010, http://www.usatoday.com/news/washington/2010-02-24-stim-jobs_N.htm (accessed October 2011).

19. Susan Pulliam, Kate Kelly, and Carrick Mollenkamp, "Hedge Funds Try 'Career Trade' Against Euro," *Wall Street Journal*, February 26, 2010, http://online.wsj.com/article/SB10001424052748703795004575087741848074392.html?KEYWORDS=soros+ (accessed October 2011) (subscription required).

20. George Georgiopoulos, "Greek intelligence probes bond speculators," Reuters, February 19, 2010, http://uk.reuters.com/article/2010/02/19/uk-greece-specu lators-idUKTRE61I4NJ20100219 (accessed October 2010).

21. Alan Crawford and Shannon D. Harrington, "Germany Bans Naked Short Selling, Some European Bond Swaps to Calm Markets," Bloomberg News, May 19, 2010, http://www.bloomberg.com/news/2010-05-18/germany-to-temporarily-ban-naked-short-selling-some-swaps-of-euro-bonds.html (accessed October 2010).

22. "Al-Qaeda plotting against European economy, report says," August 24, 2011, *M&C News*, http://www.monstersandcritics.com/news/europe/news/arti cle_1658910.php/Al-Qaeda-plotting-against-European-economy-report-says (accessed October 2011).

23. Christine Harper and Shannon D. Harrington, "Morgan Stanley Seen as Risky as Italian Banks in Swaps Market," Bloomberg, September 30, 2011, http://mobile.bloomberg.com/news/2011-09-30/morgan-stanley-seen-as-risky-as-italian-banks-in-swaps-market (accessed October 2011).

24. Mark Decambre, "Debt rumors hit Morgan Stanley," *New York Post*, September 30, 2011, http://www.nypost.com/p/news/business/debt_rumors_hit_mor gan_stanley_MRae74IGmT4XULZtyNjN3J (accessed November 2011).

25. Damian Paletta and Matt Phillips, "S&P Strips U.S. of Top Credit Rating," August 6, 2011, *Wall Street Journal*, http://online.wsj.com/article/SB100014240531119 03366504576490841235575386.html (accessed October 2011).

26. Hans Parisis, "Steps Away from Being the Next Weimar Germany," NewsMax, moneynews.com, June 3, 2009, http://www.moneynews.com/HansParisis/hans-parisis-inflation/2009/06/03/id/330689 (accessed June 2009).

27. Eamon Javers, "Four really, really bad scenarios," *Politico*, December 17, 2008, http://www.politico.com/news/stories/1208/16663.html (accessed June 2009).

28. Eamon Javers, "A sneak attack on the U.S. dollar?" *Politico*, April 1, 2009, http://www.politico.com/news/stories/0309/20723.html (accessed June 2009).

29. Stacy Curtin, "'The End of America': Porter Stansberry Sees the Future...And It's Grim," Yahoo! Finance, February 16, 2011, http://finance.yahoo.com/tech-ticker/%22the-end-of-america%E2%80%9D-porter-stansberry-sees-the-future-....-and-it's-grim-535932.html?tickers=%5EDJI,%5EGSPC,GDX,MOO, GLD,UUP,DBA (accessed October 2011).

30.   John Carney, "Wall Street Warned About a New Kind of Jihad," CNBC.com, February 1, 2011, http://www.cnbc.com/id/41370683/Wall_Street_Warned_ About_a_New_Kind_of_Jihad (accessed October 2011).

31.   Ibid.

32.   Andrew C. McCarthy, "American Taxpayer, Financial Jihadist," NationalReview. com, August 14, 2010, http://www.nationalreview.com/articles/243717/ameri can-taxpayer-financial-jihadist-andrew-c-mccarthy?page=1 (accessed October 2011).

33.   Rep. Chicago: The McCormick Foundation, "Shariah, Law and 'Financial Jihad': How Should America Respond?" 2008, pp. 21–42, http://www.saneworks.us/ uploads/application/49.pdf (accessed November 2011).

34.   2008 Current Trends in Gulf Investing Conference, Speaker Biographies, http:// www.arabbankers.org/shared/custompage/custompage.jsp?_event=view&_ id=445506_U127360__6463 (accessed October 2011).

35.   Gadi Adelman and Joy Brighton, "Exclusive: Are We Financing Our Own Demise?" FamilySecurityMatters.org, March 2, 2010, http://www.familysecuri tymatters.org/publications/id.5632/pub_detail.asp (accessed October 2011).

36.   Gary H. Johnson, Jr., "Sharia Compliant Finance Slips Past Libya Sanctions," FamilySecurityMatters.org, April 2, 2011, http://www.familysecuritymatters.org/ publications/id.9137/pub_detail.asp (accessed October 2011).

37.   Walid Phares, "OPEC War against America's Economic Independence?" Coun terTerrorism Blog, October 10, 2008, http://counterterrorismblog.org/2008/10/ opec_war_against_americas_econ.php (accessed June 2009).

38.   Uta Harnischfeger, "Dawn of Sharia-compliant gold trading," *The National*, March 2, 2009, www.thenational.ae/article/20090302/BUSINESS/186874699/ 1005 (accessed June 2009).

39.   Guy Faulconbridge and Michael Stott, "Crisis speeds BRIC rise to power: Gold man's O'Neill," Reuters, June 9, 2009, http://www.reuters.com/article/2009/06/09/ businesspro-us-bric-oneill-interview-idUSTRE5583ZA20090609 (accessed October 2011).

40.   "BRICS Target Dollar in Call For Global Monetary Reform," Reuters as reported in *Jakarta Globe*, April 14, 2011, http://www.thejakartaglobe.com/bisworld/ brics-target-dollar-in-call-for-global-monetary-reform/435468 (accessed Octo ber 2011).

41.   Sergei Blagov, "BRIC: Alternative rhetoric," ISN Security Watch, May 20, 2008, http://www.isn.ethz.ch/isn/layout/set/print/layout/set/print/content/view/full/73?id=88368&lng=en&ots591=4888CAA0-B3DB-1461-98B9-E20E7B9C13D4 (accessed October 2011).

42.   JR Nyquist, "The New Russian Threat Out of the Old Soviet Collapse," *Financial Sense*, January 28, 2011, http://www.financialsense.com/contributors/jr-nyquist/the-new-russian-threat-out-of-the-old-soviet-collapse (accessed November 2011).

43.   Disclosure statement from JP Morgan regarding Hedge Funds, https://www.jpmorganfunds.com/cm/Satellite?pagename=jpmfVanityWrapper&UserFriendlyURL=investmentinsightsQA (accessed October 2011).

44.   John Allen Paulos, "Who's Counting: Cheney's One Percent Doctrine," ABC News, July 2, 2006, http://abcnews.go.com/Technology/story?id=2120605&page=1 (accessed October 2011).

45.   Sewell Chan, "G.O.P. Panelists Dissent on Cause of Crisis," *New York Times*, December 14, 2010, http://www.nytimes.com/2010/12/15/business/economy/15panel.html (accessed November 2011).

46.   Peter J. Wallison and Arthur F. Burns, "Financial Crisis Inquiry Commission, Dissenting Statement," January 2011, p. 448, http://fcic-static.law.stanford.edu/cdn_media/fcic-reports/fcic_final_report_wallison_dissent.pdf (accessed November 2011).

47.   John Roth, Douglas Greenburg, Serena Wille, *National Commission on Terrorist Attacks Upon the United States*, "Appendix A: The Financing of the 9/11 Plot," p. 150, http://www.9-11commission.gov/staff_statements/911_TerrFin_Monograph.pdf (accessed September 2011).

48.   Alexandra Frean, "Financial Terrorists Pose Grave Risk to U.S.," *Times of London*, February 2, 2011, p. 9.

49.   Bill Gertz, "Financial Terrorism Suspected in 2008 Economic Crash," *Washington Times*, February 28, 2011, http://www.washingtontimes.com/news/2011/feb/28/financial-terrorism-suspected-in-08-economic-crash/?page=all (accessed November 2011).

50.   "About the FCIC," Stanford Law School, http://fcic.law.stanford.edu/about/staff (accessed November 2011).

CHAPTER NINE

1. Megan Davies and Walden Siew, "45 percent of world's wealth destroyed: Black-stone CEO," Reuters, March 10, 2009, http://www.reuters.com/arti cle/2009/03/10/us-blackstone-idUSTRE52966Z20090310 (accessed October 2011).

2. Elizabeth Wurtzel, "Twelve Years Down the Drain," *Wall Street Journal*, April 9, 2009, http://online.wsj.com/article/SB123923304833103031.html (accessed October 2011).

3. Shamim Adam, "Global Financial Assets Lost $50 Trillion Last Year, ADB Says," Bloomberg, March 8, 2009, http://www.bloomberg.com/apps/news?pid=newsa rchive&refer=worldwide&sid=aZ1kcJ7y3LDM (accessed September 2011).

4. Matt Apuzzo and Eileen Sullivan, "Recession, Bailout, Stimulus Pose U.S. Secu-rity Threats," Associated Press, February 26, 2009, http://www.cnsnews.com/ node/44153 (accessed October 2011).

5. "Spanish Intelligence Reportedly Probing 'Attacks' on Economy," *Spiegel* Online, February 15, 2010, http://www.spiegel.de/international/europe/0,1518,677904,00. html (accessed November 2011).

6. George Georgiopoulos, "Greek intelligence probes bond speculators –press," Reuters, February 19, 2010, http://www.reuters.com/article/2010/02/19/greece-speculators-idUSLDE61I24520100219 (accessed November 2011).

7. Joseph Fisanakis, "US Issues Financial Warfare Warning," IntelNews.org, Febru-ary 20, 2009, http://intelligencenews.wordpress.com/about/latest-analysis/ content/analysis015/ (accessed October 2011).

8. James Rickards, *Currency Wars—The Making of the Next Global Crisis*, (Portfo-lio/Penguin, 2011), p. 101.

9. John Detrixhe and Sara Eisen, "Stiglitz Calls for New Global Reserve Currency to Prevent Trade Imbalances," Bloomberg, April 10, 2011, http://www.bloom berg.com/news/2011-04-10/stiglitz-calls-for-new-global-reserve-currency-to-prevent-trade-imbalances.html (accessed October 2011).

10. "China's Yuan Could Challenge Dollar Role in a Decade," Reuters, August 30, 2011, http://www.cnbc.com/id/44326774 (accessed September 2011).

11. Ibid.

12. Fareed Zakaria, "China's not doing us a favor," CNN.com, August 14, 2011, http://globalpublicsquare.blogs.cnn.com/2011/08/14/why-china-needs-u-s/?hpt=hp_c1 (accessed October 2011).

13. "China's Yuan Could Challenge Dollar Role in a Decade," op cit.

14. Guy Faulconbridge and Michael Stott, "Crisis speeds BRIC rise to power: Goldman's O'Neill," Reuters, June 9, 2009, http://www.reuters.com/article/2009/06/09/businesspro-us-bric-oneill-interview-idUSTRE5583ZA20090609 (accessed June 2009).

15. Jack Farchy, "Dollar seen losing global reserve status," FT.com, June 27, 2011, http://www.ft.com/cms/s/0/23183a78-a0c6-11e0-b14e-00144feabdc0.html (accessed October 2011).

16. Ding Gang, "China must punish US for Taiwan arm sales with 'financial weapon,'" *People's Daily*, August 8, 2011, http://english.peopledaily.com.cn/90780/91342/7562776.html (accessed October 2011).

17. James Rickards, *Currency Wars—The Making of the Next Global Crisis*, p. 100.

18. Ibid., p. 145.

19. "How China Deals with the U.S. Strategy to Contain China," *Qiushi Journal*, December 10, 2010 (original URL: http://chinascope.org/main/PDF/R20101213A_GoogleCache.pdf), as translated by Chinascope, http://chinascope.org/main/content/view/3291/92 (accessed November 2010).

20. Ibid.

21. James Rickards, *Currency Wars—The Making of the Next Global Crisis*, p. 162.

22. Gideon Rachman, "China or the US? Make your choice," FT.com, October 3, 2011, http://www.ft.com/intl/cms/s/7885de20-edab-11e0-a9a9-00144feab49a, Authorised=false.html?_i_location=http%3A%2F%2Fwww.ft.com%2Fcms%2Fs%2F0%2F7885de20-edab-11e0-a9a9-00144feab49a.html&_i_referer=#axzz1Zm7gHItM (accessed October 2011).

23. Col. Qiao Liang and Col. Wang Xiangsui, *Unrestricted Warfare* (Pan American Publishing Company, 2002), pp. 43, 40, 127.

24. Shaun Waterman, "Internet traffic was routed via Chinese servers," *Washington Times*, November 15, 2010, http://www.washingtontimes.com/news/2010/nov/15/internet-traffic-was-routed-via-chinese-servers/ (accessed October 2011).

25. Eric Watkins, "Chinese hackers accused of cyber attacks on IOCS," *Oil & Gas Journal*, February 10, 2011, http://www.ogj.com/articles/print/volume-109/

issue-8/general-interest/chinese-hackers-accused-of-cyber-attacks.html (accessed October 2011).

26.   Ibid.

27.   Martin Gould, "Chinese TV Details Nation's Growing Cyberhacking Might," Newsmax.com, August 25, 2011, http://www.newsmax.com/Newsfront/china-cyberhacking-might/2011/08/25/id/408695?s=al&promo_code=CEB9-1 (accessed October 2011).

28.   Joseph Menn, "Cyberattacks penetrate military secrets and designs," FT.com, August 3, 2011, http://www.ft.com/intl/cms/s/0/d4f09016-bda3-11e0-babc-00144feabdc0.html#axzz1TvPkkzWH (accessed October 2011).

29.   Michael Riley, "U.S. Spy Agency Is Said to Investigate Nasdaq Hacker Attack," Bloomberg, March 30, 2011, http://www.bloomberg.com/news/2011-03-30/u-s-spy-agency-said-to-focus-its-decrypting-skills-on-nasdaq-cyber-attack.html (accessed October 2011).

30.   "Chinese hackers suspected of penetrating IMF," *Intelligence Online*, July 28, 2011, http://www.intelligenceonline.com/government-intelligence/2011/07/28/chinese-hackers-suspected-of-penetrating-imf,91750261-BRE (accessed October 2011) (subscription required).

31.   Ellen Nakashima and Jason Ukman, "Congressman lambastes Chinese cyber-espionage," *Washington Post*, October 4, 2011, http://www.washingtonpost.com/blogs/checkpoint-washington/post/congressman-lambasts-chinese-cyber-espionage/2011/10/04/gIQA5SM7KL_blog.html (accessed October 2011).

32.   "Hedge Funds Probed in EU Review of Market Abuse," Bloomberg, April 30, 2010, http://www.bloomberg.com/news/2010-04-30/hedge-funds-summoned-by-eu-commission-in-probe-of-high-frequency-trading.html (accessed October 2011).

33.   Bill Snyder, "Hackers find new way to cheat on Wall Street — to everyone's peril," *InfoWorld*, January 6, 2011, http://www.infoworld.com/print/147699 (accessed November 2011).

34.   Tom Lauricella and Jenny Strasburg, "SEC Probes Canceled Trades," *Wall Street Journal*, September 1, 2010, http://online.wsj.com/article/SB10001424052748703882304575465990082237642.html (accessed October 2011).

35.   Michael Mackenzie and Telis Demos, "Fears linger of new 'flash crash,'" FT.com, May 5, 2011, http://m.ft.com/cms/s/0/d18f3d28-7735-11e0-aed6-00144feabdc0.html (accessed October 2011).

36. Forrest Jones and Kathleen Walter, "Harvey Pitt: 'We Remain Vulnerable' to a Flash Crash," MoneyNews.com, November 24, 2010, http://news.newsmax.com/?K6IRXsju35-0iEVW-I0vSRA26trztJR1K&http://www.moneynews.com/Headline/harveypitt-federalreserve-benbernanke/2010/11/24/id/378036?s=al&promo_code=B2E9-1 (accessed October 2011).

37. Jeff Cox, "Another 'Flash Crash' Coming? Some Market Pros Think So," CNBC.com, June 21, 2010, http://www.cnbc.com/id/37780974 (accessed October 2011).

38. "High-Frequency Firms Tripled Trades Amid Stock Rout, Wedbush Says," Bloomberg, August 12, 2011, http://www.bloomberg.com/news/2011-08-11/high-frequency-firms-tripled-trading-as-s-p-500-plunged-13-wedbush-says.html (accessed October 2011).

39. Jim McTague, "Next Danger: 'Splash Crash,'" Barrons.com, May 21, 2011, http://online.barrons.com/article/SB50001424052970203869804576327391603772726.html?mod=djembwr_h (accessed October 2011).

40. Jim McTague, "How Foreigners Could Disrupt U.S. Markets," Barrons.com, September 11, 2010, http://green.lib.udel.edu/webarchives/kaufman.senate.gov/press/in_the_news/news/-id=0a760c05-5056-9502-5df6-cc9220d44e1d.htm (accessed October 2011).

41. Col. Qiao Liang and Col. Wang Xiangsui, *Unrestricted Warfare*, p. 16.

42. Jack Farchy, "Chinese Set New Standard in Buying Gold," CNBC.com, May 19, 2011, http://www.cnbc.com/id/43101618 (accessed October 2011).

43. Carolyn Cui and Rhiannon Hoyle, "China Is Now Top Gold Bug," *Wall Street Journal*, May 20, 2011, http://finance.yahoo.com/banking-budgeting/article/112783/china-top-gold-bug-wsj?mod=bb-budgeting&sec=topStories&pos=1&asset=&ccode= (accessed October 2011).

44. Ambrose Evans-Pritchard, "Return of the Gold Standard as world order unravels," *Telegraph* (UK), July 14, 2011, http://www.telegraph.co.uk/finance/comment/ambroseevans_pritchard/8638644/Return-of-the-Gold-Standard-as-world-order-unravels.html (accessed October 2011).

45. Jamil Anderlini and Tracy Alloway, "Trades reveal China shift from dollar," FT.com, June 20, 2011, http://m.ft.com/cms/s/0/2285148c-9b6c-11e0-bbc6-00144feabdc0.html (accessed October 2011).

46. James Rickards, *Currency Wars—The Making of the Next Global Crisis*, p. 163.

47. "Dollar Drop? You Ain't Seen Nothin' Yet if Yuan Jumps," Reuters, May 17, 2011, http://www.cnbc.com/id/43070668 (accessed October 2011).

48.   Terence P. Jeffrey, "U.S. Treasury: China Has Decreased Its Holdings of U.S. Debt," CNSNews.com, April 29, 2011, http://www.cnsnews.com/news/article/us-treasury-china-has-decreased-its-hold (accessed October 2011).

49.   Ambrose Evans-Pritchard, "China to 'liquidate' US Treasuries, not dollars," *Telegraph* (UK), September 15, 2011, http://blogs.telegraph.co.uk/finance/ambroseevans-pritchard/100011987/china-to-liquidate-us-treasuries-not-dollars/ (accessed October 2011).

50.   Edmund Downie, "You call Greece a crisis? Try the U.S., says China," Foreign-Policy.com, July 1, 2011, http://blog.foreignpolicy.com/posts/2011/06/30/you_call_greece_a_crisis_try_the_us_says_china (accessed October 2011).

51.   Addison Wiggin, "Don't Get Caught Holding Dollars When The U.S. Default Arrives," Forbes.com, July 23, 2011, http://www.forbes.com/sites/greatspeculations/2011/07/23/dont-get-caught-holding-dollars-when-the-u-s-default-arrives/ (accessed October 2011).

52.   Ambrose Evans-Pritchard, "Return of the Gold Standard as world order unravels," op cit.

53.   "China aims to settle nationwide trade in yuan by 2011," Reuters, March 2, 2011, http://www.reuters.com/article/2011/03/02/china-economy-yuan-idUSBJA00246420110302 (accessed October 2011).

54.   David Marsh, "BRICS Make Move to Shove Dollar Aside," *MarketWatch*, http://finance.yahoo.com/banking-budgeting/article/112563/BRICS-move-dollar-aside-marketwatch?mod=bb-budgeting%20&sec=topStories&pos=3&asset=&ccode (accessed October 2011).

55.   Abhijit Neogy and Alexei Anishchuk, "BRICS demand global monetary shake-up, greater influence," Reuters, April 14, 2011, http://www.realclearmarkets.com/news/reuters/finance_business/2011/Apr/14/brics_demand_global_monetary_shake_up__greater_influence.html (accessed October 2011).

56.   Jose De Cordoba and Ezequiel Minaya, "Venezuela Plans to Move Reserve Funds," *Wall Street Journal*, August 17, 2011, http://online.wsj.com/article/SB10001424053111903392904576512961180570694.html (accessed October 2011).

57.   Ibid.

58.   Maria Tsvetkova, "Putin says U.S. is 'parasite' on global economy," Reuters, August 1, 2011, http://mobile.reuters.com/article/idUSTRE77052R20110801?irpc=932 (accessed October 2011).

59.   Ira Iosebashvili, "Putin: U.S. Monetary Policy Is 'Hooliganism,'" WSJ.com, April 20, 2011, http://blogs.wsj.com/economics/2011/04/20/putin-u-s-monetary-policy-is-hooliganism/ (accessed October 2011).

60.   Michael O'Brien, "'No risk' the US will lose its top credit rating, says Treasury's Geithner," *The Hill*, April 18, 2011, http://thehill.com/blogs/on-the-money/budget/156747-geithner-no-risk-that-us-loses-its-top-credit-rating (accessed October 2011).

61.   "China ratings house says US already in default," AFP, June 11, 2011, available at the American Thinker blog, http://www.americanthinker.com/blog/2011/06/good_news_china_ratings_house_says_us_already_in_default.html (accessed October 2011).

62.   Deepanshu Bagchee, "China Rating Agency Downgrades US Debt," CNBC.com, August 3, 2011, http://www.cnbc.com/id/43996450 (accessed October 2011).

63.   "Dollar to Be 'Discarded' by World: China Rating Agency," CNBC.com, August 7, 2011, http://www.cnbc.com/id/44050325 (accessed October 2011).

64.   "After historic downgrade, U.S. must address its chronic debt problems," Xinhua, August 6, 2011, http://news.xinhuanet.com/english2010/indepth/2011-08/06/c_131032986.htm (accessed October 2011).

65.   "US Treasury: Dollar Could Lose Reserve Status," MoneyNews.com, August 3, 2011, http://www.moneynews.com/StreetTalk/Dollar-Reserve-Status-us/2011/08/03/id/405979?s=al&promo_code=CC42-1 (accessed October 2011).

66.   Jack Barnes, "The $1 Billion Armageddon Trade Placed Against the United States," MoneyMorning.com, July 28, 2011, http://goldsilver.com/news/the-1-billion-armageddon-trade-placed-against-the-united-states/ (accessed October 2011).

67.   Martin Crutsinger, "S&P officials defend US credit downgrade," August 6, 2011, http://finance.yahoo.com/news/SP-officials-defend-US-credit-apf-685948715.html?x=0 (accessed October 2011).

68.   Mark Duell, "Who 'made $10bn on 10/1 bet that U.S. credit rating would be downgraded'?" *Daily Mail* (UK), August 9, 2011, http://www.dailymail.co.uk/news/article-2023809/Did-George-Soros-win-10-1-return-S-Ps-US-credit-rating-downgrade.html (accessed October 2011).

69.   Michael Mackenzie and Nicole Bullock, "Insurance Cost Against US Default Hits Record," CNBC.com, July 27, 2011, http://www.cnbc.com/id/43920402 (accessed October 2011).

70. Susan Pulliam, Kate Kelly, and Carrick Mollenkamp, "Hedge Funds Try 'Career Trade' Against Euro," *Wall Street Journal*, February 26, 2010, http://online.wsj.com/article/SB10001424052748703795004575087741848074392.html?KEYWORDS=soros+ (accessed October 2011).

71. Susan Pulliam, Kate Kelly, and Carrick Mollenkamp, "Hedge funds are ganging up on weaker euro," *Wall Street Journal*, February 26, 2010, http://online.wsj.com/article/SB40001424052748703795004575087741848074392.html (accessed November 2011).

72. "You Need This Dirty Word, Euro Bonds," *Der Spiegel*, August 15, 2011, http://www.spiegel.de/international/europe/0,1518,780189,00.html (accessed October 2011).

73. "The Destructive Power of the Financial Markets," *Der Spiegel*, August 22, 2011, http://www.spiegel.de/international/business/0,1518,druck-781590,00.html (accessed October 2011).

74. Louise Story and Matthew Saltmarsh, "Europeans Talk of Sharp Change in Fiscal Affairs," *New York Times*, September 6, 2011, http://www.cnbc.com/id/44407965 (accessed October 2011).

75. Deepanshu Bagchee, "China's Wen Promises More Support for Europe, Hints at Price," CNBC.com, September 14, 2011, http://www.cnbc.com/id/44512449/China_s_Wen_Promises_More_Support_for_Europe_Hints_at_Price (accessed October 2011).

76. Deepanshu Bagchee, "Yuan Likely to Be Fully Convertible in 5 Years: PBOC Advisor," CNBC.com, September 14, 2011, http://www.cnbc.com/id/44512934 (accessed October 2011).

77. J. R. Nyquist, "When the China Bubble Bursts," FinancialSense.com, September 6, 2011, http://www.financialsense.com/contributors/jr-nyquist/2011/09/06/when-the-china-bubble-bursts (accessed October 2011).

78. Ibid.

79. "Revealed — The Left's Economic Terrorism Playbook: The Chase Campaign by a Coalition of Unions, Community Groups, Lawmakers and Students to Take Down US Capitalism and Redistribute Wealth & Power," *The Blaze*, March 22, 2011, http://www.theblaze.com/stories/revealed-the-lefts-economic-terrorism-playbook-the-chase-campaign-for-a-coalition-of-unions-community-groups-lawmakers-and-students-to-take-down-us-capitalism-and-redistribute-wealth-power/ (accessed November 2011).

80. Damon Poeter, "Anonymous Threatens to 'Erase NYSE from the Internet,'" *PC Magazine*, http://www.pcmag.com/article2/0,2817,2394071,00.asp (accessed November 2011).

81. "Stephen Lerner," HuffingtonPost.com, http://www.huffingtonpost.com/ stephen-lerner (accessed October 2011).

82. Alex Newman, "Big Soros Money Linked to 'Occupy Wall Street,'" *The New American*, October 5, 2011, http://www.thenewamerican.com/usnews/ politics/9269-big-soros-money-linked-to-occupy-wall-street (accessed October 2011).

83. Debbie Schlussel, "VIDEO – HAMAS' CAIR Wants You to Know: 'We Are Occupy Wall Street,'" October 23, 2011, http://www.debbieschlussel.com/ 43671/video-hamas-cair-wants-you-to-know-we-are-occupy-wall-street/ (accessed November 2011), and "Hamas-linked CAIR, Jew-hating lawyer Lamis Deek Plan Rally with Obama-Endorsed Occupy Wall Street to Protest Anti-Terror Activities," Conservatives for America, November 18, 2011, http:// www.conservativesforamerica.com/around-the-web/hamas-linked-cair-jew-hating-lawyer-lamis-deek-plan-rally-with-obama-endorsed-occupy-wall-street-to-protest-anti-terror-activities (accessed November 2011).

84. K. V. S. Madhav, "Inspired by Arab awakening, a silent American spring gains ground," *Arab News*, October 4, 2011, http://arabnews.com/world/article511609. ece (accessed November 2011).

85. Andrew Marcus, "Is SEIU Working With Hamas?" Big Government/Fox Nation, January 28, 2011, http://nation.foxnews.com/seiu/2011/01/28/seiu-working-hamas (accessed November 2011).

86. Fawaz A. Gerges, "Bin Laden's new image: younger, more Marxist," *Christian Science Monitor*, September 13, 2007, http://www.csmonitor.com/2007/0913/ p09s01-coop.html (accessed November 2011).

87. Ambrose Evans-Pritchard, "Gulf petro-powers to launch currency in latest threat to dollar hegemony," *The Telegraph*, December 15, 2009, http://www.telegraph. co.uk/finance/economics/6819136/Gulf-petro-powers-to-launch-currency-in-latest-threat-to-dollar-hegemony.html (accessed November 2011).

CONCLUSION

1.   "Dave Ramsey and Warren Buffett Say No to Gold," Free $ Wisdom, April 2, 2011, http://www.freemoneywisdom.com/dave-ramsey-gold/ (accessed October 2011).

2.   Maha Khan Phillips, "Politically Motivated," CFA Magazine, July-Aug 2011, cover quote.

3.   Jonathan Powers, "Oil Addiction: Fueling Our Enemies," Truman National Security Project, February 17, 2010, http://www.trumanproject.org/files/papers/Oil_Addiction_-_Fueling_Our_Enemies_FINAL.pdf (accessed November 2011).

4.   "Kudlow – 'Drill, drill, drill, so that the futures traders will flee,'" Sic Semper Tyrannis, August 4, 2008, http://turcopolier.typepad.com/sic_semper_tyrannis/2008/08/kudlow—-drill.html (accessed November 2011).

5.   "America is addicted to foreign oil," The Pickens Plan, 2011, http://www.pickensplan.com/didyouknow/ (accessed November 2011).

6.   Ibid.

7.   Jesse Drucker, "Biggest Tax Avoiders Win Most Gaming $1 Trillion U.S. Tax Break," Bloomberg, June 27, 2011, http://www.bloomberg.com/news/2011-06-28/biggest-tax-avoiders-win-most-gaming-1-trillion-u-s-tax-break.html (accessed November 2011).

8.   Ibid.

INDEX